Framed

Interrogating Disability in the Media

Framed

Interrogating Disability in the Media

**Edited by Ann Pointon
with Chris Davies**

BRITISH FILM INSTITUTE

bfi

BFI PUBLISHING

THE **ARTS COUNCIL** OF ENGLAND

First published in 1997 by the
British Film Institute
21 Stephen Street, London W1P 2LN

Copyright © British Film Institute 1997
Individual contributions copyright
© author 1997
Introductions and editorial matter copyright © Ann Pointon 1997

The British Film Institute exists to promote appreciation, protection and
development of moving image culture in and throughout the whole of the United
Kingdom. Its activities include the National Film and Television Archive; the National
Film Theatre; the Museum of the Moving Image; the London Film Festival; the
production and distribution of film and video; funding and support for regional
activities; Library and Information Services; Stills, Posters and Designs; Research;
Publishing and Education; and the monthly Sight and Sound magazine.

British Library Cataloguing in Publication Data
A catalogue record for this book is available from the British Library

ISBN 0-85170-599-5 spiral
      0-85170-600-2 paperback

Designed by Lucy Holmes

Cover collage: Stephen Dwoskin
Cover images (left to right): Stephen Dwoskin during the shooting of Face of Fear;
film still from Patch of Blue; Nabil Shaban in Flesh Fly, Graeae Theatre Co., courtesy
of Patrick Baldwin; Anthony Sher in Richard III courtesy of Shakespeare Centre
Library, Joe Cocks Studio Collection.

Typesetting by Tiger Typeset

Printed in Great Britain

Contents

Acknowledgments

The editors owe a particular debt of gratitude to Paddy Masefield for his fine judgments, unlimited and unstinted support and constant encouragement. They also join in Paddy's own thanks to the many people he mentions in the Preface, without whom the book would not have been funded or produced, and would add thanks also to all of those contributors who wrote for the book, as well as those whose pieces appeared elsewhere and were reprinted.

The magazine *DAM* was the source of many pieces that gave life and heart to the sections on disability arts and culture, and for which the editors owe more than the customary thanks to its past and present editors.

The publishers gratefully acknowledge the following for supplying photographs and illustrations: BFI Stills, Posters and Designs, Jenny Polak and Nancy Willis, Polygram/Pictorial Press, BBC, Central Television, Channel Four, GLAD, Stephen Iliffe, National Star Centre, Hugh Graham/Rex Features, Graeae/Patrick Baldwin, Graeae/Paul Armstrong, Rosalie Wilkins, RSC, David Hevey, Pam Roberts, Hugo Glendinning, Alice Dunhill, Gioya Steinke, Sandy Sham, Heart 'n' Soul, Trish Morrissey, Mary Duffy, Mandy Holland, Stephen Millward, Jo Pearson, Kate Green, Sue Elsegood, European Captioning Institute for NCI, Brenda Prince/Format.

A special thank you for the poems to GMCDP and author's estate for 'Hump' by S. Napolitano, The Disabled People's Action Network (DAN) for 'Where Were You?', and P. Campbell for 'Zeop the Centurian'.

'A Feminist Perspective' reprinted on pages 21-30 from 'Pride Against Prejudice: Transforming Attitudes to Disability' first published by The Women's Press Ltd, 1994, 34 Great Sutton Street, London EC1V 0DX, is used by permission of The Women's Press Ltd.

Preface
Paddy Masefield (OBE)

Ten years ago, I became, in middle age, a disabled person. If I had gone to sleep a man and woken up a woman, or gone to sleep white and woken up black, I might have had some understanding of my new situation. After all, more than half my world were women, I was born in Africa and I had many black professional colleagues, personal friends and teachers.

So how could it be that I was so unprepared for disability, so ignorant of any facts, so unaware of behaviour, attitudes, or experience? Strangest of all, I was a practising theatre director and a playwright. Much of my life had been spent in seriously studying the game of make-believe, the experience of living, speaking and seeing the world through the thoughts, actions and ideas of others.

Had I really, in forty-four years, never thought of disability, never worked with disabled colleagues, never travelled, holidayed, shopped or partied with disabled people? Even if this were just possible, surely at least I was used to other people's experience of disability through portrayals on the television I watched both for education and relaxation, and which informed much of my awareness of contemporary life.

Amazingly, I was apparently living in a world in which I had been unwittingly party to a conspiracy somehow to make over six million people in the UK invisible. So ignorant had this made me, that for three years I did not even know that I had become a Disabled Person.

Then I became lucky. A wise and esteemed colleague recommended me to join the Arts and Disability Monitoring Committee of the then Arts Council of Great Britain.

The person I sat next to at my first meeting was Chris Davies. Coincidentally, a man also in a wheelchair, of about my years, and also bearded! But unlike me, Chris had a lifetime's experience of disability. He also had a lifetime's experience of the media. First as a consumer, then as a television critic, presenter, producer, and as a writer. While interviewing me as an author on my life's experience, he made me realise that I had become the member of a wonderful family of disability, one which crosses any barriers of age, gender or nationality. I was welcomed with affection, compassion and humour. But if I had found a new family, I still felt I had to obtain an education more relevant than my distant university MA.

It just happened that my first real teacher was to be Ann Pointon. Despite having been a teacher and having spent many years working with young people and even teaching in a drama school, to this day I have never met a more direct, clearer or more relevant tutor than Ann. Perhaps this partly reflects her own wide personal experience; the experience of disability, of producing programmes at BBC–Open University, of being an independent television producer, a disability equality trainer, and, until 1995, a consultant on disability for Channel Four, and in addition a much respected speaker on disability. One of my earliest experiences was to ask Ann for opinions, statistics and explanations that would enable me to make my first major speech on the subject of disability, on behalf of Lord Rix's Arts Council Initiative for the Employment of Disabled People in the Arts (an initiative whose final lucid report owed much to Ann's authorship). It is a tribute to the communication skills of Ann and Chris that the speech has found its way into this book.

Later, I was to find myself sitting literally between both of them when Ann, on behalf of the British Film Institute's Disability Committee, and Chris from the Arts Council's equivalent, were instrumental in persuading the two bodies to establish a joint Disability and Broadcasting Committee from what had been an ad hoc group. The first major product of that committee's innovation and energy has been this book.

If either Ann or Chris had not existed, this book would probably still have emerged. For interestingly, each of them individually had been aware of the need for such a book for some time. As a starting point, the Joint Committee asked Ann and Chris, together with Pam Roberts, a black disabled producer, to put forward a proposal.

After the establishment of an Advisory Editorial Group, and with the promise of funding from both the Arts Council and the BFI, an editor for the first stage of research and development was appointed to move the proposal on and to identify and contact possible contributors. Tom Shakespeare, a disability activist, the Chair of the Northern Disability Arts Forum, an academic, artist and peerless television debater, brought boundless enthusiasm, energy and vision to this role, and his imprint is firmly on the finished book.

Perhaps it was inevitable that Ann Pointon and Chris Davies should be appointed for the final and longest phase of editing the book into the present version. Ann later took the lead role, with Chris acting as contributing editor.

That process was also guided and advised by the distinctive skills of Sian Vasey and Andy Kimpton-Nye of the Editorial Advisory Group. Sian has been at the forefront of the achievements made in disability television (working as a director, producer, presenter and writer with the BBC, ITV and in the independent sector). Andy is a growing voice of authority, not only in film criticism, but more recently in television experience at BBC–Open University.

To the editors was also available the publishing experience of Deborah Howell, the skills of Carolyn Axtell who has assisted Chris Davies, and the encouragement and support of Roma Gibson, the BFI editor, to whom warmest thanks are due.

Finally, none of this endeavour and determination would have seen the light of day without the deep commitment of the joint funders, the Arts Council of England and the British Film Institute. Irene Whitehead (Head of Cinema Services and Development at the BFI), Wendy Harpe (formerly Head of the Disability Unit at ACE) and Will Bell (of the Film Video and Broadcasting Department of ACE) have been champions, defenders and enablers of the editorial team's vision.

To all of these this book owes the deepest gratitude. Even more, the book is the sum of its contributors and to all of them, so many of whom are ground-breaking role models, we express our admiration as well as warmest appreciation.

The conclusion is a book that would have led me to a much speedier understanding of disability, had it been born ten years ago; a book that will inform disabled people about their status and potential in the media; a book that will inform media workers and shapers about the vision and potential of disabled people; a book that will help students of many ages to understand the interaction of disability with the media. If this book leads to more disabled people entering the media professions, and making high and handsome, proud and pertinent, the imagery of disabled people and disability in the years to come, all who have laboured on it will be rewarded beyond measure.

Paddy Masefield, Chair, Editorial Advisory Group, August 1995

Introduction

This book is intended to be an accessible 'first step' towards enabling students and devotees of film and television to develop and apply critiques and analysis to the representation of disabled people, a process that is much more developed in American media studies than here in Britain.

Parts 1 and 2 (Film and Television) demonstrate the ways in which disabled people have been manipulated by imagery and stereotyping in order to fulfil the 'needs' of the non-disabled film- or programme-maker and audience. Disabled characters abound, but the ways in which they are portrayed and the development of narrative around them is relentlessly repetitive. Frustratingly, while it can be assumed that all media studies courses will now probably contain modules that introduce students not only to the notion of cultural diversity (e.g. the representation of women, black people, gay men and lesbians) but to the work and intellectual positions of a diversity of film-makers and other media practitioners, what has not yet been routinely added to this 'diversity' is the notion of disability as open to analysis or of disabled people as artistic contributors to the culture.

Readers of the Contents may be surprised to see that approximately half of the book (Parts 3, 4 and 5) is devoted not to film and television content but to access to employment and training and the development of a disability arts movement. It is suggested that it is mainly through this area of activity that expressions of resistance to the dominant 'ablist' ideology and images are being developed. A knowledge of this infrastructure is essential to understanding future possibilities, and a function of this book is to present evidence of the crucial role of access barriers in perpetuating a situation in which non-disabled people's views of disability are still the dominant ones in the media.

Identification of the many disempowering stereotypes of disabled people portrayed in film and television is a necessary exercise, but it becomes a sterile one unless connections to the structures that give rise to and perpetuate them are made.

While it is undoubtedly too simplistic to say that the treatment of disabled people in film and television would improve if the films and other media 'products' were made by disabled people (since they are themselves conditioned within the negative cultural climate around disability), one might at least expect more variation of representation. It is also too simplistic to talk about 'negative' compared with 'positive' images because although disabled people are in general fairly clear about what might constitute the former, the identification of 'positive' is fraught with difficulty. Some accepted ideas of 'positive' may include the suspect 'triumph over tragedy' stories, often with the emphasis on physicality of a 'compensating' or fulfilling nature, whether these are stories of fictitious blind skaters or real wheelchair basketball champions.

Most of the writers in this book are disabled and some will refer to the medical and social models of disability.

Put at its briefest, the medical model assumes that the impairment or condition a person has is the key problem, the responses to which are 'cure' or 'care'. If the condition is not curable, the appropriate response of the disabled person is seen to lie somewhere on a spectrum between at one end 'a realistic acceptance of their condition' and at the other a 'denial of its existence with affirmations of "normality"'. Part of the impairment may be deemed to be the person's 'bitter' response, but what is

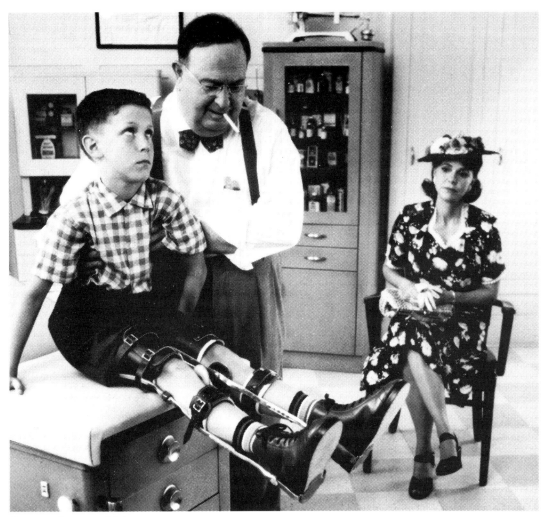

Forrest Gump, 1994

made clear is that it is the *impairment* that constitutes the disability, made worse or better by the individual's own attitude towards it.

In the social model the impairment is seen as much less important. Instead it is a disabling environment, the attitudes of others (not the disabled person), and institutional structures that are the problems requiring solution. Disability is thus not a fixed condition but a social construct and open to action and modification. One may have an impairment (or 'condition') but in the right setting and with the right aids and attitudes one may not be disabled by it.

Even in this wide range of pieces, readers may find the number of con-

tributors who refer to or explain the social model somewhat repetitive, but it cannot be emphasised too strongly how much this perspective on disability distinguishes the disabled or informed critique from the predominant non-disabled and media view.

Regarding language, the editors will use the phrase 'disabled people' rather than 'people with disabilities' which holds some problems for people committed to the social model.[1] However, some contributors use a mix of both, while in general avoiding the now outdated word 'handicap' and the offensive phrase 'the disabled'. References to the Deaf community, which identifies itself as a linguistic minority with a distinctive Deaf culture, will in some articles, as is increasingly customary, appear with a capital D. Deafness the impairment will generally appear with the lower-case 'd', as in 'deaf'/'deafness'.

With regard to images (and language) it is fallacious to assume that all disabled people think the same way, or that the critical disabled person is not sometimes entertained by images that on an intellectual level he or she rejects.[2] The complexity of make-up of the disabled audience is therefore addressed at the end of Part 4.

What this book does not tackle is the representation of disabled people in the press, although some of the ideology underpinning fictional and factual representation in television in Part 2 is clearly transferable. Nor does it attempt to cover photography and advertising. Instead, readers are referred to the major contribution of David Hevey, in his book *The Creatures Time Forgot: Photography and Disability Imagery*.[3]

What we hope to contribute, apart from a British perspective on disability portrayal, is a firmer incorporation of cultural issues. Emerging critiques of film and television have come from a political 'disability movement' fed in part by an active disability arts movement in which issues of identity and control are central.

We hope that this book will be helpful as a 'starter' for media students who are brave enough to tackle what is a complex subject. Nevertheless, we hope too that disabled people themselves will find much to argue about, or identify with. Those of us who see ourselves as part of a 'movement', understanding the commonality of our experience and trying to work in solidarity to effect change, nevertheless are also aware of the enormous differences in our experiences as disabled people, particularly where they cross those other cultural borders of race, gender and sexuality.

There are tales in the book not only of estrangement from non-disabled people, but also of estrangement between disabled people as they search for their own truths or reflections. However, we do not regard estrangement itself as negative, but rather the lack of recognition of its existence. A fundamental complaint of disabled critics is not simply that film-makers or 'the media' represent disability in stereotypical, rigid and repetitious ways, but that they fail to recognise the phenomenon of misrepresentation in relation to disability.

Notes

1. C. Barnes, *Disabling Imagery and the Media: An Exploration of the Principles for Media Representations of Disabled People* (Halifax: Ryburn with BCODP, 1992).
2. P. Darke, Introductory booklet notes, for the disability film season *Screening Lies* held at the Watershed, Bristol, June–July 1995.
3. D. Hevey, *The Creatures Time Forgot: Photography and Disability Imagery* (London: Routledge, 1992).

'Cripples' and disfigurement a speciality – Lon Chaney in *Phantom of the Opera*, 1925

Part One

Cinema Portrayal

Introduction

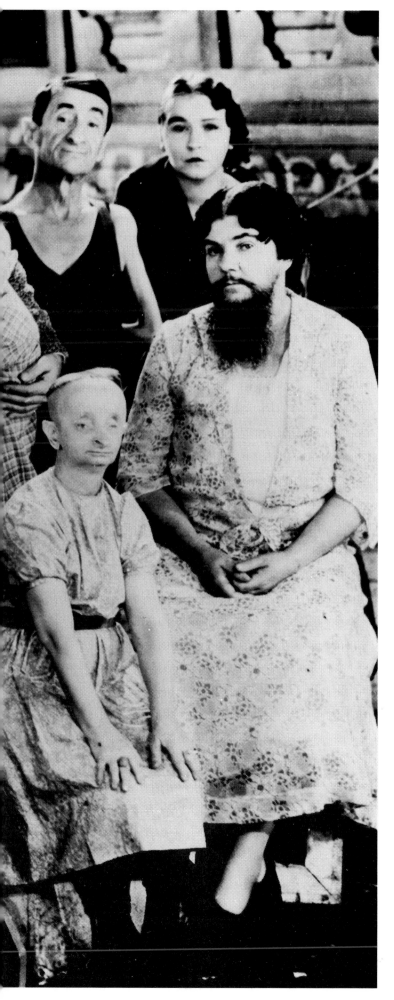

Although cinema has developed conventions of its own, much of its treatment of disability is rooted in a culture that has for centuries used the impaired body to signify sins past, sins present and the threat of future evil. The simplistic equation of beauty with goodness and ugliness with badness is intrinsic to our fairy-tales and is recycled with each retelling; and at the supposedly less primitive end we have the Greek myths and an Old Testament legacy that does not allow 'the blind man, or a lame, or he that hath a flat nose, or any thing superfluous, or a man that is broken footed, or brokenhanded, or crookbackt, or a dwarf, or that hath a blemish in his eye, or be scurvy, or scabbed' to 'approach to offer the bread of his God'.[1]

It is easy to manipulate metaphor by giving the 'good' (though powerless) dwarf a hunchback to transform him into something much more frightening and threatening. It is less easy for people, whether they are movie-makers or shopkeepers, to connect these internalised and discomfiting images with those real disabled people who are increasingly on the streets and who expect to be treated like one of themselves.

A case in point is the vast literature on the monster genre, in which there are assumed to be no parts of an audience who will be decoding these 'monster messengers' rather differently from the producers or the non-disabled audience. Disability is rarely mentioned, except perhaps, when the subject of Tod Browning's *Freaks* comes up, yet still the language of the discussion tends to call the disabled actors who took part 'freaks' and not disabled people; they have acquired a reality as something other than human even when not in role. Perhaps we

'I want something that out-horrors Frankenstein' Irving Thalberg
Tod Browning's *Freaks*, 1932

have particular problems with 'the little people'; while for instance seven blind people on stage are clearly seen as 'disabled', seven dwarfs are not.

When the monster 'problem' is considered, it is as quickly rationalised, neutralised and dismissed. Take, for example, this comment from a University of Illinois academic: 'These movies are a way of seeing our fears dealt with in a manageable way. It has a satisfying effect in the sense that we have confronted our worst fears and coped with them. We have seen these horrors and we come out okay.'[2] And Bruno Bettelheim writes: 'Those who outlawed traditional folk fairy-tales decided that if there were any monsters in fairy-tales they must all be friendly. But they missed the monsters a child knows best and is most concerned with: the monster he feels or fears himself to be and which also sometimes persecutes him.'[3] The perceived usefulness of this catharsis has questionable implications for the visibly disabled child.

What it is hoped is that some of the pieces in this section will raise 'problems' in relation to the representation of disabled people in film.

At its theoretically simplest, we can identify the five main elements of communication, according to Watson and Hill,[4] and apply these in a basic way to disability portrayal:

1. **the message** (e.g. a visual disability image) is sent, in a form initiated and encoded by the

2. **sender**, who is generally non-disabled; thence transmitted via

3. media **channels** which may be inaccessible to some disabled people, who as audience are

4. **receivers** along with non-disabled people; that message having

5. **an effect**, or outcome, on both.

One could argue that historically, disabled people have decoded the messages about disability in similar ways to non-disabled people, whether those messages appear in fairy stories, literature, film or works of art, and have come up with the same effect or result. At an unconscious level this would be true although in effect many of these messages could be said to be more dangerous for disabled people to absorb because they are so disempowering. As the phrase goes, 'we internalise our own oppression'.

When disabled and non-disabled people come to attempt consciously to decode the messages then the message is often perceived very differently, as is the analysis of effect. The difference, however, is not simply in a different decoding, but in the absolute lack of recognition by non-disabled writers, researchers, academics and practitioners that there is anything much there at all that does not more properly fit under another heading, for example medical, monster and fairy-tale.

Of course there are (what some might call) *the* disability movies, where disabled people are absolutely central (*The Men, My Left Foot*) but medical model encoding and decoding underpins any analysis. The less obvious but daily output from Hollywood or on our TV screens tends to be ignored. Cartoon characters like Mr Magoo, the Bond movie villains, Dr Strangelove and Captain Hook (not perceived as disabled) all tend to escape deconstruction from a disability perspective.

The time has come to move on, if not in terms of product at least in terms of 'knowing what we see'. That it affects our attitudes to disabled people and the attitudes of disabled people to themselves is, I believe, incontrovertible.

In this section of the book, **Paul Darke** gives an overview of Hollywood and British cinema's treatment of disability; **Allan Sutherland** discusses the use of body difference as visual metaphor; and **Jenny Morris** looks at some films from a feminist perspective.

For the purposes of analysis, there are a number of ways of classifying disability films, and the next three contributions are impairment based: **Andy Kimpton-Nye** looks at the way learning disabled characters are used, with particular reference to *Forrest Gump*; **Paul Darke** looks at *Blink*, a film featuring a blind woman; and **John Schuchman** examines the representation of Deaf people in the cinema.

Finally, **Chris Davies**, in two pieces, talks to writer **Richard Curtis** and producer **Sir David Puttnam** about commercial considerations and disability.

'NOT THE MIDDLE AGES'

Often in our seats at the cinema we are no more than a breath away from those images in our secret soul that powerfully combine in literature, myth and metaphor and occasionally these escape:

As we went along the path that leads across the tiny bridge to the cathedral we ran a gauntlet not just of beggars but of cripples and wheelchairs and of helpless mental patients, drooling and quivering and jerking palsied limbs. When I stopped to find some money the wheelchairs charged and crashed together.

An ancient woman in a brown shawl who had been standing silently watching on her crutches suddenly heaved forward, using a crutch to sweep away the legs from under two of the pressing beggars and pinioned my arm, snatching at the handful of change. A heave of her buttock and a wheelchair was skidded aside. One of the droolers howled like a dog and began to have what looked like an epileptic fit.

I backed away to the church, and left them snarling in this almost medieval scene, this cameo from Breughel in the city that had just been re-named St. Petersburg.[5]
Not a film, nor a fiction, but a straight report from the *Guardian*'s Russian correspondent in August 1991. A letter of complaint went unacknowledged.

Notes
1. Leviticus 21: 16–20.
2. Richard Leskosky, University of Illinois, quoted in John Stanley, *The Creature Features Movie Guide Strikes Again*, 4th edn. (Pacifica, CA: Creatures at Large Press, 1994), p. 9.
3. Bruno Bettelheim, *The Uses of Enchantment: The Power and Importance of Fairy Tales* (Harmondsworth: Penguin, 1978).
4. J. Watson and A. Hill, *A Dictionary of Communication and Media Studies* (Edward Arnold, 1989).
5. Martin Walker, 'Power of the People', the weekend *Guardian*, 24–25 August 1991.

Everywhere: Disability on film
Paul Darke

Paul Anthony Darke is currently finishing his Ph.D. on 'Representations of Disability in Post-War British Films', at the University of Warwick; having survived the special school system he started late in higher education. Now aged thirty-three, and married with a son, he has written extensively on images of disability in the movies in *DAM*, *LINK* magazine, *Disability and Society* and a number of other journals. He has been a consultant, contributor and jury member at numerous disability film festivals in Europe.

Darke opens his overview of disability on film with a look at the way Martin Norden in *The Cinema of Isolation* has organised and classified cinema's portrayal of physical disability.[1]

Darke himself views the representation of disability as archetypal, and of a 'naturalness' that demands challenge; he also argues that simply letting disabled people take control of the images themselves would not make as significant a difference as one might hope.

The genealogy of Western culture's disability imagery in the cinema is expertly detailed in Martin F. Norden's book *The Cinema of Isolation*.[2] His classification of disability imagery by period is quite revealing of how the images relate to disabled people's own contemporary social situation and status; the technological capabilities of the film industry at any given time; and the political climate of the day.

FOUR ERAS
For Norden the cinematic conception and construction of disability can be broken down into four main eras: first, before World War II disability is constructed as 'freakish'; then, immediately post-war, it improves to become what he terms 'rehabilitative'; in the third period from the 1950s on, it degenerates and reverts once more to a freakish perspective; and finally, from the mid-70s, there is a swing to a more enlightened and tolerant stance, linked in the USA to the returning Vietnam War veteran contingent and in Britain to left-wing liberalism, and combined with a desire for the international film industry to facilitate the rehabilitation of a divided world (the legacy of the 60s).

From the cinema's conception right up until the end of World War II, there can be no doubt that disability was predominantly seen and shown as 'freakish'. The enormous success of Lon Chaney – the man of a thousand faces – in roles such as 'Dead Legs' in *West of Zanzibar* and 'The Armless Wonder' in *The Unknown* is a prime example of this, but the rise of the horror genre also meant it was not just a trend but rather a financially expedient option for the studios. When Tod Browning (Lon Chaney's usual director) was making *Freaks*, he was ordered to top the horror of *Frankenstein*. This he easily did, and to such an extent that it was banned in the UK until the 60s. Regrettably, this was done primarily because the film was thought to be in bad taste, not because of its inappropriate and inaccurate portrayal and use of disabled people in the film.

Norden also points out in his early chapters that there are some types of representation that seem to be particularly enduring: the 'sweet innocent' (the many versions of *Pollyanna* and Tiny Tim in *A Christmas Carol* are just two examples); the 'noble warrior' (gloriously exemplified by the British silent film *Kitty* but ever-present in contemporary cinema in the guise of *Rambo*); and the 'obsessive avenger' (any portrayal of Long John Silver or Captain Hook, right through its more recent incarnation in Freddy Kruger) provide ample proof of this long enduring misrepresentation of disability.

In the period of rehabilitative representation after World War II, many films had plots that revolved around returning veterans, some of whom were disabled. The most notable of these films were the multi-Oscar-winning *The Best Years of Our Lives* and *The Pride of The Marines* with John Garfield as a blind marine. The perspective also extended to other disabled groups such as deaf people in *Johnny Belinda*: the tale of a deaf, speech-impaired, young girl who has been raped. While the treatment of the deaf girl is sympathetic and sensitive, it is the non-deaf doctor who can sign who is the instrument of her rehabilitation. Though this was an advance on the representation of disabled people typical in the first half-century of cinema, it was still fairly shallow, and was more about validating society's own conception of normality and its boundaries than accepting difference. British cinema seemed to be little different when the Douglas Bader biopic *Reach for the Sky* with Kenneth More was produced in 1956.

Regrettably – and Norden is very convincing here – under the rise of McCarthyism and the House Committee on Un-American Activities, some of those liberals who had instigated the positive changes in disability imagery were forced out of Hollywood and the 'freakish' images returned; further versions of *Treasure Island* and other literary adaptations are the best examples, with Disney contributing its enormously successful *Peter Pan*. The film *Bad Day at Black Rock* combined many elements of disability representation, synthesising the 'obsessive avenger', 'noble warrior', 'supercrip' and 'freakish' together in the guise of the one-armed Spencer Tracy character, John Macreedy.

America's paranoia movies of the cold war era facilitated an easy avenue for the simplification of complex issues. In Britain, the rise of Hammer Films and its regurgitation of formulaic horror stories ensured that disability returned to the bad old days of pre-war imagery.

ENTERTAINMENT AND SIMPLICITY

The entertainment value of disability imagery is an often forgotten aspect of the persistence of negative images that is especially relevant to any discussion of the 'freakish' image of disability. The entertainment content of such images also helps us to explain why civil rights for disabled people have been slow in coming. Entertainment works by creating a simplified world where problems are individualised (and, as such, only solvable by the individuals affected) and where social problems and groups are marginalised and deemed to be responsible for their own suffering and salvation; the medical model and the social model of disability being apposite examples of this in the social sphere. Consequently, society is absolved of any responsibility while at the same time it is left unchallenged and unaffected.

The simplest method by which the problem of disability is solved, as cinema

The Waterdance, 1991

and society see it, is for it to be remedied either by medical or miracle methods, that is, the cure (from *Torch Song* to *Monkey Shines*). Alternatively, it can be made to disappear, i.e. by death (from *The Penalty* to *Afraid of the Dark*). Either way, the audience is entertained and the problem resolved before their eyes: disability, to the non-disabled audience, remains a tragic state of being and the marginalised continue to be blamed for their own

situation. The status quo is intact.

Formula films, or genre movies, seem to have played a key part in perpetuating disability's image as one-dimensionally bad. It is interesting to note that the return to 'bad' imagery in the 50s and 60s was concomitant with the rise of the techno-films of James Bond and the Hammer Horror films (both British), in which good and evil – predominantly simplified for cinematic expediency as normality and abnormality – fight for control of the world, with good (normality) invariably being the victor. The best examples of each are perhaps Blofeld in *Goldfinger* and 'Jaws' in both *The Spy Who Loved Me* and *Moonraker*, and the assortment of characters with impairments in such films as *Asylum* and *Dr Terror's House of Horrors*. 'Normality' is thus validated at the expense of 'abnormality' in a simplified way that fulfils the audience's desire for easy, simplistic entertainment and self-validation.

Only in the late 1960s did a more liberal image emerge, one that concentrated on seeing disability as 'differently able', similar in many respects to the post-World War II 'rehabilitative' imagery of disability, or what Norden calls the 'enlightened' era of disability imagery. Though not a great step forward, it was an improvement of sorts. *Tell Me That You Love Me Junie Moon* is a transitional film that could easily pass in both the 'freakish' era and the 'enlightened' one (but then it was directed by the maverick Otto Preminger).[3] More recently the 'enlightened' perspective can be seen at work in films as apparently disparate as *The Elephant Man*, *My Left Foot*, *Passion Fish* and *The Waterdance*. This is not to say that the 'freakish' perspective has lost any of its appeal, only that variations previously not in existence have crept in to the repertoire of disability imagery.

Unfortunately, cure, death and tragedy have been a part of every era's representations of disability in cinema and in culture in general. One cannot help but feel that this is also part of the entertainment value of disability, mainly because the images are made for, and almost exclusively by, non-disabled people who wish to have their own lifestyles validated. It is, in reality, a misnomer to talk of the stereotypes of disability imagery; the stranglehold that able-bodied people have over the definition of disability makes their representation of us, 'the disabled', more akin to being archetypal in conception. Disability, to the non-disabled society and image maker, is a world-wide and eternal truth that is for them so obviously correct that it cannot be challenged. Disability has for so long been defined in the limited and archetypal manner described above that its endurance is paradoxically both baffling (in the face of our reality) and totally understandable (in the face of their hatred and fear). It is in this area of the rigidity, of the apparent 'naturalness', of disability imagery that disabled film-makers can begin to challenge the images. The persistence of archetypal imagery of disability in mainstream cinema is so strong that it must be doubted that we (or 'them') have reduced it to the level of stereotype.

In cinematic terms disability is interchangeable with impairment, and the problems that arise from the state of being are represented as being created by the individuals themselves. The disabled character who is represented as a bitter person with an attitudinal problem that needs confronting is a fairly standard type in films such as *The Men, Duet for One* and *The Raging Moon*. These films epitomise the medical model of disability whereby it is neither the environment nor society's attitude that are the problem but the disabled character's own attitude. Consequently, the disability movement, which separates 'disability' and 'impairment', is neutralised as a political force while the true causes of disability (socially constructed environs, institutions and attitudes) are left unchallenged. Almost all films with a disability element have such characteristics, yet – and this is the exciting part of any long-term analysis of disability in films – they remain entirely different in style, content and variety of representations. This enables us to explore many aspects of the images in a framework that is quite coherent.

MAKING A DIFFERENCE?

It is often claimed that the way forward is to have films about impairment and disability made by disabled people themselves, but such arguments are naive. One would be hard pushed to differentiate between the 'good' and the 'bad' with any degree of clarity or certainty, and what is certain is that some images that I don't like as a disabled person, other disabled people will see as an affirmation of their own experiences. Nor would one wish to derogate or dismiss those disabled people who have taken great pleasure from those so-called 'dodgy' images and films. Such reductionism ignores the persuasiveness of the images and the manner in which they entertain; often the pleasure I have received from watching a highly suspect film has been much greater than when I have watched a deeply earnest and 'right on' film.

The process by which entertainment reduces complex issues to simplistic individualised concerns partly explains why simply letting disabled people have control of the images themselves will not, I would argue, make the significant difference that one would hope. Disabled people are as equally socialised into seeing disability as negative as those who are non-disabled, and their own images of themselves can tend to concentrate upon their own personal triumphs or tragedies, images for which there is a ready market. Not unexpectedly, disabled people's autobiographies regularly become bestsellers and the film versions feature as 'TV Movie of the Week'. When a more difficult social, rather than personal, image is presented, it rarely reaches a wide audience; it ceases to be entertainment and, more often than not, is ghettoised as propaganda. This is one of the major dichotomies facing the disability movement and there are no simple answers.

Notes

1. M. Norden, *The Cinema of Isolation* (New Brunswick, NJ: Rutgers University Press, 1994). Surprisingly, Norden confines himself to the treatment of physical disability, which, while in itself an abundant source, leaves out the very important strand of portrayal relating to mental illness.
2. Op. cit.
3. See Norden, pp. 236–7, for a detailed story breakdown.

Hump

I hear you snigger when I say
Hump
Do you think I hadn't noticed
The shape of my own back?
Do you think I didn't wince
When as a child they said
'She's got the hump'
Do you think I didn't shrivel inside
When the Hunchback of Notre Dame
Flickered on to the T.V. screen?
Do you think I didn't hide
In the thick silence of unspoken thoughts?
Do you think I didn't learn fast
That in England
To be straight is to be good?

Sue Napolitano

(extract from 'Hump' in Dangerous Woman: Poems
by Sue Napolitano, GMCDP Publications, 1995)

The Hunchback of Notre Dame, 1939

Black hats and twisted bodies
Allan Sutherland

Commissioned as a BFI Essay and first published in DAM vol. 3 no. 1, Spring 1993.

ALLAN SUTHERLAND is a scriptwriter for radio and television, and his work for television (with writing partner Stuart Morris) has included the pilot disability sitcom *Inmates* and more recently contributions to *Eastenders*. In 1981, he programmed (with Stephen Dwoskin) a season of disability films called *Carry on Cripple*, at the NFT, and has contributed articles and reviews to a number of newspapers and magazines, including *Sight and Sound*, *Time Out* and *City Limits*. He contributed research to David Thompson's *Biographical Dictionary of the Cinema*.[1] He is also author of *Disabled We Stand*.[2]

In this essay Sutherland explores visual metaphors associated with physical difference – and the cinematic conventions that set physically different characters apart as alien or 'other'. Such differences are not, he argues, confined only to those characters who are 'overtly disabled'.

He also looks at myths associated with particular impairments and is more optimistic than Darke on the potential for disabled people to escape the portrayals of the past.

In *Screenplay*, the American screenwriting guru Syd Field urges his readers to tell stories visually. 'Pictures, or images, reveal aspects of character,' he observes, accurately enough, but then goes on to give a most curious example:

In Robert Rossen's classic film *The Hustler*, a physical defect symbolises an aspect of character. The girl played by Piper Laurie is a cripple; she walks with a limp. She is also an emotional cripple; she drinks too much, has no sense of aim or purpose in life. The physical limp underscores her emotional qualities – visually.[3]

Field's argument is in fact deeply flawed. The problem with it is that his analysis only works if one uses the same form of words. As soon as one describes the character in another way, it falls apart: she 'has an emotional limp', she is 'emotionally physically challenged'. What Field describes is the visual representation of a linguistic metaphor, which would be a very complicated, not to say inefficient, way of story-telling.

That's not what's going on, of course. Hollywood teaches writers to write in pictures ('Show, don't tell!') because of the greater emotional power and immediacy of the visual image. Any screenwriter whose images had to be translated into a specific form of words before being comprehensible would be out of a job.

Despite his sloppy analysis, Fields is by no means completely wrong. The limp does clearly provide a deliberate visual motif. It is put there to tell us something about the character, and, by its constant presence, to remind us of that facet of the characterisation. And what we are being told is fairly much as Field has outlined.

What's going on here is rather cruder than the sophisticated verbal correlation suggested by Field. The visual image has its effect because it evokes a simple negative stereotype of disability. Seeing the character limping, one is supposed to understand immediately that this is a loser, one of life's outsiders.

And it works. For a lot of the audience it works because that's how they see disability. Where the best writing creates believability based on a recognition of truth, negative stereotyping creates believability based on familiar falsehoods. Personally, I wouldn't say that was good writing. It is certainly not the sort of practice someone of Field's stature should be encouraging young writers to emulate.

More specifically, this provides an example of what David Hevey has described as 'the body as the signifier of difference for disabled people'.[4] Hevey makes the comment while discussing charity advertising: he traces its roots in the nineteenth-century pseudo-science of eugenics and Victorian 'categorisation photography', which, by attempting to demonstrate that certain physical features indicated a criminal mentality, 'sought to prove that bodily difference entailed difference in the entire psychic and social behaviour and make-up'.

This idea that visible physical difference automatically denotes a more fundamental 'otherness' is one of the most basic elements of the film vocabulary. Obviously, one can make connections with the idea of the 'twisted mind in a twisted body', which can be traced back to biblical references and is evident in characterisations such as Shakespeare's Richard III. But one should, I think, be wary of making too simplistic a link, and thereby underestimating the extent to which this is a purely cinematic convention.

The cinematic convention about physical difference varies from previous stereotypes of disability in two major ways. First, it is not confined to characters who are overtly defined as disabled. (Thus, when I speak of 'physical difference', I am not simply employing a euphemism for disability.) At its most evident in horror and science fiction movies, the convention specifies that whenever one sees a character who is basically humanoid in form, yet visibly distinct from the norm, that character is not merely physically, but also mentally 'not one of us'. From Frankenstein's monster to the 'Creature from the Black Lagoon', physical abnormality is used to denote menace.

Second, it is a purely visual convention. The language of cinema was originally the language of silent cinema. As such, it evolved an increasingly complex and sophisticated visual vocabulary, drawing upon a multiplicity of sources. Lon Chaney, the 'Man of a Thousand Faces' and almost as many bodies, was pure Americana. But European expressionism was developing an entirely distinct set of visual devices. As the rise of Nazism drove European directors (most notably Fritz Lang) to Hollywood, the mingling of these separate traditions produced a highly potent mix.

Cinema has remained a medium that is more visual than linguistic. It looks to make things visual, and to attach meaning to visual appearance. At its simplest, the bad guys wear the black hats. So when visible disability is introduced into films, it tends to carry some such meaning. It often acts as metaphor; when, in *For a Few Dollars More* (1965), Sergio Leone made Klaus Kinski a hunchback by way of indicating the irredeemably evil quality of the character, he was following in a long tradition.

Impairment is equally often used as

Lon Chaney in *West of Zanzibar*, 1928

motive. Thus, in *The Penalty* (1926) Lon Chaney played Blizzard, a gangster who had been driven to evil activity by his bitterness at losing his legs; a final scene showed a fantasy 'happy ending' with Blizzard, legs restored, whole again – but dead: the total summary of all that some would like to see for disabled people.

But film draws on received ideas, that which is in the culture. Physical impairment becomes in itself characterisation. Movies both draw on existing stereotypes and reinforce such received ideas.

One thing that is extraordinary is the variety of meanings that disability has in cinema. Every specific impairment has its own mythology. A limp, for example, indicates a deficient character, a loser. This might be Piper Laurie, or it might be Dustin Hoffman's Ratso in *Midnight Cowboy* (1969). Such characters are seen as pathetic rather than tragic. Unlike hunchbacks or blind people, they are not seen as completely 'other' but as an inadequate or incomplete form of able-bodied person. For a woman, loss of 'attractiveness' means she's a sexual loser, denied the role of wife and mother. If in a relationship, she is implicitly over-dependent on it, because she's not likely to find another.

Similarly, blind people are wise, ampu-

tees are bitter, hunchbacks are twisted. It is by no means a matter of a single blanket view of 'the disabled'.

There are even alternative stereotypes of the same disability. Blindness can be a sign of wisdom and supernatural ability (the hermit in *Frankenstein*, or the Japanese series of popular films about a blind samurai) or it may be a symbol of vulnerability (*Wait until Dark*, the 1967 British thriller that had Audrey Hepburn playing a blind woman pursued by a psychotic killer).

In examples such as these, disability stereotypes are used to give a rapidly recognisable characterisation, or to add an extra twist to an otherwise routine plot. Thus 'woman being terrorised by a killer' is familiar stuff, 'blind woman terrorised by killer' less so.

Because this whole process is largely about visual immediacy, non-visible disabilities are much less common. Where they are covered, films can often be observed working to make them visible, as with Dustin Hoffman's shambling Raymond in *Rain Man* (1988). (Though it is tricky to draw entirely hard conclusions, as Hoffman's portrayal is a kind of compendium of autism, incorporating a set of characteristics which it would be most unusual to find within a single person.)

Another tactic, particularly with disabilities that are more mental than physical, is the use of subjective or 'point of view' shots to give greater visual power – an approach exploited to the hilt in Hitchcock's *Spellbound* (1945), in which psychoanalyst Ingrid Bergman falls for Gregory Peck, who may be a killer, but, being also amnesiac, can't remember. In what was publicised as 'the first picture on psychoanalysis', the old master exploited everything from flashback to a set of dream sequences designed by Salvador Dali.

The drawback to such techniques is that they have the effect of locating disability firmly in the area of personal problem. It is no surprise, perhaps, that *Spellbound* bears strong similarities to another picture released the same year, *The Lost Weekend*, Billy Wilder's portrayal of alcoholism.

Some films of course are specifically about disability. Movies such as *Johnny Belinda* (1948), *The Elephant Man* (1980), *Whose Life Is It Anyway?* (1981) and *Mask* (1985) take disability as their central concern. Such films vary enormously in quality, from the vomit-making *Terry Fox Story* (one-legged boy hops across Canada) to the raw emotional honesty of *The Miracle Worker* (1962), Arthur Penn's intelligent film about Helen Keller and her governess.

Note, incidentally, how a key feature of most of these is the presence of an able-bodied figure, such as a doctor or parent, who provides either a cure or social acceptance. Disabled people, in such films, are almost invariably incapable of achieving independence on their own.

One should not, however, confuse films that take disability itself as a subject with movies which use disability as a metaphor. In Oliver Stone's *Born on the Fourth of July* the real subject is the failure of the American Dream, disability being simply a metaphor for that failure (albeit a metaphor that treats disability as loss). The failure to distinguish between such different approaches is one of the most frequent causes of false analyses of film by the disability community.

Born on the Fourth of July is an example of a very well-established genre, the 'home from the war' movie. Each time this century that the United States has gone to war it has given rise to a set of films about returning soldiers: *The Big Parade* (1925), *Best Years of Our Lives* (1946), *The Men* (1950), *Coming Home* (1978). The intriguing thing about many of these is that they involve disability (a fairly obvious symbol of loss), taking it for granted that disability needs adjusting to, yet regard that as merely one of a number of varying kinds of adjustment being made by returning veterans.

A somewhat more complex post-war disability related symbolism occurs in the thriller *Bad Day at Black Rock* (1954). A one-armed war veteran (Spencer Tracy) arrives in a small desert town, superficially to bring his dead comrade's war medals back to his family. But the dead man was a Japanese-American, and what emerges is a story of murder and land-grabbing, covered up by an entire community – the first film to recognise America's bad treatment of its Japanese citizens during the war.

The fact that this film chooses to make its hero an amputee is very intriguing. The film is in no way about adjusting to disability; I do not remember whether the hero's lack of a limb is even mentioned in the dialogue. Its significance is evidently symbolic. But symbolic of what?

First, it stands for the fact that Tracy's character is a war hero, someone who has been away to serve his country and seen action. The missing arm is almost a sign of moral worth. Had he, by contrast, been a wheelchair user, he would have been not hero, but victim. Or at least someone engaged in 'coming to terms' with his disability, like Brando's character in *The Men*. (The semiology of these things can get highly complex.)

But the body is still the signifier of difference. The amputation gives Tracy's character an almost non-human quality. He is in some ways a mythic figure: on one level an individual American, performing a task for his dead comrade; on another he is an avenging angel. The arm is the visible symbol of that darker side.

It is worth noting how films about disability tend to concern able-bodied people who have become disabled. Sometimes this is purely in the interest of a 'happy ending', using a disability that will be subject to an eventual cure. More often, it is simply to increase identification with the character, almost as though it has to be made clear that this story is tragic, because it has happened to a 'real' person.

Films about people with congenital disabilities are much rarer. When they do occur, they tend to present the character as tragic and isolated: *The Hunchback of Notre Dame* (1923/1939), *The Heart Is a Lonely Hunter* (1968), *The Elephant Man*, *Mask*.

Alternatively, the disabled character is of interest insofar as they affect an able-bodied person. Thus, in *Rain Man*, the film is not the story of Hoffman's character, but of the able-bodied yuppie (Tom Cruise) who becomes humanised by the growing relationship. We may threaten, we may redeem, it seems, but we are not too often of interest for our own selves. (One undervalued exception to this rule is *My Left Foot*. I have heard a lot of complaints about the casting of this film, but few attempts to assess how far it benefits from the work of Christy Brown, the disabled writer on whose

autobiography it was based.)

Is it, then, possible to escape from film history? Can we throw off this dead weight of received interpretations, to create real, interesting disabled characters, and fresh, exciting stories about disability? It is, and we can. The very fact that previous representations of disability have been narrow, confused and unimaginative leaves the way open for disabled writers and film-makers. What we can produce can blow the past away.

Look at a 40s Hollywood movie, and watch the embarrassing portrayals of black people, all rolling eyes and demeaning 'Lawdy Massa' joke characterisation. We don't see those now, because nobody believes them. Black actors, writers and film-makers have made them impossible. Disabled people already see cinematic representations of disability as being equally demeaning and unrealistic. As audiences and film industry start to see disability through our eyes, to have their perceptions of disability conditioned by our creations, tragic cripples will become as much things of the past as those rolling-eyed niggers.

Notes
1. D. Thompson (ed.), *Biographical Dictionary of the Cinema* (London: Secker & Warburg).
2. A.T. Sutherland, *Disabled We Stand* (London: Souvenir Press, 1981).
3. Syd Fields, *Screenplay: The Foundations of Screenwriting*, expanded edition (New York: Dell, 1982).
4. D. Hevey, *The Creatures Time Forgot* (London: Routledge, 1992).

A feminist perspective
Jenny Morris

From Chapter 4, 'Disability in Western Culture', in Pride Against Prejudice: Transforming Attitudes to Disability (The Women's Press, 1991).

Jenny Morris is a feminist writer and researcher. Most recently, she has edited a collection of writings by disabled women, *Encounters with Strangers: Feminism and Disability*.[1]

'Disability in Western Culture', Chapter 4 of Morris's wide-ranging book *Pride Against Prejudice*, was not written primarily as a contribution to film analysis; nevertheless, in what is a sparse field it goes further than many intentional books, with a feminist analysis that is refreshing both in its rarity and the acuteness of its perception. As a disabled woman reader one was at last able to say, feelingly, 'oh yes', as films about which one felt great discomfort suddenly became transparent. Where disabled people are present in film or in television they are overwhelmingly men. As Morris points out, this may not be surprising: disability is so often a metaphor for dependency and women are already commonly used to present images of vulnerability and dependency.

…Where am I – as a disabled woman – in the general culture that surrounds me? Generally, I am not there… [Disabled people] all experience oppression as a result of the denial of our reality. If our reality is not reflected in the general culture, how can we assert our rights? If non-disabled people would rather not recognise disability, or only recognise specific form, how can they recognise our experience of our bodies? If we do not 'appear' as real people, with the need for love, affection, friendship, and the right to a good quality of life, how can non-disabled people give any meaning to our lives?

THE MEANING OF DISABILITY IN THE GENERAL CULTURE

It is often said that disabled men and women do not conform to stereotypes of physical attractiveness. To be a disabled man is to fail to measure up to the general culture's definition of masculinity as strength; to be a disabled woman is to fail to measure up to the definition of femininity as pretty passivity. Just as white skin is presented as the norm – in the sense of being both the average and the goal to be strived for – so lack of physical and learning 'impairment' is also the norm.

In an important sense, the non-disabled world defines physical and learning disability by their absence. To be considered beautiful is to give value to the absence of physical 'impairment'. This is the case even in the classic stereotype of the 'beautiful blind girl', for the recognition of her beauty is equivocal, conditional. Otherwise, what would be the relevance of her blindness?

Status and authority are also associated with an absence of disability. A person who is revered cannot be disabled, for this would be to detract, to take away, from his (or less often, her) appeal. The clearest illustration of this was the American president Franklin D. Roosevelt. Roosevelt was completely paralysed from the waist down, yet this was hidden from the American and international public. His aides, his family and the press went to enormous lengths to hide his disability, the automatic assumption being that a politician who then became president of the USA must not be seen to be weak and dependent. In particular, the public never saw him in a wheelchair for this was and continues to be the ultimate symbol of dependency and lack of autonomy.[2]

But there is much more to the cultural representation of disability than the way in which the norm is measured by the absence of disability. The way in which the culture interprets and uses the presence of disability is the very powerful other side of the coin. Just as beauty – and goodness – are defined by the absence of disability, so ugliness – and evil – are defined by its presence.

Writers over many years, in a number of different genres, have used physical and learning disability, and mental illness, to signify evil, badness, a state of something wrong. There are obvious examples of this: from Shakespeare's Richard III to Doris Lessing's *The Fifth Child* (which uses learning disability to transmit a profound sense of threat and unease); from Captain Hook to *The Phantom of the Opera*.

The crucial thing about these cultural representations of disability is that they say nothing about the lives of disabled people but everything about the attitudes of non-disabled people towards disability. Disability is used as a metaphor, as a code, for the message that the non-disabled writer wishes to get across, in the same way that 'beauty' is used. In doing this, the writer draws on the prejudice, ignorance and fear that generally exist towards disabled people,

knowing that to portray a character with a humped back, with a missing leg, with facial scars, will evoke certain feelings in the reader or audience. The more disability is used as a metaphor for evil, or just to induce a sense of unease, the more the cultural stereotype is confirmed.

In recent years, disability, and in particular disabled men, have also been used in a more complex way as a metaphor for dependency and lack of autonomy.

MASCULINITY AND PHYSICAL DISABILITY

The social definition of masculinity is inextricably bound up with a celebration of strength, of perfect bodies. At the same time, to be masculine is to be not vulnerable. It is also linked to a celebration of youth and of taking bodily functions for granted. The BBC film *Tumbledown* about a soldier injured in the Falklands War (inadvertently) exposed the cultural representation of ability and disability. 'I hate cripples, I always have,' said the hero, in his frustration at his dependence on wheelchair and crutches. The army had promised him physical strength and perfection (and authority), not the ignominy of being told off by a ward sister for being stupid enough to leave hospital while still seriously ill. His anger was part of his denial of his bodily frailty and vulnerability – and who was a mere woman to try to remind him of it?

The absence of physical 'impairment' is so clearly bound up with popular culture's images of masculinity that film-makers are able to use visible physical disability as a clear statement about a character. In the past, the most common statement has been about evil and wickedness; children's and adult fiction alike abound with bad men whose sinister threat is signified by a physical difference. More recently, film-makers

Fiona Shaw with Daniel Day Lewis in *My Left Foot,* 1989

have used disability as a metaphor for dependency and vulnerability and as a vehicle for exploring such experiences for men.

Two films, both released in 1990, had disabled men as their central characters and received much publicity for the way that they supposedly dealt with the reality of disability. *My Left Foot* was a British film based on the autobiography of writer and artist Christy Brown, who had cerebral palsy, while *Born on the Fourth of July* was an American film based on the true story of a Vietnam soldier, Ron Kovic, and portrayed his experience on returning home paralysed.

In fact, rather than being about disability, both these films, as critic Judith Williamson writes, are actually about how awful it is for a man to be dependent, in the emotional sense as much as the physical. 'These films are about the hell of dependency for men. And maybe the men have to be in wheelchairs for that dependency to be made vivid.' The films rely on the general association of impotence with disability, and on the association of heterosexuality

with a stereotyped masculinity.

'The strongest dynamic in these movies is the sense of sheer horror, for men, in being deprived of autonomy.'[3] This is heightened by both actors', Tom Cruise and Daniel Day Lewis, being, as Williamson puts it, 'world-famous sexy pin-ups'. She goes on,

What the image of disability does in these films is to take to breaking point the pain felt in situations not exclusive to disablement. Each man loses a lover (common enough) but the devastation and helplessness that ensue enter a whole different emotional register when they're compounded with humiliation ('not being a man').This gives great insight into what it is to be a man, disabled or not.

In *Born on the Fourth of July*, the character played by Tom Cruise has to confront not only the appalling lack of resources to meet the needs of those who returned from the Vietnam War permanently disabled, but also the fear that his physical disability will destroy his relationships with others. Judith Williamson writes, 'After "dead penis", Cruise's next scream is, "Who's gonna love me?" Worse than feeling unloved is feeling unlovable; which is precisely what the wheelchair seems to explain.'

Daniel Day Lewis's portrayal of Christy Brown's cerebral palsy in *My Left Foot* never moves beyond using disability as a metaphor for dependency. The story is little more than the traditional 'overcoming all odds' portrayal of disability (indeed Christy Brown himself called his autobiography, on which the film is based, 'my plucky little cripple story').

The film is based on two expressions of non-disabled people's prejudice against disabled people. The first is the reaction to Christy Brown painting and writing with his left foot. The wonder at what he produced is not an appreciation of his writing or his art but rather a wonder that it is done at all. The second expression of prejudice is a deeply patronising attitude towards Brown's love for a woman and his reaction to her announcement that she is marrying someone else. This was the scene which most reviewers of the film focused on, making much of Brown's drunken expression of anger. At a formal dinner in a restaurant, Christy Brown abuses the woman who has just told him she loves someone else, shouting and pulling the tablecloth off the table. In other words, he behaves in an oppressive, aggressive and intimidating manner, not an unusual thing for a non-disabled man to do but film critics seemed to think it was amazing for a disabled man to behave in this way. Somehow, it was supposed to be 'progressive' that a disabled man was portrayed as behaving in a thoroughly obnoxious way.

The makers of these films are not actually portraying the lives of disabled individuals; rather the disability is a vehicle for exploring the pain of dependency and vulnerability for men. A man in a wheelchair is an easily recognisable metaphor for a lack of autonomy, because this is how the general culture perceives disabled people. It may also be the safest way for men to explore their vulnerability, for they can separate themselves quite easily from the disabled character, who is clearly 'different' from the 'normal' man. The films do not challenge the stereotype; they use it and in so doing exploit us.

The emotions explored in both *Born on the Fourth of July* and *My Left Foot* are dependent on the stereotype that to be a man in a wheelchair is to be impotent, unable to be a (hetero)sexual being, and therefore not a complete' man. The link between heterosexuality and what it is to be a man is also crucial to *Coming Home*, an American film made in 1978, which, like *Born on the Fourth of July*, was also concerned with some of the issues raised by the Vietnam War.

However, *Coming Home* was very different in that the stereotype of disability is challenged in a fundamental way. Luke Martin (played by Jon Voight) may be paralysed but Sally (Jane Fonda) enjoys going to bed with him. Luke may be physically paralysed but it is Sally's husband Bob's emotional paralysis which is more disabling – both to their marriage and to himself. (Bob eventually commits suicide.) Luke holds the moral high ground. He is able to confront not only that the Vietnam War was wrong, but that what he did as a soldier was wrong. Bob, on the other hand, finds this too painful to live with; he cannot imagine a role for himself once the framework that created his role as an All-American hero is challenged.

Coming Home was a fundamentally subversive film. It wasn't only an anti-Vietnam War film but it also challenged

American male and female stereotypes. Luke Martin had more to offer as a real person than the upright and uptight Bob. The crossing over of Sally from a frigid, rigid, pillar of the WASP community to the kind of emotional reality that Luke represented was a triumph for a set of values which runs counter to the Great American Dream. In this sense, Luke's paralysis symbolised the positive alternative.

Coming Home was an exceptional film in that the daily details of life with paralysis are shown as an integral part of a real, powerful, autonomous person. However, as with *My Left Foot* and *Born on the Fourth of July*, it is impossible to imagine a woman in the role of the disabled character. It is impossible because essentially all three films are not about disability but about masculinity; they are vehicles for the exploration of stereotyped views on what it is to be a (heterosexual) man.

FEMININITY AND DISABILITY

As part of a research project carried out in 1986, some American college students were asked to write down whatever came to mind when they heard the phrase 'disabled woman'. Many students left their paper blank, having been unable to think of anything when they heard the term. Of those who did write something the majority wrote words signifying passivity, weakness or dependency. They wrote 'almost lifeless', 'pity', 'lonely', 'crippled', 'wheelchair', 'grey', 'old' and 'sorry'.[4] The exercise was part of a research project on disabled women and the researchers were surprised at the results, even though they had been expecting negative images. When the 145 students were asked to list what came to mind when they heard the word 'woman', they wrote down terms associated with heterosexuality and heterosexual relationships, work, and motherhood. These terms were almost entirely missing from the associations with the words 'disabled woman'.

Physical or learning disability in a woman has been used in the various cultural media in the same way as it has in men to signify evil or horror. But the overwhelming association with disability for women, as these students' reactions show, is one of passivity, dependency and deprivation. Even a feminist writer such as Marilyn French has used disability to signify dependency. In her novel *The Bleeding Heart*, French explores the conflicts between autonomy and dependency, strength and passivity, which many women experience within heterosexual relationships. As Deborah Kent points out, in her analysis of the portrayal of disabled women in literature,[5] French uses the character of Edith (who is paralysed after a car crash) to portray 'the passive, subjugated woman whom according to French, men secretly desire.... Edith is submissive and asexual... [she] embodies many of the most debilitating stereotypes behind which disabled women lose their individual identities. When she loses the ability to walk, she also is robbed of her sexuality, her intellect and her sense of self. In contrast, Dolores, with whom Edith's husband has a love affair, is autonomous, strong, alive and sexual. As a disabled feminist, I feel betrayed by Marilyn French's exploitation of the cultural stereotype of disability, for she is doing nothing to challenge oppressive attitudes and everything to collude with them.

Interestingly, film-makers in the 70s and 80s have not been as interested in the use of disability as a vehicle for exploring dependency and vulnerability in women as they have for exploring the same issue about men. There seems to be no complexity to a woman's dependency

– at least not for the men who make films. Older films – such as *Whatever Happened to Baby Jane* in which Blanche Hudson (played by Joan Crawford) is 'confined' to a wheelchair and is at the mercy of her murderous sister, and *Wait until Dark* in which Audrey Hepburn plays Susy Hendrix, a terrorised blind woman – use physical disability as a fairly straightforward representation of vulnerability. The intention is to create fear, and the audience is drawn into a sense of helplessness caused by the disability (although Hepburn's character then uses her ability to 'see' in the dark to turn the tables on her aggressor).

Generally, however, women do not have to be portrayed as disabled in order to present an image of vulnerability and dependency. Not surprisingly, therefore, most disabled characters in film and television in recent years have been men. The most common representation of disability in television and the cinema is a wheelchair user because the wheelchair offers the most obvious and easiest way of presenting a recognisable disability. Most of the disabled people depicted in this way are men. Lauri Klobas looked at one hundred fictional examples of wheelchair users in film and television and found that over four out of five were men – and the great majority were white.[6]

One example of a woman's disability being used in a metaphorical sense other than to represent evil or horror or dependency was in the 1986 film version of *Children of a Lesser God* directed by Randa Haines. The stage play had been very positively received by the Deaf community because its main character, Sarah, was a strong Deaf woman who was part of a Deaf community, and who demanded that her interests and concerns be addressed by the hearing community. The story is based on the relationship between the Deaf community in a school for Deaf young people and the hearing world that surrounds them. It is also about Sarah's relationship with a hearing teacher. In the play, Sarah's strength is set within a background of other strong Deaf characters, and her struggle for her rights, including her insistence that she wants to have Deaf children, has an authority and coherence to it.

In the film, however, there are no other strong Deaf characters and Sarah's behaviour is made to seem eccentric and little more than temper tantrums. As other disabled people pointed out when the film was released, Sarah's deafness has been turned into a metaphor for the lack of communication between men and women. Mary Jane Owen wrote, 'It's a beautiful film about a beautiful couple in a beautiful landscape trying to overcome some problems they just happen to have in communication. Oh yes, she is deaf, but that's not the real problem in the director's mind. The problem's that she stubbornly refuses to recognise what's best for her.'[7] As with the cultural representation of disabled men, films such as *Children of a Lesser God* say more about what disability means to non-disabled people than anything about our real lives and concerns.

Susan Browne, Debra Connors and Nanci Stern identify two stereotypes that are frequently projected onto disabled women. 'One is the happy, humble woman who has "accepted her handicap" and is endlessly grateful for the help of others. Her counterpart is embittered, blames everyone else for her situation, and continually lashes out. Society approves of our complacency and discounts our anger. Either way, we are made invisible.'[8]

Disabled women particularly object to the way that there is no room for our anger because it can only be interpreted as individual bitterness. This is fundamentally undermining. As Dai Thompson writes:

Anger felt by women because of our disabilities is rarely accepted in women's communities, or anywhere else for that matter. Disabled or not, most of us grew up with media images depicting pathetic little 'cripple' children on various telethons or blind beggars with caps in hand ('handicap') or 'brave' war heroes limping back to a home where they were promptly forgotten. Such individuals' anger was never seen, and still rarely is. Instead of acknowledging the basic humanity of our often powerful emotions, able-bodied persons tend to view us either as helpless things to be pitied or as Super-Crips, gallantly fighting to overcome insurmountable odds. Such attitudes display a bizarre two-tiered mindset: it is horrible beyond imagination to be disabled, but disabled people with guts can, if they only try hard enough, make themselves almost 'normal'. The absurdity of such all-or-nothing images is obvious. So, too, is the damage these images do to disabled people by robbing us of our sense of reality.[9]

Some of this is echoed by Marsha Saxton and Florence Howe when they write:

Disabled women are typically regarded by the culture at two extremes: on the one hand, our lives are thought to be pitiful, full of pain, the result of senseless tragedy; on the other hand, we are seen as inspirational beings, nearly raised to sainthood by those who perceive our suffering with awe.[10]

However, the Super-Crip role poses problems for women because it requires self-confidence and assertion and is much easier to achieve with economic security. It is not surprising therefore that most 'overcoming all odds' stories concern disabled men, although a few of such stories are about women such as Helen Keller.

OVERCOMING ALL ODDS

A crucial element in this type of cultural representation of disability is a striving competitiveness. This goes together with an emphasis on the individual. Within this perspective, it is not society which disables someone by its reactions to limitations and difference but the individual who either fails to 'rise above' their misfortune or who exhibits the personal strength and will-power to achieve 'against all odds'.

Christy Brown's autobiography, *My Left Foot*, and the film made from it, fall into this type of cultural representation of disability. The non-disabled world wonders at the ability of someone who has a significant speech impediment and who can only move his left foot, to paint, to write, because these are things that normal human beings do and Christy Brown is treated as fundamentally alien to normal humanity.

In the 'overcoming all odds' model of disability, the disabled person is often presented in terms of a 'brilliant mind in a crippled body', a phrase actually applied to Professor Stephen Hawking who has a motor neurone disease. The non-disabled world finds disability, or injury, difficult to confront or to understand. Other people's pain is always frightening, primarily because people want to deny that it could happen to them. Lack of control over one's body is also very frightening, particularly as it can mean such dependence on others. 'Overcoming' stories have the important role of lessening the fear that disability holds for non-disabled people. They also have the role of assuring the non-disabled world that normal is right, to be desired and aspired to. As Pam Evans told me:

The status quo likes us to be seen 'fighting back', to resent and bewail the fact that we can no longer do things in their way. The more energy and time we spend on over-achieving and compensatory activity that imitates as closely as possible 'normal' standards, the more people are reassured that 'normal' equals right. If we succumb to their temptations they will reward us with their admiration and praise. At first sight this will seem preferable to their pity or being written off as an invalid. But all we will achieve is the status of a performing sea-lion and not (re)admittance to their ranks.

It is easy to be seduced into the role of being exceptional, of being 'wonderful', particularly as this is often the only (seemingly) positive role open to us. We can insist that people react to us as individuals and not as someone who is blind, or paralysed, or deaf, or learning disabled. The Spastics Society,[11] for example, thought that they were being progressive by producing advertisements that encouraged people to look beyond the wheelchair and see the real person, but if people are being asked to ignore our disability they are being asked to deny a fundamental part of our identity and our experience.

The 'overcoming' model of disability separates us from other disabled people; it isolates us and in any case offers no more than a very conditional acceptance. Rachel Cartwright discovered this as she grew older as a blind woman:

I spent most of my life proving that I could do everything that a sighted woman could do. I did well at school, got a reasonably paid job, got married, had children and now I have grandchildren. All that time, I pretended that being blind didn't really matter, that it was an inconvenience and that if I let my personality shine through people would treat me as anyone else. I was very successful at it. But now I'm old and what am I supposed to do about that? I can't overcome being old. I could be exceptional as a blind woman, talented, develop other abilities. But as an old blind woman, there's no positive role on offer.

THE NON-DISABLED PERSON AS RESCUER

Lauri Klobas, who writes about disability images, has identified that a common theme in films and television about disabled people is the portrayal of a non-disabled person as the wise, strong person who acts as a catalyst for a disabled person 'coming to terms with their disability'.[12] In this type of representation of disability, the disabled person has personal and emotional inadequacies, most commonly portrayed as anger and bitterness, and/or a failure to face up to disablement. As Klobas writes, 'attitudinal and physical barriers seldom confront these angry, bitter people'; instead the problems of disability are personal problems, related to individual inadequacies.

An example of this is the play by Tom Kempinski, *Duet for One*, about a violinist who has multiple sclerosis. The play is worth a detailed analysis because it is a powerful cultural representation of both women's dependency and the dependency of disability.

There are only two characters in the play, Stephanie Abrahams, an eminent violin player who has multiple sclerosis, and Dr Feldmann, a psychiatrist. Dr Feldmann is probably best described by the phrase used in the playwright's character notes as having an 'air of comforting wisdom'. Stephanie is a more complicated character:

... she had to rebel to realise her dream of becoming a musician, which has made her outspoken, often aggressive, witty, bitter and sarcastic sometimes, and seemingly confident. She has courage, now stretched to its limit with the knowledge that she has multiple sclerosis and knows her worth as an artist. Underneath she is, of course, in despair.

Stephanie can still walk, although she uses an electric wheelchair to come to Dr Feldmann's office, but she can no longer play the violin and has therefore had to give up her career. She has apparently decided to find purpose in her life by acting as a secretary to her husband, who is a world-famous conductor, and by teaching the violin. It is her husband's idea that she comes to see Dr Feldmann – 'I came because my husband thought I was fairly upset with things and might benefit from some kind of, I don't know, support or guidance, and I agreed with him.'

The essence of Dr Feldmann's role is that he is an expert about Stephanie's feelings. He is even portrayed as an expert – more expert than she – on multiple sclerosis, in a swift exchange in the early part of the play. His expertise on her feelings – his authority about what she feels and what should be done about it – takes the form firstly of prescribing drugs which are presented as necessary to her emotional and physical survival (Feldmann immediately reveals her vulnerability to suicide), and secondly, of stripping away the surface of what she says to reveal the pain and distress she feels which emanate from her childhood experiences. 'I think it is very important for you to discover your true feelings

about your position at this moment,' he tells her. And he is the source of the discovery of these true feelings.

Stephanie begins her sessions with Dr Feldmann by talking of superficialities, of presenting a positive picture of 'coming to terms with' her illness, of adjusting by becoming a teacher and her husband's secretary instead of the world-famous soloist she once was. Feldmann cuts through all this, asking her whether – since music was so important to her marital relationship – she is now afraid that her husband may leave her. In response to his skills, we learn about her childhood and its significance to her current situation. He unpeels the layers of self-deception like an onion, revealing the anger, terror and despair underneath, and the pinnacle of his expertise is achieved when she finally expresses what it means to no longer be able to make music. 'Music,' she says, 'is the purest expression of humanity that there is,' and as she confronts her loss she admits that 'you can't change this condition with determination'.

Having broken down her defences and revealed the true despair underneath, Feldmann now has the task of rescuing her, both from the very real threat of her suicide and from the nothingness of chronic depression. He describes her condition to her and sets out the goal to be achieved: 'As primitive man was the subject of the blind forces of nature, so you too are at the mercy of the dark forces of your unconscious mind; at the moment they have you in their power; you sit around, you complain, you say you can do nothing. But as that primitive man set about transforming his hostile forces to his own purposes, so you too must now engage yourself in a life activity, to master your dark forces. To succeed will be a great labour; but succeed you can and must.'

But Stephanie isn't ready yet truly to confront her loss; he has to shout at her, telling her to 'get off your arse and fight!' It is in the final scene – having in the previous week obviously done as he instructs, working on her 'inner themes and chords and progressions' – that she finally strips down to her real emotional self. 'The violin isn't my work; it isn't a way of life. It's where I live,' she says. It had become her world when her childhood world disintegrated after her mother's death. 'Everything went when she died, everything, all the normal things, everything I was used to, all the bits and pieces of ordinary life went down the black hole with Mummy... So I hung on to the only world I had: music. My violin. And I sang the song of the pain and the sorrow and loss and the awful changes, to soothe myself. And I sang for dear life literally for life, 'cos it was all I had.'

Feldmann has enabled her to see what her disability means to her. And the closing line is his assertion, through his question, 'Is the same time next week still convenient?', that he can bring her back to life from the death that her inability to make music means to her.

The play is very powerful, not least because it reflects not just the loss which is sometimes an integral part of having a condition such as multiple sclerosis, but also how the nature of that loss is determined by what went before rather than by the condition itself. The problem for disabled people, however, is that Stephanie is defined, determined and rescued by a good, strong, wise non-disabled person. She cannot find the strength from within herself even to recognise and confront her loss without Feldmann's help, let alone find the ability to deal with it and live. As a woman, and as a disabled woman, Stephanie can have no true autonomy as a human being; her very survival depends on a male expert's knowledge of herself and the alternative he has to offer her. Although the play deals in real emotions, in the final analysis it merely colludes in and confirms the stereotype of the despairing, dependent disabled woman . . .

. . . [Thus] general culture mis-represents disabled people in a variety of ways. It uses disability for its own purposes, as I have shown above. The films and plays that I have discussed are not about our experiences and our concerns; rather they are about the way that the non-disabled world reacts to disability, what it means to them. Disability thus becomes a metaphor, a vehicle for exploring what is of concern to non-disabled people.

Notes

1. Jenny Morris (ed.), *Encounters with Strangers: Feminism and Disability* (London: The Women's Press, 1996).

2. Hugh Gallagher, *FDR's Greatest Deception* (New York: Dodd, Mead, 1985).

3. Judith Williamson, 'It's Hell on Wheels', *Guardian*, 10 May 1990.

4. *Disability Rag*, Jan/Feb 1987, p. 11.

5. Deborah Kent, 'In Search of a Heroine: Images of Women with Disabilities in Fiction and Drama', in Adrienne Asch and Michelle Fine, *Women with Disabilities: Essays in Psychology, Culture and Politics* (USA: Temple University Press, 1988), p. 101.

6. Lauri Klobas, 'Hollywood', in Sam Maddox (ed.), *Spinal Network* (Colorado: Sam Maddox and Spinal Network, 1987), p. 190.

7. Mary Jane Owen, 'A Romp through Metaphor Land', *Disability Rag*, Jan/Feb 1987, p. 21.

8. Susan Browne, Debra Connors and Nanci Stern (eds), *With the Power of Each Breath* (San Francisco: Cleis Press, 1985), p. 77.

9. Dai Thompson, 'Anger', in Susan Browne, Debra Connors and Nanci Stern (eds), *With the Power of Each Breath* (San Francisco: Cleis Press, 1985), p. 78.

10. Marsha Saxton and Florence Howe, *With Wings* (London: Virago, 1988).

11. Now Scope.

12. Klobas, 'Hollywood', p. 192.

Gump and Co.
Andy Kimpton-Nye

Andy Kimpton-Nye's multiple sclerosis, combined with a lifelong passion for the cinema, shaped a commitment to analyse disability in film. His commitment led to a five-year spell reviewing movies for *Disability Now* and *DAM*, work as an assistant producer with the BBC's Disability Programmes Unit and a dissertation on 'Images of Disability on Film' to complete an MA in cultural studies.

Kimpton-Nye looks at the Oscar-winning, high-grossing film *Forrest Gump* and asks why the makers chose to portray a learning disabled character. He goes on to try to answer this by studying the appearance and actions of the main character and taking a comparative look at other recent films that also featured learning disabled people. He concludes that social and cultural convention would have us believe that people with learning difficulties are simple, childlike souls, and that this convention is repeatedly recycled. He also attempts to translate to the experience (or absence of experience) of disability Toni Morrison's view that, as a writer, the subject of one's text is usually oneself, and that where that self is alien to one's direct experience (e.g. a white American writing about an African-American) it can be a powerful exploration of fears and desires.

The 1994 film release *Forrest Gump* was an unqualified commercial success. It swept the board at the 1995 Academy Awards taking six Oscars, and, as reported in the *Guardian*, 'made 323 million dollars, making it the third highest-grossing movie ever'.[1] It tells of Forrest, a character with a 'below average IQ', as he grows up in the 1950s, goes to college and war in the 60s and finally makes his fortune in the 70s before starting a family in the 80s. Forrest's personal odyssey weaves in and out of, often interacting directly with, key moments in American history over the past four decades. In short, *Forrest Gump* made mega-bucks out of a story about the modern world as seen through the eyes of a learning disabled American male; a learning disabled American male who emanates entirely from the psychology of those involved in the commercial movie industry. The question this begs is: how exactly did the makers of this massively popular film choose to portray a character with learning difficulties to the cinemagoing public?

The best way to answer this is to study the appearance and actions of the Forrest character. As Culler observes in his article summarising semiology, characters are produced in such a way as to enable us (the viewers) 'to infer motives from action or the qualities of a person from his appearance'.[2] After all, our first impressions of a movie character are governed by what he/she looks like the very first time we see him/her. We then start to piece together assumptions about a character from what he/she actually does in the course of the film.

We are introduced to Forrest as he sits on a bench waiting for a bus. He has a seriously short haircut, a sky-blue shirt

Forrest Gump, 1994

Of Mice and Men, 1939

uncomfortably buttoned up at the neck, white socks with coloured hoops and a pair of bedraggled training shoes. All of which is worth noting because to quote Culler, '. . . to wear one set of clothes rather than another is certainly to communicate something, albeit indirectly'.[3] The moment Forrest opens his mouth we discover he speaks with a slow Southern drawl. The images of the cropped haircut, buttoned-up shirt, loud socks and battered trainers along with the 'stupid-sounding' drawl combine to suggest an adolescent nerdy-type, even though the character we are seeing is in fact a thirtysomething adult. As the story unfolds in one long flashback of Forrest's life, we learn that the boy Forrest was diagnosed at school as having a 'subnormal' IQ. The intended image of the Forrest character is now complete. The reason the first impression of Forrest is presented as being so odd, so

unfashionably attired and so 'idiot-like' is because (we eventually discover) his character has learning difficulties. The portrayal the film-makers opted for is of the adult trapped at a childlike (simple) stage of development.

The actions of Forrest throughout the film amount to the presentation of a motiveless innocent abroad in a tainted world. We see Forrest witnessing at first hand the protests surrounding the arrival of the first black students at the Alabama College, the horrors of the Vietnam War, the struggles of the Peace movement and the Black Panthers, the chicanery of Watergate and the advent of the AIDS epidemic. However, his naiveté and simplicity remain unchanged by all this; not only is Forrest made to look childlike, or 'simple', by his appearance, but his actions in the film reinforce this impression by having him remain oblivious to all the ills going on around him. The film-makers of *Forrest Gump* chose to portray a character with learning difficulties as a man-child, a loveable fool, an incorruptible 'simpleton'.

Is this 'simplistic' celluloid representation of a learning disabled character an isolated case? Unfortunately not.

Examples of learning disabled characters crop up in the 1995 release *Dumb and Dumber* (which, in its UK advertising campaign, makes overt reference to *Forrest Gump* by featuring its main characters, Lloyd and Harry, sitting on a 'public bench', just as Forrest does), *A Dangerous Woman* (1993), *Of Mice and Men* (1993) and *The Lawnmower Man* (1992).

In *Dumb and Dumber* the two main characters, Lloyd Christmas and Harry Dunn, both have learning difficulties. When we first see Lloyd he has a nerdy, Jerry Lewis-type haircut, a goofy smile which exposes a chipped front tooth and he is wearing a chauffeur's black suit which soon gets swapped for trainers, army trousers, a T-shirt and a wind-cheater. When he runs, his legs stick out sideways, again somewhat reminiscent of Jerry Lewis (clearly there are references here to the stock Lewis comic character of the inept simpleton). When we first see Harry he has a dishevelled mop of hair, scuffed black shoes, white socks, scruffy tracksuit bottoms, a T-shirt and a dirty hooded sweatshirt. He has a hunched posture and shuffles around. Both Lloyd and Harry come across to the viewer as awkward, stupid schoolboys.

The actions of Lloyd and Harry are to provide comedy of the basest kind as the duo bumble their way across America in pursuit of a 'dream' woman whose suitcase they chance to have possession of. They do not realise the woman intended to leave her suitcase at the airport as a drop for blackmailers. They accidentally kill one of the two assassins sent to retrieve the suitcase. They discover the money in the suitcase and go on a wild spending spree, thinking they can repay what they spend. They track down the 'dream' woman, help catch the blackmailers, but do not get the girl (they are presented as far too childlike to be involved in an adult relationship of any kind, let alone a sexual one). Lloyd and Harry are portrayed as loveable simpletons blundering their way through a big, bad world.

Lennie Small is the character with learning difficulties in *Of Mice and Men*. He has a large, floppy cloth cap, a scruffy denim jacket and, most importantly, massively baggy dungarees, which look like a giant romper suit (straightway making the connection between learning disability and a 'retarded' state of mind). He has a quizzical look on his face. His mouth is always open in 'dumb' amazement. His eyes dart back and forth, always struggling to comprehend what is going on. He pulls at his trousers when he is troubled, is always asking questions, forgetting things and wanting to hear stories, just like a little boy. We have, once again, the representation of an adult trapped at an infantile stage of development.

Lennie's actions underline that he is heavily dependent on his lifelong travelling companion, George; he cannot be trusted on his own because he always does something wrong, and finally, because he commits murder, he is put out of his (perceived) misery like a 'crippled dog'. He is a child motivated by simple pleasures (being with his friend George, hearing stories and touching 'pretty things') who gets in to trouble all too easily. This is the portrayal of another loveable simpleton, the only difference from the examples already looked at being that while Lennie is presented as an innocent crushed by the ills of this world, Forrest, Lloyd and Harry miraculously manage to survive.

It is Jobe Smith who has learning difficulties in the *The Lawnmower Man*. He has an unruly, haystack-like mop of hair. He has big, cute eyes, a boyish, verging on 'stupid' smile, and he speaks with a drawl.

He wears baggy dungarees and a sweat-shirt. He works as a gardener and his only friend is a young boy. The messy hair suggests Jobe has no interest in his appearance. The facial characteristics suggest boyishness and, because he is a grown man, stupidity. The baggy dunga-rees again create the impression of an overgrown baby. His job as a gardener suggests he can work with his hands but not with his head. In other words, this is the typical job for a 'dummy'. (Interestingly, Forrest does a stint as a gardener and Mel Gibson plays a handy-man-cum-gardener in *Tim*, a story about an older woman falling in love with a younger learning disabled man. Film-makers apparently feel people with learning difficulties have a natural affinity for pottering around with plants.

We do not really need to look at the actions of Jobe in the film. The poster advertising the movie in the UK said it all: 'God made Jobe simple. Science made him God.' Before Jobe was turned into a Frankenstein's monster for the 90s, he was intended, through his appearance and deeds, to represent the essence of simplicity. The film-makers evidently thought the best way to do this was to make him a character with learning diffi-culties. This is the perfect example to indicate just how the commercial movie mindset views this particular disability: as the embodiment of all that is 'simple', innocent, untainted and childlike.

It is not just male characters with learning difficulties who are portrayed in this way on screen. In *A Dangerous Woman*, the main character is Martha, a learning disabled woman. Martha wears extra-thick glasses, blouses done up to the neck with cute winged collars, knee-length skirts, white ankle socks and flat shoes. She is often tight-lipped as if she has been naughty and must not open her mouth. There is a slightly lolloping move-ment to the way she walks. The unsexy specs, the blouse denying any glimpse of exposed female flesh and the girly ankle socks all reduce Martha the woman to a child. One of the other characters in the film refers to her as a '. . . primitive thing who's never been spoiled'. Martha is presented as a girlish, unspoiled, virginal (even though the film highlights her abuse) woman-child, yet another example of learning difficulties being used to suggest a childlike, simple state.

In terms of her actions in the film, her primitiveness and simplicity are, as mentioned, abused (physically, verbally, sexually) time and time again, and yet somehow remain intact. The childlike Martha is bizarrely, and simultaneously, the 'dangerous woman' of the title and held up as a shining example of innocence in a crooked world. For these film-makers the supposed simplicity of people with learning difficulties is conceived as both fault and virtue.

Why does this cinematic 'simplifi-cation' of learning disabled characters occur with such regularity? To return to Culler's comments on semiology, we can say that '. . . every means of expression in a society is based, in principle, on a collective norm − in other words, on convention.'[4] Similarly, Barthes observes that the viewer of any given image '. . . receives at one and the same time the perceptual message and the cultural message',[5] that is to say, the actual image and what that image has come to mean in society, or to a particular culture. There-fore, the images of learning disabled characters on film and the messages being given off by these images, which amount to 'means of expression', are based on social and cultural conventions, or collectively held beliefs.

Social and cultural convention would have us believe that people with learning difficulties are simple, childlike souls. The commercial-sector film-makers, who are after all part of society and share in its collective ways of thinking, choose to trade in these conventions and thus help to perpetuate them.

But how has this conventional view of learning disabled people come about? I think there is an answer to be found to this question in an essay by the Nobel Prize-winning novelist Toni Morrison entitled 'Black Matters'. This looks at how the white literary imagination produces black characters in American literature, and can be used to shed light on the workings behind the creation of disabled characters on film.

Morrison concludes the extract by stating that as a participant in creating literary characters herself she came to realise that the subject of the writer's dream, or text, is the dreamer, or the writer him/herself. Morrison goes on to add that for this reason the creation of an imaginary character alien to the writer's direct experience (such as, for example, a white author writing about an African-American) can be 'an extraordinary meditation on the self; a powerful exploration of the fears and desires that reside in the . . . [writer's mind]. It is an astonishing revelation of longing, of terror, of perplexity, of shame, of magnanimity.'[6]

If we transfer this idea to the creation of learning disabled characters in the movies, we come to realise that these simple, childlike characterisations represent the film-makers' own feelings of fear, desire and shame about this particular disability. The non-learning disabled film fraternity fear the mental impairment of the learning disabled: they themselves would not want to be so disabled and mentally 'incapacitated'.

But, at the same time, they feel shameful about such uncharitable feelings towards those whom they perceive as being 'less fortunate', and so portray characters with learning difficulties as (for the most part) cute, overgrown children. This is out of a sense of magnanimity and, perversely, a sense of desire. For film-makers, these overgrown children suggest a state of unspoiled adulthood, reminiscent of a mythical time in the garden of Eden before life became complex and tainted. The problem is that this is not actually referring to the real lives of people with learning difficulties.

We can finish by saying that 'what becomes transparent', to re-apply Morrison's words, are the '. . . self-evident ways that . . . [film-makers] . . . choose to talk about themselves through . . . allegorical, sometimes metaphorical . . .' but always simplified representations (in terms of the real lives of learning disabled people). Characters with learning difficulties on film are exploited as thinly coded messages for portraying blessed, loveable simplicity.

Notes

1. The *Guardian*, 20 April 1995, p. 13.
2. Jonathan Culler, 'Semiology, the Saussurian Legacy', in *Culture, Ideology and Social Practice* (Open University Press, 1981), p. 141.
3. Ibid., p. 137.
4. Ibid., p. 130.
5. Roland Barthes, 'Rhetoric of the Image', in *Image – Music – Text* (trans. London: Fontana, 1977), p. 36.
6. Toni Morrison, 'Black Matters', *Playing in the Dark: Whiteness and the Literary Imagination* (London: Pan Books, 1993).

1.5

Eye witness
Paul Darke

PAUL DARKE is currently finishing a Ph.D on 'Representations of Disability in Post-War British Films' at the University of Warwick. (For other biographical notes see Part One, Chapter 1.)

In 'Eye Witness', Paul Darke explores the cinema's treatment of visual impairment. Visually impaired female characters are more negatively treated than their male counterparts, in the sense that they are more often portrayed as good and/or inspirational, but essentially dependent and often as victims of terrorisation; men, by contrast, sometimes acquire their blindness in an act of heroism. The transition into blindness (or 'disability') and out again is an ever-present problem. As Frances Simister says 'types of disablement... imposed by war are badges of courage, displayed to others and accepted by them... It says nothing about life at the mundane level for people who happen to be blind from birth or otherwise, but presents visual impairment as a danger, waiting to be inflicted upon the sighted by disease or injury.'[1] Paul Darke takes a general look at 'blind' movies, but then focuses on *Blink* (1994), a film which features a female blind character; and by way of illustration he uses one short point-of-view scene in the film.

'BLIND' IMAGERY

Visually impaired characters are a regularly used stereotype in movies and are invariably generalised under the blanket term 'blind'. It is usually assumed that 'blindness' is most often attributed to female characters but, in fact, just as many men – if not more – have been portrayed as visually impaired. In real life, visual impairment has many degrees. In the movies, such degrees are only referred to as the process of going totally 'blind' or regaining perfect vision, and then only as a plot device or an attempt to do some unusual point-of-view shots (of which more later). As is the case with most images of disability, visual impairment is used on screen to reinforce the idea/ideals of normality, which in the case of 'blind' movies is the ability to see. One such film is *Blink* (1994), which I will shortly analyse to indicate how visual impairment is wrongly denigrated and 'normality' falsely validated as the only path to a decent quality of life.

As there have been well over a hundred movies with 'blind' characters in them, it is worth asking the question, what lies at the root of the cinema's obsession with visual impairment? There is in the first place an obvious dramatic appeal: many a film has 'added' an impairment to a character to beef up a weak narrative or suspect motivation. Secondly, because movies are a predominantly visual experience, film-makers are enchanted with the paradoxical idea of representing the unrepresentable: 'blindness'. The point of this chapter is to show that what you see on the screen should not be believed because it is a visual distortion of visual impairment that mainly serves, however subconsciously, the misconceptions of sighted audiences. The numerous representations of visual impairment are as much a big lie as any other representation in movies (women, gay people, black people, Deaf people, people with learning difficulties, and disabled people in general, to name but a few).

In an age in which audio description[2] is almost never utilised, the average audience member will invariably be sighted. Film-makers have enjoyed playing with the idea of a film as a visual experience, as this exploits the audience's own fears of not being able to do in the future that which they are doing at that very moment: *seeing* a film. The visual nature of film as film has ensured that visual impairment is, and always will be, a mainstay of the film-makers' repertoire. The movies' and the spectator's voyeuristic tendencies, that is, seeing and watching without being watched or seen, have no greater power or force than when watching the unable to watch and seeing the unable to see. Visually impaired characters on the screen reassure the audience, society and the film industry in their own delusions that 'seeing is believing'.

'BLIND' TYPES: SUPER MEN AND SAD WOMEN

'Blind' male characters can be categorised within a fairly limited range of types. For instance, there are beggars, frauds and villains, who use their impairment to exploit sighted people for their own evil schemes *(Saboteur, Victim, Dark Eyes of London, No Trees in the Street, The Boy Who Stole a Million, Tiger in the Smoke)*. Alternatively there are characters who are 'supercrips', perhaps detectives, who always outwit the bad guys . Such films often include a climactic scene in the dark where the 'blind' character is supposedly equal to the opposition *(Eyes in the Night, 23 Paces to Baker Street, A Man on the Beach, The Great Escape* and *Blind Fury)*. Then there are the saintly sages, usually returned from a war, who are so full of wisdom that the corn pops *(The Bride of Frankenstein, The Enchanted Cottage, The Dark Angel* and *Pride of the Marines)*. Finally there are the musical types who, directly or indirectly, do their best to prove the fallacy that the loss of one sense leads to the miraculous improvement of the other four (most obviously *Night Song* and *Torch Song* but also, amazingly, almost all films that have 'blind' characters).

Like other impairments used in films 'blindness' is usually portrayed, according to the stereotypes, as making the individual bitter, dependent, lonely, tragic, somewhat misguided and infantile. The use of visually impaired children only heightens that sense of tragedy: *Afraid of the Dark* and *Ballad in Blue* for example. *Ballad in Blue* is a film about a 'blind' child who spends the entire film waiting to be cured. The use of Ray Charles (the jazz pianist), himself blind, legitimates the stereotype of the visually impaired and disabled as people who sit around waiting for someone (a doctor) to cure them; a fallacy in the extreme. The 'cure' climax of a majority of 'blind' films ensures that the medical model of impairment, that is, impairment as lacking and in need of rectification by medical professionals, is falsely validated and the 'blind' individual is denigrated and dismissed as not being fully human.

In contrast to men, female 'blind' characters come in only two types, although occasionally the two types are combined. First there are the tragic terrorised victims *(Union Station, Blind Terror, Wait until Dark, Witness in the Dark, Blink* and *Jennifer 8)*, who, just like the blind detective type mentioned earlier, often reach the story's climax in a dark room or space, thus 'levelling the playing field' – supposedly. The second type (often combined with the 'terrorised') are those perceived as tragic and inspirational whose main purpose is to leave the spectators feeling good about themselves (examples to be found in the thrice made *Magnificent Obsession*, Chaplin's *City Lights*, in *Mask*, and, in conjunction with deafness, *The Miracle Worker* and *The Story of Esther Costello)*. If creating a darkened scene as a means of placing the visually impaired on an equal level with the sighted characters is a movie cliché, so too is the practice of 'face feeling'. Yet almost without fail, all 'blind' movie characters go round feeling peoples' faces; to such an extent that it is not uncommon for sighted people to offer their face for feeling when they meet someone who is blind. Other clichés abound: not surprisingly, the musical ability of blind women is as equally amazing as that of blind men. *Blink* is no exception to this as its 'blind' character is a violinist. Also, as with men, female 'blind' characters are always portrayed as dependent on sighted people for either their salvation or happiness, and without fail, they would always rather be sighted that 'blind' (however tragic that makes them seem!).

Black or Asian 'blind' characters are a rarity in Western cinema – except perhaps as extras in Western movies about the poverty of the Third World, where the tragedy of visual impairment (and the Third World!) is given as self evident. However, in *Patch of Blue* the myth of 'blind' people as seeing beyond the visible (closely related to the saintly sage stereotype) is used to critique the bigoted views of 'white trash' America. Lesbian or gay people with a visual impairment, in the world of mainstream movies, simply don't exist.[3]

The only other type of 'blind' character one could identify is the comic one *(Proof, Blind Fury, See No Evil, Hear No Evil, Young Frankenstein)*. In *The Woman in Red* a whole scene (stolen from W.C. Field's *It's a Gift)* is given over to the supposed comic potential of 'blindness' by having a sighted character play the 'blind game', where one goes to a public place, wearing dark glasses and destroys everything around, finally driving away in an automobile. Nevertheless, I consider the comic 'blind' character to be a positive portrayal of visual impairment because it only works if one is aware of the conventions of the earnest representation of visual impairments (the stereotype in other words) and, as such, that convention is undermined by its exaggeration.

The social barriers faced by visually impaired and other disabled people are generally ignored by film-makers in order to reassure the audience, society and the film-makers themselves that 'blindness' is its sufferer's problem and not anything to do with society. Thus the terrorised 'blind' women in, for example, *Blink, Jennifer 8* and *Blind Terror* are given as dependent and liable to be terrorised solely because they are 'blind', not because society has created those dispensing terror, or whole groups of people (doctors, social and charity workers) who see visually impaired and all disabled people as second-class citizens. The culture and techniques of film have subscribed to the general view that visual impairment is the disability (i.e. a negative stage of physical loss from which you suffer – the medical model of disability) and not that the impairment is *only* an

Blink, 1994

impairment which results in the individual being disabled by a disablist society. The trouble originates in perceptions and definitions of disability. Traditionally our society, including those in the film industry, has chosen to subscribe to the view that visual impairment is a negative state of physical loss which is suffered and therefore should be avoided – that is, the medical model of disability. The alternative social model is to perceive the limitations inherent in any impairment as being significantly less than those imposed upon people through attitudinal, behavioural and environmental barriers.

BLINK: VISIONS OF VISION

In *Blink* the eye surgeon who restores the leading lady's sight states at one point that 'Seeing isn't something that happens to you; it's something you do. I gave you the equipment'. Consequently we can see, from these few words of dialogue, how visual impairment is given as passive and dependent upon the medical establishment (the medical model again), whereas conversely, vision must be active. Also, such dialogue equates vision with movie-going and, as such, the audience is encouraged to see them-

selves as active: being in the cinema has not just happened to them because they have *gone to see* a film. The 'blind', however, are marginalised as passive and sad.

Blink is a thriller about a visually impaired woman who, on regaining her sight, is the only witness to a murder. The only complication – and the entire plot – is that her newly restored vision only registers fully in her brain many hours later (labelled in the movie as 'retroactive vision'). As is the convention in such popular films, the police detective (Hallstrom) investigating the case gradually falls in love with the visually impaired, violin-playing 'eye witness', Emma. Significantly, their love grows as her sight improves and the final scene implies that it will last because she will have complete visual recovery; in *Blink,* seeing is believing.

The scene I wish to discuss in detail is immediately after Emma and Hallstrom have first made love, and is about two thirds of the way through the film. It consists of nine shots that last a total of 55 seconds and the whole scene takes place on the roof of Hallstrom's apartment block; where they, with others, are watching a distant baseball game.

THE SCENE

Shot 1

A dark low angle shot, from floor level, looking up at the silhouettes of Emma and Hallstrom (drinking a bottled beverage) sitting on a wall, against a darkened sky with bright lights below the other side of the wall. The camera moves forward, rising as it goes, to reveal that they are overlooking a Chicago Cubs Baseball match in a large impressive stadium. As the camera tracks forward and rises, the crowd's roar and the stadium's lights become apparent. Thus, the shot starts in the dark and ends in the light. It lasts 21 seconds, which compared to the total length of 34 seconds of the other eight put together makes it the key shot of the scene. As the camera reaches Emma and Hallstrom, in medium close-up, the crowd's roar and the music on the soundtrack subsides, and we hear Hallstrom say: 'Oh yeah. There was one time, me and my friend Dennis – were about nine, ten years old – sitting in front of grandstand and I had a coke in my hand.'

As the camera reaches Hallstrom, having tracked forward and up, he pours the bottled drink he is currently drinking over the edge to signify that this is what he and Dennis did as kids. We then cut to shot 2.

Shot 2

A head and shoulders (medium close-up) of Emma looking, lovingly, at Hallstrom. Meanwhile, off screen we can hear that Hallstrom is talking but the crowd and music drown his voice.

Shot 3

A medium close-up of Hallstrom talking to Emma (part of a dialogue shot-reverse-shot sequence in fact). We then hear Hallstrom's dialogue more clearly again. He goes on: '[a]nd I said, right there

and then, I am gonna live in one of those buildings; with a view like this!'

Shot 4

A cut away shot of the baseball match taking place in the stadium behind Emma and Hallstrom. In this shot the batsman is thrown a baseball which he hits, and his bat shatters into many pieces and the crowd cheers.

Shot 5

A medium close-up, shot-reverse-shot, of Emma listening, starry-eyed and longingly, to Hallstrom. As in all the shots in this scene, the stadium, or its lights, are visible in the background.

Shot 6

A medium close-up, shot-reverse-shot, of Hallstrom, leaning forwards, who asks Emma: 'What?' One presumes she appears bored with his talk and wants to get straight down to some more sex.

Shot 7

Of Emma (as in shot 5).

Shot 8

Of Hallstrom (as in shot 6): who asks, with a strong sense of a sexual undertone, 'You want to go inside?'

Shot 9

Of Emma (as in shots 5 and 7): leaning forward and saying in a sexy voice 'Ohhhh, yeaaah!'. The scene ends.

The subsequent scene is one of Hallstrom and Emma making love in his apartment; only this time with the lights on and their eyes open.

THE ANALYSIS

What are we to infer from such a scene? Plenty. Obviously it must be taken in the context of the film – and in this case I would argue that the whole scene is indicative of the entire movie – and, as such, the scene is perfect for analysis. The thrust of this analysis is to show how the scene is constructed in such a way so as to demean visual impairment; achieved, specifically, by creating a virtual eulogy to normal vision (sighted people). First, we can see that by the very juxtaposition of a magnificent image of a major spectator sport to a story about a 'blind woman' – in competitive comparison – visual impairment comes across as a very poor second best. The film has thus highlighted one above the other: the visual as magnificent and good and 'blindness' as lacking and bad!

The *mise-en-scène* (construction by the film-maker) of the opening shot of the scene – camera tracking forward to reveal the spectacular view of the base-ball stadium and its action – is a wholly *visual* experience. So the whole imagery of the opening shot is designed to compare the bad vision of the impaired (the shot opens darkly and with a low-level view of the silhouetted couple) with the good vision of the sighted, the dawning spectacular view from the roof-top. The soundtrack's use of the crowd's roar, combined with the extraneous music increasing in time with it, make passive involvement with the sequence impossible. The opening shot does not invite competitive comparison between being sighted and being 'blind', quite the opposite, it forces it down your throat (and eyes).

When Hallstrom is reminiscing about a happy memory, which culminates in us only being able to get the punchline by being able to see Hallstrom pour his drink over the edge, the film implies that a happy childhood (and life) – with all its memories – is only possible if one is sighted. That, in the narrative of the movie, Emma has had a miserable child-hood (she was 'blinded' by her own mother) merely goes towards confirming such a stereotypical view of visual impair-ment. 'Memory' is itself here constructed as being only possible for sighted people. The bizarre view *Blink* has of visual

impairment is quite astounding. That the opening shot of the scene is so long, in comparison to the other shots of the scene, only serves to reinforce its power; that the image of the stadium is so magnificent clarifies, in the film-makers' eyes, the absolute superiority of being a sighted person.

With the rest of the scene done in shot-reverse-shot style, that is, people looking at one another in conversation in sequence, the status given to being sighted is enhanced as it seems to be at the root of all decent social interaction (that is, in the logic of the film). The development of a special effect creating visual distortions – called Emmavision by the film's-makers – in order to give Emma's point-of-view shot of many key moments in the narrative, only serves to place visual impairment as an individu-alised problem. The point-of-view shot in 'disability' films is one of the key tech-niques of film-making that de-politicises disability and places it firmly in the mould of the medical model of disability (where the individual's impairment is the sole cause of their disability problems). That Emma, and most disability film characters for that matter, is reliant on or in hospital only makes the point more obvious and literal.

Hallstrom's second piece of dialogue, in shot three of the scene, which culminates in the phrase 'with a view like this', only serves to leave the film's viewer in no doubt of the superiority of the sighted over the sightless (though to the seasoned disability critic it borders on labouring the point). The dialogue of this shot is enough in itself to get the mis-guided message across. However, a com-parison between this sequence and that of the view from Emma's apartment, a large, dark, warehouse type building that only overlooks other similar dingy buildings, demonstrates that the whole question of life for sighted people versus that of the visually impaired is raised to further put down the 'blind' as the film portrays them.

Having the rest of the shot-reverse-shot sequence filled with a degree of sexual innuendo that can only be deciphered by looking at (seeing) the characters – Hallstrom saying 'what?' in shot 6 is only translatable in the context of his and Emma's looking at (seeing) one another – reinforces the impression that the whole sequence is about the joy of vision, and by extension, the misery of being visionless. But the only shot of the scene I have yet to mention, the zoom shot of the baseball players, leaves us in no doubt of the film's philosophy of the meaning and value of 'blindness' and sight. In its extreme, visual impairment, for *Blink*, is nigh on un-American as it can't enjoy (see or play) baseball! Seriously though, the zoom shot of the baseball game is quite interesting because, first, it is not accurate (it is a closer, zoomed-in, view that does not reflect the true situation of the distance between the actors and the stadium), and secondly, the action is unusual and rare (the player's bat shatters). Thus, the action's significance is over emphasised to enhance the imagery beyond reality that the scene would imply, and the actual image contains an incident that needs to be seen to be believed.

CONCLUSION

Overall, as I have shown, one must try to read a film to decipher as much as possible of what it perceives others (i.e., 'normal' people) to be in order to fully comprehend how it sees, marginalises and degrades disabled people. The use of the point-of-view shot is a good place to start as it puts the impaired at the centre of the image; the point-of-view shot, particularly in movies about visual impairment, is the great de-politiciser of disability, and the simplifier of its reality, which is (in reality) complex and far from simple. If it sees impairment and disability as interchangeable concepts – as is almost always the case, and exemplified by the point-of-view shot – or as the sole factors in motivating the disabled character's behaviour, it is a bad sign. The point-of view shot and the competitive comparison of normality to abnormality must be identified in any attempt to analyse the disablist philosophy behind any specific film, or group of films, as they are the most widespread techniques used, and are the easiest to comprehend.

Finally, in reading this chapter over again, one is struck by the constant emergence in its language of the metaphors of the superiority of sight. One must remember that because film is a visual medium it uses its language to also highlight the superiority of sight as it sees it, however far removed that may be from the reality. Having a visual impairment is not how the movies portray it; but then, what is?

Notes

1. Frances Simister, 'Shadows on the Screen: Disabled Characters in British and American Films, 1935–1993 (unpublished thesis, Manchester Metropolitan University, 1995).
2. A system whereby an audio soundtrack gives non-verbal information, fed via headphones, to visually impaired cinemagoers. (See also Part 4, Chapter 20.)
3. Outside of the mainstream there are notable exceptions, for instance Derek Jarman's *Blue* (1993), which reflects his personal experience of AIDS and the onset of blindness.

Deafness and the film entertainment industry
John S. Schuchman

From John S. Schuchman, *Hollywood Speaks: Deafness and the Film Entertainment Industry* (University of Illinois Press, 1988).

JOHN SCHUCHMAN is a child of deaf parents and has been active in the Deaf community for many years. He has taught at Gallaudet, a prestigious university for deaf students, since 1967, and in 1981 he turned his attention to the history of the Deaf community for which he has been developing videotaped oral history interview techniques. He has lectured on Deaf images in film and television at the National Film Theatre, most recently in 1994 and 1995.

The Golden Age of cinema for deaf people was the silent movie era. As Schuchman says in *Hollywood Speaks (The Silent Movie Era),* 'The history of the early film industry reveals that [it] inadvertently included deaf people to an extent unknown today. Deaf people participated in the industry as equal members of the audience, as pedagogical beneficiaries at school, as actors on the screen, and as subjects for film scripts . . .' Unfortunately, the deaf actors did not, he says, play roles as deaf characters and had little opportunity to influence the popular images. So stereotypical images of deaf people as 'dummies' (hearing trumpets and sign language transformed into visual gimmicks designed to elicit laughter) were passed on, along with the alternative deaf characterisation of cantankerousness, ill humour and lonely isolation. In this piece from *Hollywood Speaks* he argues that the film industry, more than any other medium, has popularised simplified views of deafness, contributing little to a better understanding of the Deaf community.

What is the Hollywood image of deafness? In her analysis of the image of women in films, Molly Haskell uses the term 'the big lie' in concluding that the movie industry has served as a popular agent to foster and perpetuate the myth of women as the weaker sex.[1] Is there a comparable 'big lie' in the Hollywood depiction of deaf characters? If so, one must conclude that a collective Hollywood is guilty of the perpetuation of a pathological view of deafness as a disease and of deaf individuals as abnormal. At the same time, it is only fair to observe that the film industry did not invent this perspective.

Film-makers reflect the prevailing American cultural bias toward disability and deafness. There certainly exists a large network, both in the United States and abroad, of educational, rehabilitation and medical professionals who are dedicated to the proposition that deaf people, particularly children, have special needs that require their expertise. Unlike the professional who can take the time to deal with the complexities represented by deafness, movies try to convey their messages as simply as possible and, in doing so, often turn to formulas and stereotypes in their depiction of deafness. It is at this level that films have so much potential for harm. More than any other medium, they have popularised simple-minded views of deafness. This survey of film and television entertainment programmes clearly demonstrates that the deaf community has every right to complain about the practices of Hollywood in the industry's depiction of deafness up to the present.

Often described as the invisible handicap, deafness remains a mystery to most Americans. The motion picture industry has contributed little to a better understanding of the deaf community. Historically, Hollywood's ideal deaf person has been truly invisible – other than the inability to hear, the stereotyped movie ideal invariably speaks clearly and reads lips with unfailing accuracy – both unrealistic exaggerations. Talking motion pictures have continued the negative image of deafness established in silent films. Often, a movie ends with a cure through an experimental drug (And Now Tomorrow), an operation (Flesh and Fury), or a psychologically traumatic event (The Story of Esther Costello). When the character's deafness cannot be cured, the film ends with the character acquiring speech, the symbol of success for the 'dumb' individual (The Miracle Worker). In common with the depiction of other disabled figures, the deaf character contemplates suicide (Sincerely Yours); and like his or her literary brethren, the deaf character often serves as a symbol for loneliness and alienation (The Heart Is a Lonely Hunter). Hollywood has avoided deaf couples or families, and movies very rarely have more than one deaf character. With two exceptions, in 1926 (You'd Be Surprised) and most recently in 1986 (Children of a Lesser God), actors who

could hear always played the role of the deaf persons in theatrically released films. Until 1979, in the movie Voices, audiences had not heard real deaf speech from a deaf adult character. Only deaf children, usually portrayed by a class from nearby schools for deaf children, have difficulty with speech.

In Hollywood's view there is little or no humour in deafness. This has been particularly true since the demise of silent motion pictures. Of the more than one hundred movies and television programmes produced since the advent of sound technology, only three associate a deaf character with humour.[2] Westerns and horror films constitute less than a half-dozen films involving deafness; all of the rest are melodramas. In the movie houses of American, deaf people are usually victims, either to be pitied or cured. It is clear that the Hollywood stereotypes of deaf persons as either 'dummies' or 'perfect lipreaders' represent the extremes, which rarely are encountered in the real world.

Deafness is a disability in a society that communicates primarily through sound and speech. Deaf persons have been killed by oncoming automobiles and trains that they could not hear, shot by policemen with whom they could not communicate easily, incarcerated in mental institutions and jailed by professionals who misunderstood and misdiagnosed them and their deafness. They have been denied equal employment opportunities by individuals who equate good speech and English skills with intelligence. It is on this aspect of deafness that Hollywood has focused its camera lens.

There is another view, however. In the past, some deaf people accepted the fact that they would never hear and, as a result, developed cultural responses to a dominant hearing society that could not and would not assimilate them. At least as early as the antebellum 19th century, there emerged a deaf community replete with its own social organisation, schools, churches, clubs, self-help societies, newspapers and magazines, and language. In spite of the fact that the American deaf community is considered to be the most independent and progressive such community in the world, and that within the United States the Los Angeles (the spiritual if not geographical centre of Hollywood) deaf community is considered to be one of the most assertive and politically astute groups at the local level, the normal activities of this community are largely unknown to the public, and no movie or television script has dealt with its existence or activities at a substantive level. It is clear that the movie industry has been a primary vehicle for the transmission and perpetuation of an American cultural view that depicts deafness as a pathological condition. The deaf community does not exist in film or television, only deafness and deaf individuals do.

The reason for this is clear. Hollywood cannot or will not deal with the issue of language in the deaf community. Individual deaf characters are excellent victims. Like their blind counterparts, these characters look good; and since film-makers value a pleasing physical appearance, this explains why deafness and blindness predominate among disabled characters in film. It is no accident that in more than eighty years of film there have been no multiply disabled deaf characters depicted, with the exception of deaf-blind portrayals (of course, the deaf-blind characters have met the test of good looks). It is only when two deaf characters appear in a film together that communication difficulties are experienced. Even if they are physically attractive, how will the audience understand them?

As a practical matter, Hollywood treats the deaf community as a linguistic minority; and as such, it has avoided substantive depictions of American Sign Language. At the individual level, Hollywood consistently has its deaf characters speak orally or simply lets the audience guess at the meaning of the deaf character's limited signs. The 1948 film *Johnny Belinda* used a hearing character, the doctor (played by Lew Ayres), to provide contextual clues to the signed dialogue with the deaf character (played by Jane Wyman), but at the time this was an exception to the general film practice. Another thirty-eight years passed before film-makers again used this technique, in *Children of a Lesser God*. Although this is not unlike the situation for Hispanic characters who must speak in accented English, it does explain why there are almost never two deaf characters in the same film. (The two notable exceptions are *The Heart Is a Lonely Hunter* and *Voices;* but in both films, when the two deaf characters communicate in signs, the audience is left to guess at the meaning of the dialogue.) Note that in *Children of a Lesser God,* when James (William Hurt) appears lost and isolated at the party of deaf people, the audience has no idea what the deaf characters at the party are saying since he is not interpreting their signs.

The obvious solution to this dilemma is the use of captions, but the movie industry consistently has rejected their use since the transition from silent to talking motion pictures in the late 20s. In spite of occasional use of captions for foreign-language dialogue in such films as *The Longest Day* and *Patton,* theatrical films and television have opposed the use of open captions with the rationale that general audiences dislike them. This result has reduced the ability of scriptwriters to

Deaf child learns to speak in *Mandy*, 1952

get beyond simple-minded dialogue for non-speaking deaf characters and has perpetuated the practice of separate viewing for deaf audiences. In *Johnny Belinda* and *Children of a Lesser God*, the dialogue is complex, but the deaf person is wedded to a hearing person's voice, which reinforces the image of the deaf person as dependent.

This image has not been exclusively negative, however: *Johnny Belinda* did make a difference by demonstrating that deafness could be portrayed substantively and still turn a profit. After the film's success, there was a significant increase in the number of deaf characters in the movies and on television during the 50s and following decades.

Although many of the stereotypes continued unabated, there were films and television episodes that provided information to the general public about new developments in medicine, education, hearing-aid technology and telecommunication devices. In 1968 *The Heart Is a Lonely Hunter* presented an English-literate non-speaking deaf person, and finally, in 1979, the first professional deaf person, a teacher, appeared in *Voices*.

Unfortunately, the only three theatrical films produced in the first half of the 80s that deal with deafness appear to have returned to some of the old formulas. *Eyes of a Stranger* once again shows the cure of a deaf-blind-mute female victim through the device of a traumatic attack by a rapist. And although the screen-

writers wrapped *Amy* in a historical guise, its story celebrates the triumph of articulation (lipreading and speech) over dependence on sign language and a parochial deaf community. Finally, the most powerful and potentially independent deaf character to appear in motion pictures, Sarah in *Children of a Lesser God*, is a cleaning woman who is dependent on a man who earns his living as a speech teacher.

In contrast, television has broken many of the prevalent stereotypes about deafness. A wide range of deaf adult characters have appeared as attorneys, illiterates, dancers, prostitutes, stunt-women and teachers; and they have been allowed to speak with clear voices or speech-impaired voices, or to remain mute. Although loneliness prevails in the continued predominance of melodramas, deaf couples have appeared in two television movies: *And Your Name Is Jonah* and *Love Is Never Silent*. The most significant and hopeful sign has been the appearance of deaf actors in the roles of deaf characters: since 1968 they have appeared with increasing frequency, capped by the December 1985 Hallmark Hall of Fame presentation of *Love Is Never Silent*, starring deaf actors Phyllis Frelich and Ed Waterstreet and produced by Julianna Fjeld, who is also deaf.

Even though many of the earlier and more pejorative filmic views of deafness will continue to appear on late-night television and on videotape recorders (through rentals), there has been a discernible change in the direction of the depiction of deafness in the 80s, led by television programming.[3] Since much of television continues to be produced in Hollywood, we can only hope that theatrical films will reflect these positive changes within the near future.

Some credit for this recent change in direction for television must be attributed to the presence of deaf persons as actors, technical advisers, and, most recently, as producers. Although most film-makers would not accept the analogy of white actors in blackface, many in the deaf community perceive the continued use of hearing actors in the role of deaf characters as a present-day example of that silent era practice. When Daniel Wilson, the producer of the television programme 'Mom and Dad Can't Hear Me', responded to charges of discrimination by deaf actress Audree Norton, he argued that film-makers should not limit deaf roles to deaf actors. Even though the facts are that less than 10 per cent of the deaf character roles have been played by deaf actors and that virtually all of these have been on television, his argument struck a familiar and responsive chord in Hollywood. While the evidence makes his argument shallow, his rhetoric reflects a basic principle: actors should be free to play any role. Certainly, the testimony of the actors is clear.

Anthony Quinn, referring to his role as Deaf Smith, observed (or at least his publicist did) that 'if every actor could play a deaf-mute once, it would be the best thing that could happen to him. I had to react to everything and everyone round me. It was a terrific experience for an actor.'[4] Alan Arkin recognised that deaf people are as 'multicolored and varied emotionally as they can be', but the 'one thing that the affliction does seem to cause is a great sense of isolation'.[5] In an effort to replicate the experience, Arkin watched television without sound and learned that a deaf lipreader watches the face, not the lips.[6] Jane Wyman worked hard to capture the look of deafness, stuffing her ears with wax and arranging for a young deaf woman to visit her regularly. She strove for a look that tried to anticipate and guess the meaning of

the spoken word.[7]

All of this, of course, misses the point, because these excellent actors focused on the absence of hearing, not the deafness. Although there are actors who are oriented to a visual mode of communication, there have been few of them since the silent era. To use recent examples, the deaf actresses Phyllis Frelich and Marlee Matlin have few peers, among their hearing colleagues, in the use of facial expression and body language, not to mention sign language itself. Their portrayals of the charming deaf prostitute in *Barney Miller*, the deaf mother of a hearing daughter in the television movie *Love Is Never Silent*, and Sarah in *Children of a Lesser God* exemplify the best of a long tradition of deaf actors and expose the shallowness of weak imitations by hearing actors.

Perhaps the silent film actor Lon Chaney understood this better than anyone else. Even with the high-tech gadgetry of modern film-making, few actors have been able to surpass Chaney's ability to master the look of a character. Although he was gifted at make-up artistry, he understood that characterisation was more than cosmetics. This son of deaf parents understood, instinctively and experientially, what it meant to be different as well as to look different. Accordingly, he created memorable characterisations that remain classics today. So far, Hollywood has had limited success with the look of deafness.

Although some of the films discussed in the survey demonstrate insights into individual aspects of deafness, none of them deals with deafness in a way that reflects a cultural understanding of deaf people. Until film-makers portray the existence of an active and healthy deaf community, it is improbable that Americans will get beyond the pathological myths that make daily life difficult for deaf individuals. In this sense, films continue to serve as a major source of public misinformation about deafness and deaf people. The deaf community awaits the next step in the industry's portrayal of deafness.

Earlier, I observed that the deaf community has a right to complain about its treatment by film-makers; at the same time, I have been puzzled by the comparative absence of complaints. A few petitions in 1929 and a boycott fifty years later, in 1979, hardly represents significant protest. Much of this, I believe, can be attributed to our national policy of segregated film and television viewing for deaf audiences. Deafness is a disability of communication. And it is my opinion that the deaf community literally does not appreciate how badly they have fared at the hands of the entertainment industry. For most of the period covered by this survey of film and television, deaf viewers have not been given precise information about the dialogues that accompany the images on the screen. For example, within the past several months, *Beau Bandit* (1930), *Charlie Chan at the Olympics* (1936), *No Road Back* (1957) and *For the First Time* (1959) have appeared on television stations in the Washington, DC area. Despite the presence of what is considered to be the best-educated deaf community, Washington deaf audiences had no information about the audio content of these films because, like most past and current films, they were not captioned.

Even though most current prime-time network television programmes are captioned for use with television decoders, the overwhelming majority of the films and episodes described in this survey are not captioned. And, as exemplified by the appearance of old films in the Washington, DC television market, this backlog of films and episode reruns will continue to haunt the deaf community through the depiction of misinformation about deaf people. Simple equity requires that the industry, or the federal government, if need be, correct this communication imbalance with the provision of captioned versions so that the deaf community is fully informed. A society committed to a policy of equal access for all of its citizens can do no less.

Notes

1. Molly Haskell, *From Reverence to Rape: The Treatment of Women in the Movies* (New York: Penguin Books, 1974), pp. 1–41.
2. The three are: *Pocketful of Miracles* (United Artists, 1961), *Good Times* (CBS, 1975), and *Barney Miller* (ABC, 1981).
3. Although I do not agree that this has occurred with commercial films about deafness, this positive change has been observed for other disabilities. See Paul K. Longmore, '"Mask": A Revealing Portrayal of the Disabled', *Los Angeles Times Sunday Calendar*, 5 May 1985, pp. 22–3; and Longmore, 'Screening Stereotypes: Images of Disabled People', *Social Policy*, Summer 1985, pp. 36–7.
4. '*Deaf Smith and Johnny Ears*: MGM Pressbook', C-37, Motion Picture, Broadcasting, and Recorded Sound Division, Library of Congress.
5. Alan Arkin to Virginia S. Carr, Personal correspondence, 22 September 1970, Manuscript Department, Duke University, Durham, NC.
6. Robert E. Miller, Transcript: American Film Institute Screenwriting Workshop, 22 March 1977, Beverly Hills, CA, Center for Advanced Film Studies, 1977, pp. 26–7.
7. Joe Morella and Edward Epstein, *Jane Wyman: A Biography* (New York, Dellacorte Press), p. 115.

Disability on sale: I Four Weddings and a Funeral

An interview with Richard Curtis, by Chris Davies (OBE).

RICHARD CURTIS made his reputation in television co-writing the *Blackadder* series, creating *Mr. Bean* and producing and organising *Comic Relief* for the BBC, before writing the screenplay for *Four Weddings and a Funeral*.

Four Weddings and a Funeral was an extremely profitable British-made film which in 1994 came highest in the ten top-grossing films, at £27.4 million.[1] An unusual feature was the entirely natural and non-negative way that a Deaf character, played by deaf actor David Bower, was incorporated into the narrative. The deaf character was the brother of the main protagonist, Hugh Grant, and their sign language exchange in the final scene was an important element in the story's resolution. While some disabled people would not see contact with charities, such as Comic Relief, as the best way to learn about disability, Richard Curtis's sensitive incorporation of the deaf storyline was much praised. Chris Davies was interested in how this developed.

CD: When you were writing *Four Weddings*, did you always intend for David to be a deaf character or did the idea come in the second or third draft?

RC: I can't remember the order in which the characters came into my mind but by the time I actually put pen to paper he was already deaf.

CD: How come?

RC: Firstly it was a subject I was interested in as a result of Comic Relief, although it wasn't one that I felt I *needed* to write about, and secondly, I was very interested in this idea of a secret language between people. Because when I was young, my sisters used to speak Swedish in front of everybody and all our friends were English, so they had a way of communicating that meant that they could talk very quietly in Swedish and nobody else would understand them. And I thought what a wonderful idea that would be, to have two characters who could communicate across conversations

where people can't understand what they're saying. And I thought, anyway, that I'd like to portray a deaf character, so immediately I started thinking about how I could make that work in the film.

CD: I noticed that you didn't take the easy way out of having another character speak the words being signed: instead you had it subtitled. Was there any pressure to be more conventional?

RC: I wrote the script and handed it in and that was the way it had to be done, because in a way that was the joke, that you, the public, read what was going on, and if anybody else had vocalised what was going on, it would have destroyed the joke.

CD: If you didn't have any pressure about subtitling, did you have any about casting a deaf actor as a deaf character?

RC: I told the director that one of the things I would absolutely never give way on was not casting a deaf person in that role because it would be inaccurate and

David Bower, the bridegroom's deaf brother, *Four Weddings and a Funeral,* 1994

ridiculous and also wrong. That was always taken with a pinch of salt by the production; they thought, 'oh well, we'll probably make a bit of an effort, but chances are we'll end up with a hearing actor who can pretend.' But I was so firm about it that in the end they allowed extra time for it to happen. I mean it's probably the first time your casting director's had to do that. My director, who is an extremely good soul, was particularly unconvinced and thought that it would not work. We organised an audition with seven or eight deaf actors and Mike [the director] changed his mind about the situation within thirty seconds of the first person coming into the room, because he suddenly saw that there's a whole different cultural world and form of expression for deaf people which as a film-maker he found absolutely intriguing. So Mike found it an extraordinarily interesting two days. And then we got lucky insofar as David was really good, really right for the part and so we found someone. The interesting thing would have been if we hadn't found anyone in that group.

But it was complicated and an education for us. For instance, I thought I was responsible for making sure that the subtitles would work in frame and for making sure that anyone deaf who was watching the film could see David's hands, as there's no point saying, 'I'm going to make a film which says that deaf people operate normally in society' and then sticking big letters in the way. Mike would make a beautiful frame and I'd suddenly think, 'But wait a minute, you're not going to be able to see David's hands below the edge of the frame,' and I'd say so. It's kind of a battle, and I think the important thing is to declare your ground right at the beginning and say, 'This is a real priority, that we're accurate and that it's accessible.'

CD: So is there a formula whereby any kind of disability can be brought into a storyline? Is the best way to make it an integral part of the story with no big issue?

RC: Well it depends, I mean the point of my film was not to make a big issue of anything. That's why the gay character didn't die of AIDS, and everyone didn't keep saying 'ooh you're gay'. It was all just about attempting to say friends are friends.

CD: And do you think that's the best

way forward?

RC: I think it's kind of half the story, since people with disabilities in society do often lead fairly unexceptional lives, as most of us do, so there's no reason to represent them always as some exception – it's the same thing as basically 80 per cent of gay men in the movies die of AIDS these days, they kind of go for the dramatic point. The thing about the character in *Four Weddings* is that there was a trick at the end, I can't remember whether or not I decided I'd definitely keep the character *because* he solved the end of the movie, or whether I developed him because he was going to solve the end of the movie – I think I knew he was going to have a deaf brother and then we worked out that that would be fantastic at the end. But I would have thought the normality, just sort of having disabled characters in things, adds a great deal of colour when you're writing it. It's an interesting thing to do. So if people can and will do it – but that I suppose will depend on people having experience of disabled people in their lives so they can write about it.

CD: Do you think that's the only reason why people don't do it?

RC: Because they don't have enough experience of it? I think it's one very big reason. People often write about friends and colleagues basically, and if they had more friends and colleagues who were disabled, then it would be easier for them to write about it. It's a complicated thing. It wasn't a bitter battle for me to fight but I had to be aware of what the battle was. So it's good to have some sort of enlightenment on the issue, so that when the first argumentative person stands up against you and says, 'Isn't this going to be difficult? we aren't going to be able to find an actor who can really do this, isn't it going to make it complicated around the set?', you can actually say, well no, not really, because it's no more complicated than a temperamental actor, someone who's going to take two hours in make-up every day or whatever. I think maybe some level of political awareness is important because that's definitely the bedrock on which my arguments were based and that's because I'd worked with Comic Relief.

CD: Without Comic Relief do you think you wouldn't have had that awareness?

RC: I don't know, because you never know which way round you get an idea, but it definitely made it much easier for me because I sort of knew the arguments. I know now, for example, that some of the disability movement is based on a parallel with the race movement. If you know that then that's part of your arsenal of arguments, so that when the director says, 'But surely we can get a hearing actor to play that part', you can immediately say, 'Would you get a white actor to play a black part?'; then of course he goes, 'Oh no, of course you're right', because that's such an obvious example. So in that way knowledge is powerful because you've got one or two arguments that you can martial that make it obvious that you're in the right.

CD: The other way of course is to write a character that's not specifically disabled and then cast a disabled person in that role.

RC: I do think there are lots of cases where one writes and one's thinking about, let's say, a powerful headmaster, a corrupt policeman, something like that where it wouldn't make any difference. If you could write a general part and then cast a disabled actor then it would of course need commitment from the director and the producer to that idea.

CD: So which way is guaranteed to get results – by saying, 'I definitely want a disabled person playing this character', or by leaving it to the director?

RC: I think definitely by the writer specifying. The director has a very complicated job and has a lot of worries, and if the writer's made it very clear and in some ways easy for the director to make the choice to hire a disabled person, then that's the easiest way to do it.

CD: Most of your work has been in comedy. Is there a reason why disability doesn't often appear in comedy?

RC: My instinct would be that because people don't have that much knowledge about disabled people, the chances are that if you were to take ten good writers who write good comedy, the probability that they would have any experience of writing about characters with disabilities is pretty low. And then I think that people are probably frightened of being funny on the subject.

CD: But the joke doesn't have to be at the expense of the disabled person.

RC: No, but what I'm saying is they're frightened by the possibility that it might be. One of the things I tried to do with the character of David, right at the beginning, was to have Hugh Grant's character, Charles, take the piss out of him and joke about the disability because I thought that must be legitimate, between two brothers who've grown up together.

CD: And do you think you'll continue to include disability in your work?

RC: I've been thinking about it but obviously I've got to be careful that I don't appear to repeat the formula of *Four Weddings*. There are various issues on the edge of my consciousness that it would be great to deal with, disability is one of them and colour or race is another. I suppose because they're there I look around and if I find a character or an area where those issues would be useful or interesting, if I'm able to make some kind of point, then they will come in. But then I'm not a political writer. I'm political

in a personal way, personal politics are what I believe in.

The moment you do come in contact with disability is the interesting thing because it's such a rich brew, particularly at the moment because there's so much going on in terms of politics and progress. There's so much that the public are just becoming aware of, like the basic shock of the contrast between a badly made, charitable film and the protests in the street. In one case you've got a portrayal of people as being very sweet and helpless and then you've got the realistic image on the news footage which is definitely not sweet and very powerful and aggressive. I would have thought that anyone who does make contact would get quite a lot of opinions quite quickly on the subject.

Notes

1. Source: *Screen International*, quoted in the *Guardian*, 5 April 1995. Interestingly the list also included *Mask* and *Forrest Gump*.

Disability for sale: 2
The writer and the producer

Compiled from an interview with Richard Curtis by Chris Davies and written replies from producer Sir David Puttnam (OBE).

Like *Four Weddings and a Funeral*, many films 'featuring' disability have also been critical and sometimes financial successes. For instance, the 'disability' movies that are essentially war genre and transformation stories (*Coming Home, Born on the Fourth of July*) have found willing audiences, while the nomination queues for Oscars for disability portrayal are getting ever longer (*My Left Foot, Rain Man, Forrest Gump*). There clearly is a fascination in watching non-disabled actors play the alien 'other', and as contact with disabled people is limited both at school and in the workplace, one can understand the actor's own commitment to meeting the unusual challenge. Horror movies, though full of 'disabled' characterisation are paradoxially not seen as 'disability films' and continue to be popular. But however we choose to identify a 'disability movie', are they usually commercial? What makes a commercial film? And is disability a plus or minus factor in the commercial equations? What too is the future for disabled actors in big-budget feature films?

Sir David Puttnam responded in writing to questions from Chris Davies, and on the question of the essential commerciality or otherwise of disability he was very clear:

DP: As has by now been established in many movies, from *The Best Years of Our Lives* to *My Left Foot*, the subject of disability is not inherently uncommercial, but it does very much depend on the emotions that the film is designed to evoke.

As with one of my favourite films, *The Miracle Worker*, the emphasis is most likely to be placed on the interplay between the disabled and the 'helper' and, in turn, their relationship with society in general.

But like most things – it's all in the telling!

CD: For disability to be commercial, should it be a) on the margins of a film? b) an heroic story of the *Reach for the Sky* type? c) made acceptable by an able-bodied star portraying a disabled character?

DP: The issue of disability doesn't have to be on the margins of the film and is, in fact, probably best addressed head on. Two good examples of this would be *Coming Home* and *Born on the Fourth of July*.

Among my own work the best example (although still not yet seen in this country) is *Without Warning*. This is the story of Jim Brady, who was very badly injured at the time of the Reagan assassination attempt and who, despite a severe impediment, was able to contribute massively to the turnaround in the US government's attitude to gun control.

CD: For a main disability storyline, must there be an element of tragedy and pathos if it is to be commercially viable?

DP: I think it's inevitable that the main storyline of any film regarding disability would have to allow the audience an opportunity to understand the nature of disability, and inevitably the able-bodied audience would regard the fact itself as something of a tragedy.

As to pathos, I think that's just a dramatic facet of the story you decide to tell, but what is certain is that the issue of disability clearly evokes sympathy and it would seem to me to be a wasted opportunity not to optimise the emotions of the audience in watching someone overcome any form of severe disability.

Whether the 'tragic and brave' portrayal is the only way that disability can be made into a commercial asset was something that writer Richard Curtis thought started from a 'dodgy' premise:

RC: From my point of view, you don't try to write commercial films. You try and write films which you think are good or funny or entertaining or true, and then see whether or not someone else can sell them commercially, or whether or not they turn out to be commercial. So my argument is that you're probably better off telling the truth, being more interesting, more complicated, and more funny, and not using clichés which only make for boring inconsistent film-making.

CD: And as to whether it sells?

RC: Nobody can ever know what will sell. If you look at the American charts this summer, they're full of movies which people have spent fifty or sixty million on and they've made almost no money at all. Other movies which haven't been expected to make much money have made a lot of money. I think it's up to the film-makers to believe in what they're doing and to be consistent. My basic tenet as a writer is that if you even begin to think about what will please other people, you're doomed . . .

But I think the downside is that people have often taken integrity to mean seriousness and gravity and social issues,

whereas I think you can have a lot of integrity in writing a very stupid joke movie or a light romantic comedy, or even a sentimental story about a horse.

CD: So were there problems around casting, when it came to the deaf character that he had written into *Four Weddings and a Funeral?*

RC: I told the director that one of the things I would absolutely never give way on was not casting a deaf person in that role because it would be inaccurate and ridiculous and also wrong. [See Part 1, Chapter 7 above.]

However, the deaf character in *Four Weddings and a Funeral*, while essential to the storyline, was not the central one, and the view put by Sir David is probably quite typical of today's successful when the question is raised of whether a part should go to an able-bodied actor or not:

DP: It's worth remembering that for *The Best Years of Our Lives* William Wyler was able to find a genuine amputee, who you may recall went on to win an Oscar for Best Supporting Actor, but in today's more pressing commercial environment, there are two undeniable realities. One is that the hero or central figure of any reasonably expensive film is *required* to be an acceptable star name and, almost by definition, that would preclude anyone seriously disabled.

Second, the process of a starring role in a feature film over a period of fifty to sixty days can be enormously debilitating and one would always have to take into account the stamina of the actor and the attitude of the insurance company to his or her hiring. There is no right or wrong about any of this, it's just the way the industry works and it's very doubtful that an industry such as the film business would be likely to adapt itself in any way that would be specifically helpful.

Unfortunately it does contain the catch-22 – without experience how does the talented disabled person become the star name that the film company 'must have'?

Whether or not a political approach to disability such as many disabled people favour is uncommercial, Sir David thought the simple answer was yes:

DP: I don't believe you would ever make a commercially viable film which majored on the issue of the *political* issues surrounding disability.

He did, however, make a concession:

DP: It would, however, be perfectly possible on television, as to an extent was proved by Brian Gibson's wonderful TV film *Joey* in the mid-1970s or, more recently, Stephen Frears' *Walter*. [It is true that although *Joey* and *Walter* were about institutionalisation they were also very much centred around the eponymous.]

CD: So could you see a film which is up front about disability (that is, not just about a single person's life but about disability matters generally) succeeding and, if so, how?

DP: I can well imagine a successful film of the type you describe being made for television, although with the ever narrowing demands and inevitable pressures of the feature film, it's unlikely (although not impossible) that such a film might succeed at the box-office.

Perhaps the process has to start before a producer has the responsibility of getting a film financed and moving, and disabled people themselves have to either come up with 'the product' or recognise a greater dependency on the writer. The producer and financiers are, however, the ultimate arbiters.

CD: So can writers engage in disability in a different way?

RC: From a writer's perspective, the way that you make writers write about a topic is to make them interested in it. Firstly, writers are very hard to get together because they don't band together instinctively, and secondly, they're very curious about the world, so my instinct is that it's worth making an effort to try and engage writers in thinking about it.

CD: Possibly by bringing writers together with disabled people?

RC: Maybe by bringing writers together and presenting them with an argument about disabled people. The one thing I know for definite is that one successful programme or film can change everything. If there were one or two sitcoms with disabled characters which suddenly appeared and everybody felt completely comfortable with them and saw that it would be easy to do, that would radically change the landscape as far as writers are concerned. I suppose there aren't that many writers in this country and one could either have some kind of conference, which would be pretty hard, to get them all to pay attention, or at least compile a video putting forward the points: 'Look at these characters and how they've been used, have you ever thought about putting a disabled character in what you do?'; this is an issue.'

'Heroic' portrayal, *Journey to Knock*, 1991, (BBC)

Part Two

Television – Fact and Fiction

Introduction

The problem of disability images in film is essentially one of type, or quality, and not one of quantity; there are plenty of 'images' available, albeit of unacceptable kinds. In television, however, there is a relative absence of disabled people on screen,[1] both in factual and in fictional programmes (particularly in the latter if one removes the feature film and American made-for-TV components of the output).

Preethi Manuel, a writer and producer, became conscious of this absence of images, particularly of disabled children, when she had a disabled child.

I am a parent of a disabled child and also a writer. Seven years ago, at the hospital when the consultant pronounced my daughter was 'handicapped' (that was his term), it was not just the shock of a parent's expectations that froze me. I could not visualise in my mind anything, any picture, any person that would even vaguely resemble what my little girl was going to be. That vacant image of what my baby was going to grow up to be was one of the biggest traumas of my journey in parenting.

And yet, it need never have been. Disability is a normal part of life. I have learnt that only from meeting other disabled people. In this barrage of images fed to us today in the information highway that we are approaching (some say we are already on it), try as you might, where is the picture of the happy seven-year-old that my daughter is today? Where is documented the power, the strength, the vulnerability, the sheer humanity of thousands of children like her?

In that cold hospital room I badly needed an image of that reality. I realised that I was suffering because it wasn't there. The fact is, we all need that image too. We don't realise how deprived we all are because of the lack of it. Images of invisible children. As an eager parent I combed the Mothercare catalogue, pretty pictures all of them, but none of the model little children was disabled. The message to my daughter was clear – they are not very important people and even, do they really exist? The message of the omission is loud and clear. As an ex-teacher and media resources officer, no one need to have tried to convince me of the importance of images in our lives, particularly during those formative years when opinions and ideas are shaped.[2]

Even more problematic is the dearth of research work available in this area, compared to the amount of work that has been done, for example, on the representation of women and race.

There is also a neglect of factual output analysis in relation to disability, compared to that done on television drama. Although part of the Cumberbatch and Negrine study *Images of Disability on Television* (1992) covered factual output and produced some useful statistics, coverage was limited compared to the effort devoted to drama.[3] In their qualitative research, that is, research that involved interviews with producers, their selection seemed almost wholly to come from drama. Yet, of the 1,236 programmes looked at in the study period nearly two-thirds were factual programmes and one in six of these contained someone who could be classified as disabled. The rationale for dealing much more briefly with factual programmes was that 'the characteristics of non-fictional programmes can be summarised more succinctly and they do not usually have the richness of treatment, theme and storyline which a proper account of fictional genres

One in Four presenters Chris Davies, Isabel Ward, Simon Barnes, 1990 (BBC)

necessitates.'[4] One might argue that lack of recognition of the importance of factual coverage goes along with an uncertainty about what questions should be being asked. Certainly in news and documentary, camera angles, locations and interview style, programme format and the actual relationships between producer and participant are powerful mediators of the message.

Their study did quantify types of storylines and themes ('treatment' being the top percentage in both news and documentaries), and they analysed language for its acceptability and 'offensiveness'. But what was missing, for instance, was any breakdown of how many reporters, presenters and contributing 'experts' were appearing and how many of them were themselves disabled. Had the study been of representations of women, or of ethnic minorities, it is hard to imagine such a key question being neglected.

The question of whose voice is represented is a crucial one, and there has always been a tendency for documentary and current affairs producers to seek opinions on disability from the medical 'experts', social workers, paramedical professions and 'carers'. Further work commissioned by the Broadcasting Standards Council over the period 1992–5 did include some coding of disabled people appearing in major, minor or incidental interviewee roles, and perhaps this signals more detailed studies in this area.[5] However, the figures for roles depicted are not separated into factual and fictional programmes.

This Broadcasting Standards Council study revealed other changes in the distribution of the appearance of disabled people throughout the programme genres. In 1994, for example, there was a marked increase in appearances by disabled people on national news and a marked decrease on film, a phenomenon which was not surprising, however, given the activity in and outside Parliament around the Civil Rights Bill.[6]

In the Cumberbatch and Negrine study, the news category contained the greatest percentage of reporting on disability. However, it was distributed in news of a regional type, probably because 'disability' is generally seen as a 'soft', 'caring' type of story, not hard national news. This distribution somewhat misleadingly indicated that BBC2 and Channel Four (neither of which runs regional news) appeared to be the channels least interested in news coverage of disability.

The first contribution in this television section is an overview by **Chris Davies** of programmes featuring disabled people since the 1950s, particularly the specialist strands for disabled people. **Tracey Proudlock** then looks at disability in children's television and **Tom Shakespeare** reviews progress in the soaps.

An extract from **Anne Karpf**'s 1988 book *Doctoring the Media* is helpful in the absence of statistics if one wants to try and assess degrees of change. This is followed by **Ann Pointon**'s look at documentary and disability, with its emphasis on the personal rather than the political, while **Angie Carmichael** traces coverage of the Civil Rights (Disabled Persons) Bill. Finally, **Chris Davies** talks to producer **Terry Riley** about programming for Deaf viewers.

Notes

1. Ann Karpf, in Chapter 5 of *Doctoring the Media: The Reporting of Health and Medicine* (London: Routledge, 1988), an extract from which is included later in this section (see Chapter 2.5), comments on the sins of omission on the part of television producers.
2. Preethi Manuel speaking at the Invisible Children Conference, April 1995, organised by Richard Rieser and Michelene Mason, with the Save the Children Fund. Richard Rieser and a number of actors, writers and producers later founded the 1 in 8 group.
3. G. Cumberbatch and R. Negrine, *Images of Disability on Television* (London: Routledge, 1992).
4. Ibid., p. 27.
5. Communications Research Group, Aston University; findings published in Section 2 of *Perspectives of Disability in Broadcasting, Research Working Paper 11* (Broadcasting Standards Council, 1995), pp. 74–5.
6. Unpublished BSC figures, as at September 1995.

Window on the world – almost!
Chris Davies

Chris Davies has written articles on disability in the media for the *Guardian*, *The Times* and the *Independent*, and since 1986 he has been television critic for the monthly publication *Disability Now*. As a freelance broadcaster and producer, he was co-presenter of the BBC2 disability magazine programme *One in Four* and originated the BBC Select series *Disability Agenda*. He has founded two independent companies, each specialising in disability programming.

Outside television and the print media, Chris Davies has worked in disability arts mainly for the Arts Council of England. He is also a member of the British Film Institute's Disability Committee.

Chris Davies who has been watching and participating in disability television since its inception gives his overview of television output and its changes. He takes a particular look at the role of specialist programming for disabled people and raises the question of how far disability issues can move into the mainstream.

OUTSIDE THE WINDOW

In the early 1950s, *Panorama*, then, as now, the BBC's leading news and current affairs programme, carried the subtitle 'Window on the World'. Even as a child the phrase caught my imagination. Doubtless it wasn't meant to be considered literally, but for me as a disabled person, television *was* a window on the world for most of my life. It was only later, when my viewing began to be filtered through a political disability perspective, that I realised the window only permitted a partial view. The perspective I gained showed me how subtle and sophisticated television was in its selectivity, but well before my adulthood I was aware that television didn't show 'people like me'.

The 50s and 60s are pretty dim memories in terms of detail, but general impressions remain. In the early days of television, as in post-war cinema, escapism was the watchword. Then as now,

television informed (hence programmes such as *Panorama*), but the BBC, at that time the only channel, veered heavily towards panel games and light entertainment. *What's my Line?*, *Hancock's Half Hour*, *The Billy Cotton Band Show*, *Café Continental*, all these and many other similar programmes were the staple diet of the service, which in those days had fewer broadcast hours and relatively small audiences. My memories are of a screen that was unashamedly middle class in which men wore black ties and women evening dresses. Even the supposedly lower-middle-class and 'ordinary' family in the early soap opera *The Grove Family* was very well spoken.

As more films and American drama imports reached the screen, disabled people were in a sense 'present', but that is not the same as characters identifiable as useful role models. The effect then, in the early television mix, was of an absence of disabled people, but with the greater institutional segregation of the time fewer people had direct experience of disabled people, and that absence was therefore inconspicuous.

FLANDERS AND SWAN

While Robert Newton as *Long John Silver* in the TV series of that name sticks in the memory, the most well-known disabled person of the time was Michael Flanders, of the humorous duo, Flanders and Swan. Donald Swan and Michael Flanders staged a succession of very successful revues, accompanied by equally successful recordings (LPs). They performed and wrote their own songs, some serious, most humorous, linked by witty repartee. That Michael Flanders was a wheelchair user had very little to do with their success or their material, although reference was occasionally made to disability in their 'conversations'. Nevertheless, as a highly successful act, it for once gave a disabled performer an instant high profile, although he too wore a black tie, was white, middle class, articulate and debonair.

CHILDREN'S PROGRAMMES

The first major breakthrough in terms of regular programming came through children's television with the advent of *Vision On* (1964, BBC). One of its stars, Tony Hart, is still well known to today's children. The programme was originally designed as a vehicle for Deaf children and its original presenter came from a background of Deaf education. Yet it entertained everyone. The programme is probably known to millions who don't remember it as being mainly for a specialised audience of Deaf viewers, but with a mixture of art forms and a very visual style, it made access for hearing and Deaf viewers equal. There are still people who believe that programmes intended for a particular audience cannot be made accessible to others, something long ago disproved by *Vision On*.

Even in the early days, charity played a part. Although it may not have had the airtime it does today, the yearly appeal for *Children in Need* (BBC1) still informed (or misinformed) the public about disability. In addition, the BBC's children's TV had an annual appeal on its flagship programme, *Blue Peter* distinguished by its characteristic of not asking for money from children but reusable objects that could be exchanged for money.

IRONSIDE – THE SERIES

The late 1960s saw the creation of a character that put disability on the map in the shape of Chief of Detectives Robert T. Ironside who had been shot down and paralysed. Having become a wheelchair user he was expected to relinquish his former occupation, but being a bloody-minded character before the accident, he remained so afterwards and refused to accept a passive role. He then became a consultant to the Police Force, the first case being to find his own murderous assailant. There are disabled people today who ridicule *Ironside* (1967, BBC), and, as the character was played by a famous non-disabled actor already known for as previous able-bodied character, Perry Mason, it is very easy to dismiss the series as 'Perry Mason in a wheelchair'. And it is true to say that Ironside rarely encountered access hazards, so it was hardly a 'warts and all' portrayal of disability. Nevertheless, the character was thwarted occasionally by steps and mobility difficulties and did have to rely on his assistants, and the fact remains that here we had a hero who was a wheelchair user who was not only a central character but was successful by being assertive and authoritative. Such characters remain rare. For all its faults, this American series did provide a character capable of being a role model for other disabled people.

SANDY – SOAP OPERA

I suppose for some people, Sandy Richardson, from the ATV/Central soap *Crossroads* (1964), could also have been a role model; certainly he is always remembered whenever disability and television are discussed. I didn't follow the series, but Sandy to me was a much weaker character than Ironside. Like his American counterpart, Sandy acquired an impairment in the 70s and became a paralysed wheelchair user. Having been a non-disabled character, he was of course played by a non-disabled actor – at least initially. It was planned that he recover, until it was pointed out to the producers that because this was such an unlikely event it would cruelly raise the hopes of viewers who also had spinal injuries. In the event, fate also conspired against this as the actor became a genuine wheelchair user with spinal cancer, thus turning fiction into reality. Sandy's presence in *Crossroads* was the first example of disability in this soap, but it wasn't the last. Years later, via the influence and assistance of MENCAP (some would say ironically, given that this is a charity run by non-disabled people), a young person with Downs' syndrome became the centre of a story-line. And then, of course, there was Benny, a character who was 'slow'. He was never identified as being in any way disabled but there is a valid argument for saying that this ATV/Central soap beat *LA Law* (USA/ITV) in having the first regular character with a learning difficulty.

JOEY – DRAMA-DOCUMENTARY

Apart from these two examples, very little significant disability drama stands out from the late 60s to the early 70s. However, there were two notable examples of the hybrid drama-documentary type, both from the BBC. The similarities do not end in style because they were both dramatisations of real stories and featured the people whose stories they were telling. The award-winning *Joey*, directed by Brian Gibson, was an edition of the usually scientific documentary series *Horizon* and was broadcast in 1974 on BBC2. Based on the autobiography of Joey Deacon, it was ahead of its time because in addition to showing Joey and his disabled friends (who had cerebral palsy) as they were in real life, it featured other disabled actors in the flashbacks showing Joey's childhood and early adulthood. Yet like *Scallagrigg*, a 1994 BBC drama also featuring people with cerebral palsy, one of the incarnations of the central character was not played by a disabled actor. Nevertheless, it was strong stuff and well deserving of the acclaim it received.

So too was another BBC2 drama-documentary, *On Giant's Shoulders* (1979). Though its nominal stars were Judi Dench and Bryan Pringle, the real centre of attention was Terry Wiles, who had no limbs because of the drug thalidomide. Based on his own story, it told how a childless couple adopted the disabled teenager and how his adoptive father invented a wheelchair (among other aids) that could rise in height, enabling Terry to be more independent. This was a very sentimentalised version of reality, and not a favourite with all disabled people because of the strong 'parental carer' line, but undoubtedly the intelligence and presence of the disabled star was what won critical and viewer favour.

A WATERSHED – 1981

The International Year of Disabled People (IYDP) in 1981 triggered a surge of programmes about disability and marked a watershed. During that year the airwaves were crowded with disability factual programming, much of it poor, but nevertheless opening up long neglected topics.

Since then, in the ten years that I have been writing monthly television reviews, I have never been short of choice. But that choice is from a very mixed bag containing a certain amount of true gold and a great deal more televisual 'dross'.

Undoubtedly the most problematic programmes are those which exist to fundraise. Although the biannual 27-hour ITV Telethon was axed in 1992, the BBC still holds the admittedly less blatantly manipulative yearly *Children in Need*. *Children of Courage*, much criticised in the past for its voyeuristic use of disabled children 'demonstrating' their impairments, finished in 1993. And there is the notably more politically correct *Comic Relief*.

Other problem strands include *Hearts of Gold* (1988, BBC1) and *The Visit* (1983, BBC1). Often, these put 'carers' of various kinds on pedestals, and when disabled people are featured there is a tendency to show them as extraordinary people bravely overcoming the odds in order to be 'normal'. But it's not just emotive programmes such as the two just mentioned that promote 'normality' as the prime goal of disabled people. 'Normalisation' as an aim of scientific progress is often the angle on disability chosen by programmes such as *Horizon* (from 1964, BBC2), *QED* (BBC1) and *Tomorrow's World* (from 1955, BBC1).

Most of the 1981 programmes were definitely made from a non-disabled perspective and therefore had an in-built flaw. However, one very noticeable exception was a programme from the BBC2 popular documentary series, *Man Alive*, called 'Very Independent People'. This took three very different disabled people and showed them just getting on

with life. Most of the words were theirs and the narrative was mercifully free of emotive value judgments. One of the three people, Alison French, a young teenager with cerebral palsy who was shown preparing to leave school, made such an impression that two follow-up documentaries were made focusing entirely on her in the years that followed (*Alison* [1981] was about her beginning an independent life, and *I, Alison* [1988] about her marriage.)

While some of the 'gold' in disability terms appeared in mainstream programmes, most of it in my judgment was in the specialist programme strands across the channels.

SPECIALIST PROGRAMMES – ITV

Link is the only regular disability strand on the ITV network, and it goes out each Sunday morning across the network, fifty weeks of the year.

Started in 1976 by the then ATV and continued by Central Television, it began as a half-hour programme which initially alternated with a programme aimed at elderly people. It was also the first dedicated disability programme, although its scheduling has always been marginalised. It at least has a steady and full network time now, but for some years it appeared at different times on a Sunday, depending on the region, and did not appear in the north-west at all until the mid-80s. Being brought up in Merseyside, I had no idea of its existence until 1981, but having subsequently seen the first programme I can honestly say that it was well ahead of its time. In 1976 few people were familiar with the social model, and many still do not know about it. Yet, there in that first programme was a detailed explanation of the model and a discussion with presenter Rosalie Wilkins and Open University lecturer in disability studies, Vic Finkelstein. Initially it was

Michael Flanders and Donald Swann, *At the Drop of a Hat*, (BBC)

merely made *with* disabled people, but nowadays it is made *by* disabled people through an independent company for Central/Carlton Television.[1]

WE WON'T GO AWAY

Then came the IYDP in 1981, and *Link's* contribution, which was an hour-long special carried across the whole ITV network. Presented by Rosalie Wilkins, *We Won't Go Away* chronicled the early days of the American Civil Rights movement of disabled people. I surely can't be the only person whose life has been changed by this then truly revolutionary programme, fronted by a disabled person and showed disabled people acting through civil disobedience to attain legal equality. These days, when such demonstrations are relatively frequent in Britain, such material is less remarkable. The IYDP watershed in disability programming was for me a personal watershed, showing me that I could actually use the medium to which I was addicted and giving me a purpose for using that medium – to benefit my community.

SPECIALIST PROGRAMMES – BBC

In 1976 the Continuing Education Department at the BBC transmitted a series of ten programmes called *Contact* about disability, or 'handicap' as the popular terminology was at that time. Whether the series was meant to be a rival to *Link* is unsure and certainly there was no indication that the programme would extend beyond its initial run. Looking down the list of programme titles for *Contact*, it seems to have been intended as a self-contained package. The other difference appears to be in outlook. *Link*, right from the start, worked uncompromisingly for a disabled audience. In its assumptions and lack of explanations, it paid little heed to any non-disabled viewers who might be watching. *Contact* on the other hand, though being mainly for disabled people, had programmes on topics that while common knowledge to disabled people themselves were probably new to a non-disabled audience. This difference of outlook still distinguished *Link* from any of its competitors.

In 1979 the BBC also transmitted *Lost*

65

for Words, about people with communication impairments; *The Handicapped Family* followed in 1980. Since then the Education Department has made other excellent series, including *Disabled Lives* (1992, BBC) and *Denied the 9–5* (1994, BBC) about disability employment, but the bulk of the BBC specialist programmes now comes from the Disability Programmes Unit (DPU). *One in Four* predated and was a factor in the setting up of the DPU, and was replaced later by *From the Edge* (1993). Both series had magazine formats and both generally had off-peak late afternoon or early evening transmission. Later the *From the Edge* magazine was supplemented by an occasional late-night documentary strand called *Over the Edge* (1993), giving the team more opportunity to explore topics in depth. *See Hear* is the weekend strand for deaf viewers and has run on BBC since 1981 (see Part 2, Chapter 7).

**SPECIALIST PROGRAMMES –
CHANNEL FOUR**

Channel Four also began its specialist programming with a magazine strand *Same Difference* which like the BBC series was transmitted outside the evening slots. This was replaced by the documentary strand *People First* (1992), and later *Inside Out* (1995), both of which have two six-programme series each year. Channel Four's first series for Deaf viewers, *Listening Eye* (1984), was also replaced in 1992 with *Sign On*.

The most significant change, however, was that *People First* was the first regular disability series (as opposed to single programmes) to be allowed out of the ghetto, scheduled in 7.30 or 8 p.m. transmission slots.

WAYS INTO THE MAINSTREAM?

One hears frequent complaints from disabled people about ghettoisation in specialist programmes of important disability topics, which may sometimes be covered in the mainstream but in a quite different way. Even if one agrees that they achieve their aim of providing a specific service for a specific audience, the question always arises as to how well or badly they are doing this, and whether they are able also to provide information and entertainment to an eavesdropping audience of non-disabled people.

Much of this specialist programming is deliberately not balanced, covering topics either neglected or distorted in other media. But to differing degrees they recognise that the disabled audience itself is a wide one.

They have also tackled topics that appear in mainstream programmes, but with a different stance. Thus, *From the Edge* has featured disabled ex-miners, disabled casualties of Middle Eastern warfare, and disabled people facing discrimination from insurance companies. It is the perspective of direct experience of disability which no one else fully uses that really makes specialist programming unique, useful and valid. And there is no doubt that disabled people cannot find the same depth of coverage on their issues anywhere other than in their own programmes.

The content of most specialist programmes differs mainly in the degree to which they are willing to concede to a non-disabled viewership. *Link* has always made no bones about the fact that it wastes no time giving explanations that would make the programme more accessible for non-disabled people. The programme that emerged on BBC to challenge *Link* was *One in Four*, with a brief which was quite precise – to be the exact opposite to *Link* and appeal to the widest possible audience. Next came Channel Four's *Same Difference*, which lay somewhere in the middle, making more concessions than *Link* but less than *One in Four*. What the programmes shared was marginalisation in the schedules and if they got any consistent audience at all, it was a minor miracle.

But quality and a determination not to deter should mean that a wider audience is obtainable. This being the case, why not push them into the limelight of evening mainstream television? This is, in fact, just beginning to happen. From 1995 *From the Edge* went out early evening, the ground having already been tested with *The Invisible Wall* (7.30 p.m., BBC1, for three weeks in 1995) which used hidden camera techniques to illustrate discrimination in action. Autumn 1995 also saw four programmes on education called *Old School Ties* (scheduled at a peak time of 7.30 pm, BBC2).

While this movement into the mainstream might be considered brave, it has to be said that it is something that could and should have happened long ago. Channel Four deserve the credit for taking the plunge, with *People First*, but unlike its predecessor, *Same Difference*, it (and its successor *Inside Out*) is made by a variety of independent production companies, not all of which have disabled people playing a significant part in the production. In two six-programme series every year since 1992, it has handled a wide variety of topics, each given its own half-hour documentary. Though the programme-makers are encouraged to work with disabled people as much as possible, there is no obligation to do so. Therefore, the input of disabled people can't be guaranteed to be consistently high. The only factor that binds the programmes is that they are disability oriented and this is, in itself, widely interpreted — there have, for instance, been impairment based-programmes on asthma, epilepsy and sickle-cell anaemia. Whether or nor this diversity equates with dilution is a moot point. Certainly some *People First* programmes had harder edges then others, while some came dangerously close to being medical explanations.

But the omens are good. A less marginalised choice of transmission time will mean that more people, including disabled people, will at last have the chance to become more acquainted with disability issues. It is no longer the case that one has to make a choice — disability specialist programmes or disability in mainstream programmes — because specialist programmes are becoming more part of the mainstream. The final frontier will be the move from BBC2 and Channel Four to BBC1 and ITV, but maybe crossing this final frontier isn't the task of the specialist programmes. After all, *Tomorrow's World* has been on the air for long enough and with large audiences. Yet, given the numbers of people who really understand the science behind it, surely this is a specialist programme? As the song says, 'It ain't what you do, it's the way that you do it'.

But what is the mainstream future when it is clear that the 'brave and/or tragic' stereotype is still with us, for instance in *Journey to Knock* (1991, BBC2), *Goodbye Cruel World* (1992, BBC2) and *Keeping Tom Nice* (1990, BBC2)?

Well, apart from the specialist programmes, the window on the world does give occasional accurate glimpses of disability. Fictionally, the best most recent examples have been *The Count of Solar* (1992, BBC), *Scallagrigg* (1994, BBC) and *Deptford Graffiti* (1991, C4) . However, on a sustained level, I consider that the best example of drama ever to come out of Britain was the fifty-week reign of *Eldorado* (1992, BBC1). The character of Nessa Lockhead never went beyond teenage shallowness, and life in expatriate Spain is hardly one with which many can identify, but even given this it was a sustained attempt to incorporate a disabled character as a member of the core cast. It was a year's brave experiment that deserved to be continued, or at least followed by others.

Factually, my window on the world has also shown me *Don't Just Sit There* (1988) and *Go for It* (1989), both Channel Four programmes aimed at motivating young disabled people); *D'art* (1992), again Channel Four, encouraging the artistic talents of Deaf people, and *Disabled Lives* (1992, BBC2), which, together with *Rights Not Charity* (1988, BBC2), not only provided political role models but explained the purpose of the movement of disabled people.

THE PRESENT PICTURE

So does my window now show all that it ought? No, noticeably not in comedy and not in game shows. Humour and disability appear to be difficult to handle, in case the laughter is at the expense of disabled people. However, that doesn't mean that these difficulties shouldn't be challenged. To the best of my knowledge, there have only ever been three attempts to write a situation comedy around a disabled character and all stopped at the pilot stage. The other blank spot, game shows, is connected to the physical characteristics involved with the mechanics of the game. There have been disabled contestants on a few shows such as *Going for Gold, Big Break, Blankety Blank* and *Every Second Counts* (BBC1), but because of the requirements of the programme, these tend to be physically self-sufficient and therefore 'normal' disabled people – if you can't stretch or co-ordinate your movement, how can you press buttons, bells, etc.? The other problem with game shows is that the presenters tend to be show business oriented, mainly comedians, for whom being patronising is arguably a way of life.

In 1995 I reached fifty. Most of that time I have spent obsessed with that square window on the world. Though the window is now more oblong and has digital style, the quality, as far as representation of disabled people is concerned, still has much room for improvement. When it finally reaches and realises its potential to minimise if not eliminate the disabling factor in our society, I for one will die happy, and, at last, it will be an actual fact that television is a Window on the World – on all of it.

Note

1.   See Part 3, Chapter 6 for an interview with Kevin Mulhern who currently produces *Link* for Central Television.

2.2

For generations to come
Tracey Proudlock

Tracey Proudlock was born in the north-east of England, the youngest of four children. On graduating from university in 1986, she moved to London to work in the voluntary sector. She is a private pilot and founder member of Delta Foxtrot, the disabled pilots' association, and is on the National Executive of ASBAH (the Association for Spina Bifida and Hydrocephalus). She is a member of the Institute of Personnel and Development and currently works for an Inner London local authority. Her first pregnancy (she has two children) was the subject of 'Mother's Pride' (BBC2, 1993), an *Over the Edge* programme, and she has subsequently presented *From the Edge*.

There have undoubtedly been many excellent television programmes that have featured disabled children in the best possible way. However, much of the television we watch is forgotten, and people are left with their all too fallible memories and only a general 'sense' of what television has told them. The understated wheelchair-using actor in *Press Gang* (1992, Central TV) left a positive impression in my own mind, precisely because of the lack of fuss made. But television is also as powerful as it is ephemeral, and a memory that persists just as strongly is of a *Blue Peter* programme, many decades old, where a group of disabled children were being loaded onto a red and white bus with Sunshine Coach written on the outside. As a young disabled person, I was uncomprehending and angry that donors should think it a happy and dignified experience for disabled people to travel around in labelled transport. And I am disturbed even now, whenever I see just such a patronising charity coach on the road, or watch programmes that feature them.[1]

Tracey Proudlock, now the mother of two children, has her own memories, as well as suggestions for better representation of disability on children's television.

Billy and I are wheeling around the supermarket. In and out of the aisles, it's just an ordinary day, but the two of us are having fun doing mundane chores. I am jolted out of mother-and-baby domestic bliss by the loud voice of another, older child: 'Look Daddy, that woman has no feet, tee hee hee.' Immediately I am hurled back to my own childhood of classroom teasing. This time my hurt is quickly replaced by raging anger and I desperately look at the 'offending father'. I cannot and will not blame the child for her comments, it is the father I blame. But he averts my eye, refusing to catch my stares, for I have already decided I will challenge his child's behaviour, not for my sake but for my own child's. The moment is lost, he dashes to the cheese counter and I am left deflated.

Children, in their early years, speak with remarkable innocence and truth. It is the adult world that corrupts. In a child's very early years, undoubtedly home is the prime influence; this is quickly overtaken and replaced by school and television. It

'Sandy' in *Crossroads*, (Central Television)

would seem that children watch so much television, it could be argued that they take more notice of it than they do of their parents! If we are to educate children about disability and include disabled people in all aspects of life, then surely television – specifically children's television – is the prime tool.

As a disabled child I do not remember seeing disabled characters on children's television, but I do remember pestering my parents to allow me to watch *Crossroads* and *Ironside*. I was a political innocent, and Sandy, the tragic disabled son of hotelier Meg Richardson, spoke volumes to me. Sandy was in a wheelchair but never seemed to have problems getting around, he wore a shirt and tie and, like every other adult I knew, had a job. I soon became bored with Sandy, in fact he rarely left the hotel or did anything dangerous or offensive. My tastes matured and I moved on to *Ironside* – now there was a man to emulate! He had his own wheelchair-accessible van with chauffeur and a team of agents to boss around. While these programmes were aimed at the non-disabled adult consumer, they were speaking to me. These are my only memories of disability on television in the 70s.

When I am at parties, non-disabled people often try to make small talk: 'I suppose', they say, 'over the years you've noticed things getting better for the disabled?' Yes, I must admit certain aspects of our environment are more accessible to disabled people, but nothing can be taken for granted. We, disabled people, have no rights of access to everyday facilities. I am still regarded as a fire hazard and banned from my local cinema when using my wheelchair, and in all probability I will be physically excluded from my children's school. If I am a fire risk in cinemas, how can I take my children to the Saturday morning cartoon shows? It's quite simple – we won't go to the cinema and we will be confined to home viewing.

If I am excluded from major aspects of life, how can I honestly say things are 'looking up' for disabled people, and what hope is there for children and young people looking for a lead on how they too should respond to disability? There has been a small increase in the number of disabled characters on television, but precious few are on children's programmes. Perhaps this is because producers think disabled children do not do things independently, that they just have things done to them and therefore quite legitimately can only be featured when their condition is the storyline or issue. So we have a position where disabled children's characters are brought in and out of programmes at will and disability is not part of life's natural jigsaw.

The BBC children's drama unit has made brave attempts to tackle this situation: *Byker Grove* and *Grange Hill* have both featured disabled characters with varying degrees of success. In *Grange Hill* a disabled actress portrayed a young schoolgirl with cerebral palsy, and we are told by the producers that they drew on the young actress's direct experience of disability in the storylines. Here we are in a catch-22 position. A young disabled person portraying disability on screen can be a powerful message to the viewing public. However, I would challenge the wisdom of relating a young person's experience of disability to issues within the wider disabled community itself. For instance, it would be naive to expect a young person to appreciate the subtle ways that society excludes and discriminates against us when we apply for jobs or assert our right to be sexual beings. There is of course a need for disability equality training for disabled and non-disabled children alike. I remember my own valiant efforts to pass off as 'normal' at school and social functions in my early teenage years. How my anxiety could have been eased, had I been given the opportunity to speak more with disabled adults and appreciate some of the positive aspects of my disability.

Perhaps I would not be so concerned if I were not a parent myself. I have selfish motives to bring about a change in children's TV. By reaching out to young people I will not just be helping to secure a better, and better-informed, future, I will also be smoothing the path for my own children who inevitably will be the topic of many pitying conversations, for having such a 'terribly disabled mother'. I am conscious of other older children pointing and staring at me, and indirectly their abuse is aimed at my children.

So how would I change children's programmes? Perhaps the most obvious but apparently difficult hurdle is to introduce disabled actors and characters into programmes. Programmes ought to reflect what actually happens in the High Street. One in four consumers either have a disability or are close to someone who does. Exciting things can and do happen to disabled people.

Blue Peter, the BBC flagship children's programme, has been watched by millions of children for decades. As a child I remember desperately longing to win a Blue Peter badge, but I could not do Scottish Highland dancing or play the violin so my chances were slim to say the

least. If I could not win a badge, at least once a year I could join their patronage of 'others less fortunate than myself' — yes I am talking about the Blue Peter Special Appeal! I remember collecting balls of old wool, old aluminium tincans and used stamps to save the African children threatened with famine and disease and, quite possibly, for their famous appeal 'Riding for the Disabled'. The appeals were always straightforward enough: here is a problem, make a small sacrifice or donation to make the situation better. The traditional Blue Peter Appeal can and should be an opportunity to examine in greater detail issues of charitable giving and how young people can work together to change situations. Perhaps in years to come the Blue Peter Appeal will be launched by a disabled presenter, blowing a hole through the traditional, worn-out charity campaigns. The real breakthrough will come when *Blue Peter* launches an appeal in partnership with organisations controlled by disabled people with an agenda to empower and not, as we have at the moment, one that enables the non-disabled community to feel smug and worthy at our expense. I and many other disabled people are not against wealth sharing, but we do oppose charitable giving which undermines our existence and rights to everyday facilities.

Children's gameshows offer other opportunities. Some shows concentrate on physical challenges of strength and dexterity, which would not automatically rule out all disabled children, but there is little positive encouragement for such children to come forward. Disabled children with a talent for anagrams and puzzles are rarely given the opportunity to shine like their peers. I am therefore suggesting positive action on behalf of TV researchers to go out and find talented disabled young people for their programmes. I recently saw a young girl on a school quiz programme whose rapid responses to questions on everything from medieval history to Greek mythology could not fail to impress. Her blindness was only mentioned when she claimed her prize of a wrist-watch – it had been brailled so she could read it herself.

Lack of media representation cannot simply be blamed on the entertainment industry itself. Young people who have been segregated in their education and leisure pursuits or who are living in institutions will not naturally present themselves. At this point it should be noted that segregated facilities are not bad per se; sometimes we want the option of being separate to talk among ourselves. The injustice creeps in when we have no choice or alternatives and we are planned out of schools, clubs and services. Here there is a role for documentaries and educational programmes. Where there is injustice or denial it should be uncovered in an informed manner and I do not mean Desmond Wilcox features about 'triumph over adversity'. Within the children's arena we are looking at *The Lowdown* and *Newsround* type programmes telling other children about such things as disabled youngsters going to the courts fighting for a place at a mainstream school.

Educating young people about disability does not always have to take the form of drama and documentaries. Children love escapism and we can open up many options to inform them through cartoons and science fiction. Disability is not and should never be a tedious issue, if anything it enables people to explore exciting possibilities beyond their own experience.

When we are young we look for role models, someone to dream about and hang on our bedroom walls. Whoever we are, we are never quite like our idol but we still want to do and say the same things they do. So few disabled people are held up as non-patronising role models, that it's no wonder that disabled children have little self esteem and their non-disabled peers grow up thinking disabled people are dreary! As a teenager I wanted to be a dancer with Pan's People on *Top of the Pops*, but then I met Eileen. She was a disabled teacher from a nearby village who took me out in her car, an automatic with hand controls. I soon forgot about miniskirts and dancing and I wanted a car just like Eileen's!

Like most parents, I want the best for my children. As much as anything I want for them a world that values difference, and one that therefore respects the rights of disabled people. Such inclusiveness would open up opportunities and enrich lives, not just for those of us with a disability, but society at large. Through children's television, disabled people can reach out to young people, who are still open to a new understanding of disability. Of course, no matter how well informed children's programmes may become, children increasingly have access to prime-time adult television, with all its stereotypes, gimmickry and catchphrases. Television has the power to play a part in the formation of social opinion and ultimately the removal of discrimination and barriers to disabled people. It is not children that irk disabled people, but the bad behaviour of our television industry.

Notes

1. A programme for children 'Bring Me Sunshine', in the *Lowdown* series (BBC1, 1989), was shot around the donation of a Sunshine Coach to a special school. It was entirely and 'warmly' naive about both special schools and the role of charity in donating what was clearly essential provision.

Soaps: The story so far
Tom Shakespeare

Tom Shakespeare is a Research Fellow at the University of Leeds, and is actively involved in the Northern Disability Arts Forum. He has written and reviewed for numerous periodicals, including *Disability and Society*, *The Times Higher Educational Supplement* and *Critical Social Policy*, and has broadcast frequently. His CV describes his 'other activities' as: compere, comedian, story-teller, fire-eater, and safer sex educator.

As his starting point, Shakespeare takes Cumberbatch and Negrine's[1] Broadcasting Research Unit study, based on work done in 1988 when the representation of disabled people in soaps was not only low, but particularly so in contrast to the other strong social and political storylines that soaps were running. His trawl through some more recent soap developments indicates that there has been some improvement.

Among genres of fictional television entertainment, the soap opera is predominant. In Britain, domestic series such as *Eastenders*, *Brookside* and *Coronation Street* regularly head the audience ratings, and even the recognisably weaker Australian imports such as *Home and Away* and *Neighbours* are extremely popular, reflected in the celebrity status accorded stars such as Kylie Minogue, Mark Little and Jason Donovan. While the sensationalism and sentimentality of the genre may dismay cultural purists, exciting storylines and a willingness to deal sensitively with controversial issues suggest that shows such as *Eastenders* and *Brookside* represent British television at its best. Above all, soap operas are about entertainment, forming a cherished part of the lives of millions of viewers.

Guy Cumberbatch and Ralph Negrine's 1988 research led them to critical conclusions regarding the place of disability in soaps. Finding that only 8 per cent of programmes portrayed disabled people,[2] they contrasted this neglect with the strong coverage of other social and political issues. In their conclusions they argued:

There do need to be series written and produced in which people with disabilities are among the leading characters. Should this occur, then the public would be regularly confronted with the experience of disability in a perfectly ordinary context. The most ordinary context is presumably that of the realistic soap opera and we strongly urge writers and producers of soap operas to accept the continuing challenge to provide such roles.[3]

Certainly at that stage disabled people had played little part in the life of British soaps, and then usually in stereotypical roles. For example, 'Sizzler' was a villain character in *Brookside* and had a stammer. Colin, the pioneering gay character in *Eastenders*, developed a mystery illness, first thought to be AIDS and later revealed to be multiple sclerosis. Like wheelchair-using Owen from *Brookside*, Colin was soon written out. More progressive was the development of Nina, the young woman with learning diffi-culties in *Crossroads*, a soap which had also featured Sandy, a wheelchair user, and Benny, a character with mild learning difficulties, in previous years.

More recently there is evidence of slight improvement in the coverage of disability, both in the number of charac-ters, and in the variety of issues covered. *Coronation Street*, which is characterised by a less realistic, more exaggerated style, has featured Don Brennan, who has had a car accident which led to a leg amputation. After an initial failure to cope, Don has recently developed a more positive outlook and formed a new relationship. Interestingly, Don's impair-ment led to a shared bond with another character, Denise. The actress playing this character has an impairment of the hand, and playing Denise she was able to give encouragement to Don and argue strongly that 'disability doesn't matter'. Another storyline involved Tracy Barlow, who developed kidney failure after taking the recreational drug Ecstasy. Eventually she was able to have a transplant, after the death of her mother's boyfriend and donation of his kidney, and is now able to live a normal life. And then there was Maud Grimes, the cantankerous owner of the corner shop. Maud is as equally bad news for portrayal of elderly people as she is for disabled people. She used a wheelchair but her main characteristic was dogged awkwardness. The women in the cartoon strip *Andy Capp* or those in *Last of the Summer Wine* are no more of a caricature of elderly women from the north of England than Maud. The melodramatic coverage of disability in *Coronation Street*, typical of the series, is similar to the regular use of health crisis in Australian soaps, usually to write out characters, and is equally medicalised.

Eastenders takes a more realistic approach to modern life, strongly centred on characters. However, it has failed to develop major disabled roles. Minor dis-abled parts have included Lloyd Tavernier, who had the condition sickle-cell anaemia, which was seen to prevent him enjoying the same freedoms and lifestyle as his school friends: he was written out after a short time when most of his family moved on from Albert Square. A positive use of a disabled actor in a 'roll-on' role came during a storyline about the demolition of the youth club, in which the council official – represented as being officious, but not entirely negative – was a wheelchair user. However, the major success of *Eastenders* in this area has been the character of Mark Fowler, who is HIV positive. His diagnosis, the reaction of his family, and the death of his wife Gillian, have all been portrayed sensitively and effectively, and his story continues to unfold as he has now formed a new partnership and is considering starting a family.

Brookside takes the same realistic approach as *Eastenders*, with a grittier style which focuses on social issues. However, again there has been only a limited treatment of disability. For example, one storyline concerned a main character, Sheila Grant, who became a dinner-lady at a Deaf school and be-friended one of the children there. This enabled the programme to feature Deaf people and British Sign Language and was generally a positive treatment. However, this storyline was not further developed after the girl left the school. More significant was the exploration of the issue of prenatal testing through the pregnancy of Patricia Farnham. Having had one child with Max, she discovered after amniocentesis that their second child had Downs syndrome. The issue was handled very realistically: after an initial reaction of acceptance at the time of the diagnosis, the father, Max Farnham, reacted very negatively at the time of the birth, refusing to see his daughter or accept that she was disabled. After a major row between husband and wife, he managed to come to terms with the situation, and they subsequently became a model family, with baby Alice often featured in the programme. Apparently, the original plan of the producers was to write Alice out of the series after about three months, but she was so popular that there are now plans for her to be an ongoing character.

Among the minor soaps, *Emmerdale* has recently featured several positive portrayals of disabled people. For example, an actor with visual impairment played a young blind student in several episodes, after one of the characters went to college in Leeds. More importantly, a main character, Chris Tate, became impaired after the ludicrous storyline in which an aeroplane crashed into the village. Initially, Chris seemed to be the stereotypical bitter and twisted wheelchair user, but subsequently a storyline developed in which he had an affair with a friend who had been supportive. More recently they have had a child together. While not condoning his behaviour, this is a more interesting representation of disability than is conventional, especially given the fact that disabled characters are usually either asexual or sexually deviant. Most positive of all was the development of a young disabled character on the soap *Eldorado*, played by an actress, Julie Fernandez, who herself uses a wheelchair. Unfortunately, the programme was not well received and was short-lived: this was a rare example of a well-thought-out character, integrated into the life of the soap, who was treated as an ordinary individual and not as a stereotype defined by her medical condition.

Having explored the chequered record of British soap opera producers, I will conclude by discussing some of the opportunities for building on the example set by *Eldorado*. While it seems that the producers and writers pass the buck over their responsibility for developing disabled characters,[4] the time for soap operas to represent communities appropriately and fairly is long overdue. Given that disabled people comprise one in eight of the population; given the rise in disabled people's self-organisation and the increasing success of disabled people in a wide range of public spheres; and given the slow but steady increase in the number of skilled disabled actors, there is no excuse for continuing failure.

Three major developments are necessary at the outset. First, a willingness to use disabled actors to play disabled roles. Without this, any increase in such roles is meaningless. Second, the development of disabled characters central to the community life of the major soap operas, especially older disabled people and disabled women. These must be characters who can develop and grow during the years, in the same way as other non-disabled characters, not people to be written out or killed off after a few months. Third, disabled people should also be seen in the background, and in incidental and walk-on roles. Given the diversity of the British population, the failure of soaps to show this variety and difference is problematic for programmes which aim to be genuinely realistic.

However, these character and role developments do not exhaust the possibilities. With new characters, new storylines become possible. In the past, disability has been medicalised and narratives have centred around traumatic accidents, death-bed crises and other dramas of diagnosis and disease. However, disability is about far more than

Yesterday's 'Soap' – learning disabled Benny in *Crossroads* (Central Television)

Today's 'Soap' – baby Alice and the Farnham
family in *Brookside*. Courtesy of Channel Four

this focus on impairment. Disabled people face discrimination in modern societies. For example, people face major obstacles to gaining employment; parents of disabled children have to fight for them to be educated in mainstream schools; disabled people face violence and prejudice in the streets and in social settings such as pubs; housing, transport and other services are inaccessible. All these are dramatic situations, often involving major interpersonal conflict. It is easy to imagine an issue-based programme such as *Brookside* developing a gripping storyline around such experiences. Critically, this would have to involve more than one disabled character, and would have to offer a disabled person's viewpoint. Such a radical shift in orientation would also open up the possibility of representing the increasing militancy and radicalism of disabled people and disability groups, who are no longer prepared to endure discrimination, but are effectively organising and demonstrating against it.

One precondition for this type of narrative development is actually talking and listening to disabled people themselves. If television news can represent new developments around disability, so can soaps. If researchers and writers were to witness some of the experiences of British disabled people, they would be far better placed to write about them. Better still, disabled people could be employed as consultants or writers for soap operas. There are many writers within the disability arts community who are equal to the challenge of scripting soap operas: just as gay writers are now being employed, so we should expect to see disabled writers, because this is the key to fairer and more appropriate representation.

I believe the situation is improving, and it is vital that it does so, because soap operas are a key part of contemporary television scheduling. Britain's six million disabled people form a major part of the TV audience, and we have every right to see ourselves, and our issues, on popular programmes. Representing disability fairly is not a matter of political correctness, and it certainly is not incompatible with exciting entertainment. I look forward to the day when we can watch the Greater Manchester Coalition of Disabled People protesting against the inaccessibility of the Rovers Return. I know that *Brookside* would only be improved were disabled actress Mandy Colleran to be given accommodation in the Close. And I am deeply surprised that the Disabled People's Direct Action Network have still not targeted Albert Square. It's only a matter of time.

Notes
1. G. Cumberbatch and R. Negrine, *Images of Disability on Television* (London: Routledge, 1992).
2. Ibid. p. 46.
3. Ibid. p. 140.
4. Ibid. p.130.

Block Telethon demonstration outside LWT, 1992. Courtesy of GLAD

Where were you?

Telethon last year,

We were there

Children in Need,

We were there,

Cheltenham by-election,

We were there,

Morris Cerullo, evangelist

fascist,

disability is payment

for your sins,

We were there

DAN's next action

Where will you be?

Disabled People's Direct Action Network

2.4

Crippling images
Anne Karpf

From Chapter 5, 'Crippling Images', in *Doctoring the Media: The Reporting of Health and Medicine* (London: Routledge, 1988).

Anne Karpf is a journalist, sociologist and the *Guardian*'s radio critic. She has had a particular interest in medicine and television, and *Doctoring the Media* was probably the first book about British television to look critically at the output of telethons. She grounded her work in the critiques that were already a feature of the growing voice of disabled people in Britain.

In this extract from *Doctoring the Media* Anne Karpf takes a look at factual programmes, at a time when the the use of disabled people on screen was even more strongly medical model-based than it is today. Her treatment of telethons makes useful reference to their American origin. She also looks at what she terms 'consumer' programmes, by which she means specialist disability programmes rather than general consumer output. The general consumer programmes of the time generally did not perceive disabled consumers as 'out there', and have only relatively recently begun to recognise this sector of audience in the occasional item in holiday, sports, gardening or motoring series.
 In this chapter Karpf identifies some of the 'real' issues surrounding disability, using the social model derived from her awareness of a growing disability voice, which, as she indicates, was being by-passed by the media. What is depressing is that some eight years later recognition of this voice by other journalists and media workers is still so limited.

DISABLED BY WHOM?

The images of disability on the big and small screens are mainly medical and seemingly natural, uncontroversial and unchangeable. In the medical approach, disability results either from a cruel accident of nature (a genetic gaffe) or from fate (causing riding accidents, sporting mishaps or car crashes). People with disabilities are courageous or long-suffering; we're invited to praise or pity them. They're applauded in 'aren't they wonderful' stories for triumphing over their disability, and for performing tasks as proficiently as the able-bodied (or even better). A blind woman climbs Everest,[1] a deaf woman is an award-winning professional percussionist.[2] Medicine offers them the possibility of a cure, or helps them function more 'normally' by supplying increasingly sophisticated technological aids, and charity is its sidekick, raising money and hope. The medical approach also encourages the take-up of prenatal screening and rubella immunisation to prevent handicap.[3] Programmes using the medical approach are usually presented and produced by able-bodied people, for the medical approach speaks to the able-bodied (and shows disability as seen by them); 'the disabled' are its objects.

The consumer approach, by contrast, addresses people with disabilities them-

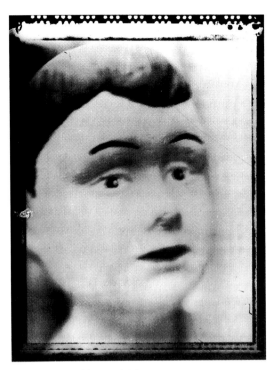

courtesy of David Hevey

selves, or their carers. Consumer programmes, often aimed at people with a
specific disability like visual handicap or
deafness, offer information about goods
services, and welfare benefits, reviewing
new aids and equipment, and tackling
problems such as access. They're strong
advocates of self-help, acting (on air and
off) as a clearing-house for self-help
groups and charitable organisations.
They're often presented by people with
disabilities, and are broadcast either in
afternoon magazine programmes or the
'ghetto' weekend morning slots reserved
for minorities and education
programmes.

The look-after-yourself programme,
when it looks at disability, speaks of its
prevention. It proposes personal ways of
maintaining health and avoiding disabling
conditions, for instance through precon-
ceptual care.[4] It offers advice, given or
endorsed by doctors, aimed at the able-
bodied. In the environmental approach,
disabled isn't a noun or adjective, it's a
verb. People are disabled by the society

they live in: social institutions and
practices disable them more than their
physical or mental handicap. The environmental approach explicitly challenges the
medical approach, rejecting the notion of
handicap as a 'natural' condition or a
medical fact of life inevitably bringing
other problems. 'If a person in a
wheelchair is unable to take an office job
because there are steps up to an office
building are we to assume that the fault
lies with the wheelchair user for not
being able to climb steps? I would say the
fault lies in the architecture.'[5] Similarly,
the absence of sign language interpreters
at public meetings or events denies deaf
people access to the hearing world. In the
environmental approach, attention is
shifted from people with disabilities to
the wider culture: the problem is no
longer the disability, but rather the failure
of the able-bodied community to accom-
modate it. Social interaction, rather than
an intrinsic physical condition is to blame.
In the environmental approach, people
with disabilities aren't spoken for by
others: they speak for themselves.

BRAVING THE MEDIA
The past two decades' quiet revolution
by people with disabilities has gone
largely unrecorded by the media. Able-
bodied broadcasters are still (and
increasingly) enthralled by the dominant
medical approach. 'Cure' stories are
favourites, like 'the miracle of the man
who got his sight back after 36 years',[6] or
the sick child whose leg was amputated,
and her heel reattached as a knee fixed
to an artificial leg. The disability movement argues that:

**we celebrate deaf people, but they
celebrate people who aren't deaf any
more. They love stories about
children who have been given
marvellous new hearing aids, deaf
people who've learnt to play**

instruments... **The emphasis is always on becoming as much like hearing people as possible.**[7]

Courage is their defining characteristic. Children with disabilities must always be smiling, since 'a happy child seems to be the only acceptable image of disability'.[8] They achieve Douglas Bader feats of fortitude, as if individual acts of heroism represented the solution to their daily problems and disability was only an individual and psychological challenge, not also a practical and collective one. Exceptional disabled people are particularly popular, notching up achievements impossible or irrelevant to most people with disabilities – hence the blind mountain-climber or runner – even though the average British blind person is elderly, female and usually hard up.[9]

This kind of coverage was especially prevalent in the International Year of Disabled People (1981), when 'children received bravery awards for lying in bed and undergoing operations. A thalidomide 'heroine' made headlines for passing her driving test. Television news showed a compulsive tendency to film us struggling to make a cup of tea with an able-bodied commentary overlaid.'[10] Television often uses these images for its leave-'em-happy final news story, usually occasioned by a visit from Royalty.

TELETHONS: CHILD APPEAL

Telethons, fund-raising television marathons, are the annual opportunity for celebrities and audiences to have fun while doing good. Simultaneously glitzy and worthy, they're usually 12- or 24-hour affairs with celebrities dropping into the studio to chat or perform, and filmed inserts of charities needing money or showing what past recipients did with theirs. Viewers and listeners phone in to pledge donations and the presenters, regularly announcing the total to date,

exhort the audience to the finishing-line – the target sum.

Telethons demand enormous organisation – one used 650 telephones staffed by British Telecom telephonists. The BBC telethon *Children in Need* ropes in every BBC local and national radio station, as well as the BBC TV networks. And the 1985 Thames Telethon completely displaced the station's regular schedules for twenty-four hours. Telethons originated in the United States, where the best known is comedian Jerry Lewis's Labor Day telethon, which has raised large sums for muscular dystrophy charities for nineteen years. When the BBC borrowed the idea in 1980 they decided that the British public wouldn't stomach the full American revelry, with its unrestrainedly heart-tugging appeals in a 24-hour non-stop variety show. The BBC version is a more muted affair, aiming to reach the (smaller, local) charities the other appeals don't reach. Its recipients are children with mental or physical handicaps (who get some 40 per cent of the grants), or those with behaviour disorders, in care, hospital or living in under-resourced or stressful places. The sums raised by telethons are sizeable. Between them in 1985, the BBC and Thames TV telethons raised over £5 million, and in 1985/6 British commercial radio stations raised over £2.6 million in cash for charity through events like a Walkathon (a 25-mile charity walk).

But although the receiving organisations are understandably pleased to have the money, telethons have been roundly indicted by American disability activists for perpetuating damaging stereotypes of disability that outweigh the financial gains. While acknowledging both organisers' and donors' good intentions, they argue that they arouse 'there, but for the grace of God' feelings in their audience which oppress people with disabilities.

In order to get their money, they have to humiliate me ... to me, a wheelchair is a solution, not a sentence. Because I use a wheelchair, I am able to do many things I otherwise could not. I am not 'confined to a wheelchair'. I don't 'face a life without meaning', and I'm not a 'poor, unfortunate cripple who needs your help'.[11]

Although British telethons are more subtle, their images usually more positive and optimistic, the British disability movement too deplores:

... fund-raising at a distance ... the twentieth-century version of the beggar in the streets. Even the begging bowls are no longer in our own hands ... [It] gives people a sense of doing something for us without bringing them into contact with us.[12]

Most British telethons focus almost exclusively on children, since cute youngsters undoubtedly head the hierarchy of tele-appeal with less cute oldsters at the bottom. There's a total mismatch between the age of those people with disabilities who appear on telethons (and TV in general) and the age of the majority of people with disabilities in the general population. Moreover, although the BBC's rules specifically forbid them giving grants to relieve a statutory body of its responsibilities, disadvantaged groups are especially disadvantaged at a time of cuts, and telethons (since they rarely collect for luxuries) can't help but contribute to the idea that it's the job of private organisations and not the state to provide or collect essential funds. They also reinforce an image of people with disabilities as dependent on charity. Even where telethons increase the visibility of people with disabilities, their one-off oc-currence inevitably smacks of tokenism.

For whose benefit are telethons organised? It's not always clear. Parts of the 1985 Thames Telethon were commercially sponsored, causing one TV critic to observe that:

no shove ha-penny contest went unsponsored. This made for wall-to-wall advertising and a steady line of executives crossing the stage like ants, each carrying a large cardboard cheque. 'Give a big hand to the chairman of Burtons' ... 'Sponsored by those lovely folk from Panasonic'.[13]

Commercial companies gain a whiff of worthiness and all are beyond reproach when the vulgarity's for charity. Since telethons make the able-bodied feel bountiful (and many would be affronted to hear that people with disabilities feel oppressed by their pity), telethons may really be for the able-bodied. As the Controller of BBC1, who authorised the first British telethon, said, 'It makes me feel warm.'[14]

Could telethons be different? In 1979 United Cerebral Palsy (UCP), an American organisation known for its 'look, we're walking' telethons, decided to change them. They wrote up the speeches the celebrities were supposed to make, asked people with disabilities to monitor the telethon, and set out guidelines stressing that telethons should show both adults and children and should reflect the degrees of disability typical among people with cerebral palsy. Celebrities were to be thoroughly informed about the condition and use appropriate terminology, avoiding terms like victim, poor, cripple, unfortunate, tragedy and other words arousing pity rather than respect. They were also to avoid asking viewers to give out of thankfulness that their own children were born healthy, and UCP outlawed images that placed undue emphasis on people with cerebral palsy walking and talking, leading to unrealistic public expectations and damaging the self-image of people with cerebral palsy who would never be able to do either. They also wanted to draw attention to the organisation's advocacy role in helping people with disabilities realise their own desires and needs, like gaining access to public education, barrier-free buildings and transport, housing and jobs.

When people with disabilities monitored the telethon, they found it a significant but limited improvement. Though the main issues emerged the celebrities are tuned to seize on the theatrics of the moment. Given national television exposure, they are not going to be held to tight, pre-drafted scripts. So when they see a moment of possible drama, they seize it.[15]

Notes

1. *Woman's Hour* (BBC Radio 4, 7 January 1986).

2. *The Glennie Determination* (BBC Radio 4, 7 January 1986), and Wogan (BBC1, 24 January 1986).

3. The medical approach often grossly inflates the proportion of congenital abnormalities, detectable by prenatal screening. In reality, most people acquire disabilities later in life, as the result of an accident or chronic illness like a stroke, where prenatal screening is irrelevant.

4. The spread of the look-after-yourself approach and its emphasis on the perfectability of the body has created a climate in which disability is even more deviant.

5. Allan T. Sutherland, *Disabled We Stand* (London: Souvenir Press, 1981), p. 15.

6. *Six O'Clock News* (BBC1, 14 July 1986).

7. Maggie Woolley interviewed by Julienne Dickey, 'Deafness and the Media', *Women's Media Action Bulletin* no. 19, January 1983, p. 3.

8. Keith Armstrong and Wendy Moore, 'Shut out by the Media', *Journalist*, October 1985, p. 2. So, 'despite [the fact that she has brittle-bone disease] and the fact that she's broken one or other of her legs nine times, Sharon keeps smiling', or else she wouldn't have got into the *Radio Times*. ('Raising Hopes, Raising Laughs, and Raising Money', *Radio Times*, 15–21 November 1986.)

9. Tony Macaulay, 'Disability and the Broadcasting Media' (The Volunteer Centre Media Project, December 1985).

10. Maggie Woolley et al., 'That Was Our Year Was It?', *The Times Health Supplement*, 22 January 1982, p. 9.

11. Diane Lattin, 'Telethons: A Remnant of America's Past', *Disabled USA* vol. 1 no. 4, 1977

12. Woolley et al., 'That Was Our Year Was It?'.

13. Nancy Banks-Smith, 'Just a 'Thon at Twilight', *Guardian*, 31 October 1985.

14. Quoted by Mark Patterson, 'Children in Need', *Media Project News*, September 1984

15. Diane Lattin, 'United Cerebral Palsy: Communicating a Better Image', *Disabled USA* vol. 2 no. 7, 1979, p. 5; this also describes some innovative UCP TV ads featuring a married couple with cerebral palsy.

2.5

Disability and documentary
Ann Pointon

For biographical notes see Part 3, Chapter 2.

This piece argues a neglect of critical analysis of the treatment of disability in factual programmes, and particularly in documentary. It tries to identify some elements of documentary that enable us to look in a more systematic way at the treatment of disability, that is, its 'actors', their 'roles' and the way they contribute to four (sometimes overlapping) themes, termed 'transformation', 'tragedy', 'normalisation' and 'spectacle'.

However, there is much scope for future work on other important aspects of disability and documentary, for instance in the way different factual genres may represent disability, on the key differences that distinguish the 'medical' from the 'disability' documentary (apart from the 'medical' being essentially about a condition) and developments in the way disabled film- and programme-makers are beginning to deal with the subject.

When the subject of disability representation and stereotypes is raised, it is writers, producers and directors of fiction (film and television) who are most commonly asked to look at their practice. In factual programming, producers and directors have generally been spared systematic investigation that moves much beyond attacks on telethons and a generally expressed dislike of intrusive documentaries with overt 'cure', 'supercrip' and 'tragic' themes. Discussions of stereotyping find more comfortable homes in feature films and drama.

The result in British television is a tradition in which the documentary and other factual portrayers of disability have been held less accountable to disabled people than their fictional counterparts. That this has happened is also partly a function of the lack of recognition of a growing disability movement or 'subculture'. The resulting lack of political sensitivity in this area of some producers and analysts is coupled with a deliberate avoidance by others, with dismissal of 'minority' disability voices as irrelevant or as representing the voice of political correctness that they do not want in 'their' programmes. Programmes that have covered disability in new ways, with fresh issues, do exist but have generally come from community programme, education departments and specialist disability strands rather than from producers in the main documentary feature tradition.

'REAL PEOPLE'
In relation to non-documentary film Lauri Klobas writes:

An immense chasm exists between disabled people and their screen counterparts. People with physical limitations are fighting for civil rights in a 'disability rights' movement. They strive to effect change in political definitions and legislation. They attempt to draw the camera lenses away from a voyeuristic study of their

physicality to such realities as their denied physical access to public buildings, public transit, and other facilities supported by their taxes. They often face discrimination in education and the workplace.[1]

This could however, just as easily apply to the treatment of disabled people in documentary. The subjects of documentary are 'real people', but despite the fact that producers of disability programmes frequently say that they are precisely in the business of challenging stereotypes, this does not really happen. Indeed, it cannot happen where the programme is underpinned by the presentation of the body as the 'signifier of difference'.[2]

The focus of the traditional 'disability' documentary is the experience of the disabled *individual*, there is rarely a challenge to the system within which that individual operates. There is, on the contrary, a broad belief that in general the 'system' works, evidenced perhaps by the slowness with which the 'rights not charity' argument has gained ground. And whereas disabled people themselves (and/or their family) might not always be happy about that system, their solutions are naturally often personal, and they may play to the stereotypes or allow themselves to be used in a non-challenging way. This is partly because there is a tendency for 'therapeutic relationships' to develop between subject and producer. This comment by Alison French, who was the subject of two documentaries made with the same producer, is not untypical:

It was thanks to her [the producer] that I was able for the first time in any depth to express how I felt about being a disabled person in an able-bodied world. Making that programme was an enjoyable

experience and another personal landmark. It made me realise that I was a good communicator with a possible contribution to make to society.[3]

Similarly, Charles Rose, father of Emmett de Monterey, who has cerebral palsy and who was the subject of a television documentary, says of their relationship to the media:

In a strange way it felt for the first time as if someone was interested in the detail of of how Emmett's having cerebral palsy had altered our lives, how our expectations had been changed and how we had responded to the challenges. Both Fran and I found it refreshing to let out many of the feelings we had had over the years but had only really expressed to each other.[4]

A desire to communicate the stresses of one's situation is entirely understandable. Indeed, the person may have been 'found' by the producer through an organisation or self-help group to which the disabled person or family member is connected and the communicating/therapeutic relationship around the impairment is simply a further step in this process.

The therapeutic relationship may sometimes appear to be naive, but often this is not the case. Disabled people (or organisations) frequently 'find' the media, in a self-motivated effort to use it as part of a personal campaign, 'message', or fund-raising initiative. The media is therefore to be used by them as well as they are to be used by it.[5] Where the subject and the producer have the same goal it is thus easier for the producer to describe his/her role happily as a progressive one of partner with the subject.[6] Since these subjects become the disabled people the producers know, and with whom the audience is familiar and comfortable, it is not surprising that defending programme content, and contesting the 'chasm' referred to by Klobas, are easy. But important aspects of 'real life' are usually left outside the narrative.

There is a temptation to feature individuals because producers recognise that they are attractive to the general audience and to the publicity machine, and keep the narrative simple. There is less incentive, unless one is already part of a network, to enter alien territory and work with groups of disabled people. Not only are they much less media attractive and controllable, but they entail a recognition of the 'personal as political', and as already recognised in black, women's and gay/lesbian film-making, this movement comes from participation on the inside.

THEMES OF DISABILITY DOCUMENTARY
While I accept both the general premise that 'documentary' is not 'actuality'[7] and Michael Renov's statement[8] of four tendencies of documentary (i.e., to (a) record, reveal, preserve (b) persuade or promote (c) analyse or interrogate and (d) express), I do not intend to explore here what constitutes documentary or to ascertain, for instance, which of the many 'styles' of documentary might best mediate the disabled voice. (However, I would suggest that particular resonance for disability is found in Renov's argument that '[documentary] employs many of the methods and devices of its fictional counterpart'.[9]) Rather, I shall attempt to outline four possible subtexts (or underlying themes) that can be identified in disability documentaries, irrespective of format.

The four main themes I outline are transformation, tragedy, normalisation and spectacle, although elements of each may overlap considerably in any particular programme. *Transformation* and *tragedy*[10] are familiar themes in disability

cultural and media work. *Normalisation* is a term I have chosen reluctantly because of its particular conceptualisation in social work, and its pejorative connotations for many disabled people. However, finding an alternative is difficult. *Spectacle* begins to speak for itself, in suggesting voyeuristic intent and effect, even though some of the programmes I choose to discuss in this category might not be obvious candidates.

These are not fixed categories but themes which are often present and may be dominant or contributory, but they help us to look at the perceived aims and role of the producer in a more systematic way.

However, first it is useful to ask who the main actors are who help the producer 'illuminate' these themes. In the case of disability the actors generally include therapists, 'carers', disabled people and organisations (usually impairment-based charities).

The roles taken on by these actors will generally include those of 'saviour' and 'victim'. Despite the fact that documentary may purport to relate a story that is precisely not that of victim (the contrast is usually of 'independence'), the notion of 'victimhood' is inseparable from the implicit or explicit denial. The saviour role may be taken by therapists and/or family 'carers', but can also be adopted by the disabled person themselves. It is a role which attracts the label 'saintly', for instance of staff of a Camphill school for disabled children: 'What he [producer Jonathan Stedhall] found was an astonishing and heart-warming continuity of commitment by people who are, by any reckoning, secular saints.'[11]

The other significant voice or unseen 'actor' is that of the director/producer, who often becomes very close to their subjects — indeed most programmes would not be made if they were not —

and, as indicated earlier, subjects of the documentary, and producers themselves, often identify a substantial role played by the producer and production team as 'therapists'. They are also often part initiator, of that which they film, as well as witness; sometimes they are 'saviour'.

Many successful producers 'succeed' precisely because of the extent to which they identify with their audience. The effect on 'disability', around which there exists so little widespread cultural challenge, is that prejudice, stereotypes and other preconceptions are played to rather than changed. For instance, most disabled people (radical and conservative) protest that what they most dislike is pity, but the word triggered most often in previews, reviews and publicity around the disability documentary is 'moving'. However, the 'moving' is that of the emotions rather than a movement of mind, to which a documentary too rarely appeals.

TRANSFORMATION

Where transformation is the main theme, we, the audience, are persuaded that not only will we see a change, but that it will be a change for the (perceived) 'better' rather than 'worse', and it is transformation of the body that is central to the narrative.

The Visit and *QED* (BBC) are only two of numerous series which are attracted by transformation, although *QED* as a science strand has the more medical bias. In two programmes for *The Visit*, PC Olds, a policeman paralysed by gunshot wounds, went to the USA to be treated with an electronic walking aid, and this is perhaps one of the best-remembered examples. As Vanessa Perkins, his friend and sometime partner said in her book *Sorry, Vessa*, 'Philip would shock people by referring to himself as "cripple of the year". He didn't want to be associated

with any disabled group. All he wanted was a cure, to be back as part of the system and everyday society, to be considered normal – whatever that really means.' On the other hand, this response is not typical. She also says, 'Of all the people you could name with the ability to accept life in a wheelchair, no one could have made a worse adjustment than Philip.'[12]

This particular story, as was the *QED*[13] story covering Emmett de Monterey's trips to the USA, was very much media led, with PC Olds' costs and living expenses in the USA being met by the *Daily Mail*. The less exciting story of a police officer injured in a road accident, who was in the Spinal Injuries Unit at the same time and who responded rather differently than PC Olds (related in one of three BBC Education Department documentaries called *Disabled Lives*, 1992), clearly did not offer the same media excitement and possibility of event and action.

In 'transformation' stories the disabled subjects may be the ostensible subject, but often the real 'hero' and central actor is the 'transformer', a role very often given to a doctor. Dr Petrovsky in the case of PC Olds and Dr Gage in the case of Emmett (both based in the USA) played major roles. The scientific elements, or overall utility of the techniques, are rarely held up to hostile analysis. For instance, disabled people's challenge to conductive education was virtually confined to specialist programmes.

So what is their intention? What do they think is going on? Of *The Visit*, programmes covering forty stories, journeys and groups of people, Desmond Wilcox says:

... we have travelled with them, shared their experience and then shared it further with a television

audience, millions of other families watching, sympathising, perhaps learning; not entertainment but still compelling; not education but nevertheless a lesson for all of us.[14]

But what kind of 'lesson'? It is not usually founded on dispassionate observation. It is revealing of the philosophy behind The Visit to read of the case that was Wilcox's inspiration. On reading an article by a mother making a weekly journey to see her child who was in residential care, he says:[15]

She went on to write clearly and so precisely, that it made me weep when I read her article... Her real purpose had been to draw attention to the need for more such homes, so that the difficulties of a long journey to visit a loved one (particularly for parents without a care) could be softened ... her article had taught me something thing of the strains, and the rewards, of a life I didn't know – and I was the better for it.

The documentary solution he followed, however, was to choose another such mother and not to examine why such facilities are not more locally available, or to question their usefulness and standards.

There is a 'reality' in these programmes but also a real world that gets left out. PC Olds describes his wheelchair as a 'prison' and the producer concurs. But external factors such as the difficulties of attitude and environment for wheelchair users in Britain compared with the USA (specifically referred to by PC Olds' fiancée, Vanessa, in her book) are rarely of interest to the television producer, perhaps because there is being no 'moving' transformation to observe. The service that television has now found 'exciting' is computer provision, but this is regarded as 'transformational' in the way that an adapted Ford Escort or a ramp to the front steps is not.

TRAGEDY

Stories of 'tragedy' are unfailingly popular. These are stories which do not have 'happy endings'. The focus of the 'tragedy' documentary is often the progressive impairment – the failing body. The approach to the tragedy tends to be concerned with the compensatory spiritual development of the actors. The saviour is often the 'self' (i.e. the disabled person). However, the 'carers' are likely to take central roles as 'saviours' and 'victims' in programmes that are often, even if not ostensibly, about them and how they are 'coping' with their burden; a 'plight' with which the non-affected audience is invited to identify. 'Incurable' conditions that have particularly interested film-makers have included motor neurone disease, cystic fibrosis and multiple sclerosis. The justification for such 'tragic' programmes is sometimes 'identification of a need', e.g. QED: When it Happens to You (1992, BBC), which featured a man dying from a brain tumour and was supporting the extension of hospice care. More medical research, more support services may be identified by family ('carers'). Medical professionals and therapists may well be featured (if only to ask questions about research for cures) but they will tend to be shown as helpless and marginalised.

The carer as victim may appear in programmes such as 'Looking after Mum' (Cutting Edge, 1993, C4) which looked at the child carers. It simply 'showed' a problem in relation to two disabled mothers and their children, who were carrying out many care duties to the detriment of their own social lives and schooling. The producer was concerned to explore the feelings of the children who were performing both the 'saviour' and 'victim' roles. The mothers were used to emphasise physical dependency rather than non-physical aspects of the 'mother' role. There was no challenge to the status quo, no language that indicated a scandalous lack of support, no journalistic desire to explore options, or to contrast these two 'sad' mothers with other disabled mothers who had better support systems in place and more apparent awareness of the risk of exploiting their children.[16] While disabled people were necessarily important actors in this programme, the key background organisation was one looking after the interests of 'carers'. In contrast, a later Channel Four programme on disability and parenthood (from the specialist *People First* strand, and made by a disabled producer) gave a more positive view, without ignoring the difficulties.

NORMALISATION

The therapeutic relationship may also be present in the category I have called 'normalisation'. The theme of 'normalisation' took hold from the early 80s (after the 1981 International Year of Disabled People). Part of its (crude) message is that disabled people are 'just like other people' and part of its function in documentary, it could be argued, is to persuade and convince us that the disabled 'victim' (easily identifiable in 'transformation' and 'tragedy') is no such thing.

Alison, a young woman with cerebral palsy was the subject of two BBC documentaries and made several other television appearances. She says, of the first documentary:

The BBC approached me to appear in their *Man Alive* series (on TV) to help promote positive images of disabled people. There were two blokes and myself, all from different colleges, and the programme explored our attitudes to disability and to life in general. The main aim

was to encourage the able-bodied population to regard disabled people in a more enlightened and less patronising way – to bridge gaps between these two sectors of the community.[17]

In such documentaries we see *process* (eavesdropping on the disabled person performing small tasks like making tea or changing the baby, which are 'marvellous' because the person has no arms). This replaces dramatic surgery or arduous physical therapy. The *resolution* of the problem offered is the disabled person giving us their very positive and personal philosophy of life, occasionally denying that they are disabled; and we recognise *progress* because this person has tackled the problem themselves and removed the burden on society. No burden; no problem.

The saviour is essentially self, but in order for this documentary to work, many of the services the disabled person needs will have been substantially provided. But because such provision as adapted housing, transport, etc. is 'boring' these services will be effectively invisible in the programme to the non-disabled viewer. (One might guess that disabled people, on the other hand, are 'clocking up' what this person on TV has that they are still struggling for.)

Unlike the 'transformation' documentary, the central subject is usually the disabled person him/herself; if therapists or 'carers' appear, they will tend to have a much more subsidiary role.

While the focus is initially the impairment, the developing narrative tells us it is all about the social skills, personality, powers of acceptance and adaptation of the disabled person themselves, that is, the overcoming of disability and the denial of 'victimhood'. But usually there are elements of transformation; in the case of *Forty Minutes: I,*

Alison (1988, BBC), for example, the most memorable (for the media) was Alison's marriage. And while Alison herself had an engaging and very down-to-earth approach to her life and her marriage (her partner was a vicar, so she says she had little option), it presented yet another unfortunate image for disabled people of how to be normal.

When society accepts disabled people genuinely as 'of themselves' and not alien 'other' then perhaps the popular disabled wedding may cease to lose its fascination for the media. Paradoxically, the wedding as an important indicator of 'normality' can serve to tell us the opposite. As a programme preview put it after saying that Alison fell in love and walked up the aisle, 'It's no fairy story, for Alison is an athetoid spastic . . .'[18]

SPECTACLE

The wedding of Louise, one of the people affected by thalidomide, features in at least two documentaries on the progress of this group of people. No doubt the producers and others would contest the inclusion of these two documentaries under the heading 'spectacle', but there is enough ambivalence in both to justify this.

The first programme, *World in Action: Born Survivors*, features three people: Louise; Ken, a single man working as an advice worker; and Liam, who, of the three, was the most severely affected by thalidomide. As well as having no upper limbs, Liam has neither sight nor speech.

This is a follow-up 'progress' programme, but it is not clear whether Liam was featured in the first (we see old film of the other two). The commentary tells us that his speech might have been surgically correctable if lack of a palate had been diagnosed at an early stage; he was also assumed (incorrectly) to be unable to walk, and he was (initially and again incorrectly) diagnosed as 'mentally handicapped'. Despite *World in Action's* general track record as an investigative programme, all criticisms of the professionals are suspended in this programme, no issue of compensation was raised, and we see only loving, caring therapists now working with Liam. Why we are watching, except perhaps out of sheer curiosity, is unclear.

The other documentary, in two parts, is called *The Tin Lids* (1991, Anglia).[19] The first programme is titled 'Childhood' and the second 'Thirty Years On'. Unlike *World in Action: Born Survivors*, which uses minimal commentary to move the story on, *Tin Lids* has a strong authorial commentary voice. It is challenging in the ground it attempts to cover, but sweeping comments about 'the disabled' are derived from the experience of the particular people featured and their impairments. Sometimes the commentary uses the phrase 'the tribe' (i.e., those with thalidomide-caused impairments), pointing out that people did not want to belong to this 'tribe' and wanted to be 'normal'. 'Childhood' contains a doctor's observations on the analogies between the way animals treat their 'deformed' offspring and how the parents of the thalidomide-affected group acted. The language in 'Thirty Years On' is particularly dehumanising – some interviewees being described as 'this four-limbed deficient' and others, as 'thalidomides' (the noun).

An apparent lack of familiarity with the disability 'subculture', or a range of other disabled people, means that, for instance, the total failure of the medical profession to predict accurately the future quality of life for their young patients is presented as a unique insight and is not translated into other disabled people's experience. Similarly, the 'torture' that the children were exposed to as appliances and artificial limbs were developed to make them look 'whole' and more 'normal', and which they later abandoned for the more efficient use of their own bodies, is not referenced out.

The programmes' great strength is the disabled people themselves, and they cover interesting ground in contrasting the experience of the children who stayed at home and those who were put into institutional care. However, the repetitive use of medical film and photographs draws us into voyeuristic intrusion; for instance, the use of a full-frontal image of a naked, limbless baby more than once within the body of the programmes and re-featured in the end credits can only be construed as indulgence in 'spectacle'.

The more sensitive portrayal of conjoined twins in *Katie and Eilish: Siamese Twins* (1992, Yorkshire) can be contrasted with the portrayal of a pair of orphaned conjoined twins brought to Philadelphia for treatment in the BBC's flagship science documentary, *Horizon* (1995). The programme showed a disturbing lack of respect for their bodily privacy. One could argue that this was essentially a 'transformation' programme, but the 'spectacle' element was equally as large and was built up further in the publicity.

Although the word 'freak' is not often used by producers, the presentation of 'freakishness' is present in many programmes (not all of them about disability), and, like thalidomide-caused conditions, some impairments are seen as more 'freakish' than others. 'Dwarfs', for instance, tend not to be seen as disabled people.

Even if its participants aver 'normality', the 'spectacle'-driven programme tells us something else. Like programmes with a dominant 'normalisation' theme, they hold up for our admiration people's social skills, but usually offer no analysis of how or why the 'general public' fail to 'understand'. Similarly programmes around 'facial disfigurement' can be characterised by meaningless pieties, and have no stronger a message than the platitudinous 'if only people were more understanding'. The only action indicated is for the disabled person to be burdened further with the responsibility of gaining confidence (and even more social skills) through self-help. The recognition that 'they are not alone' is very limited and impairment-based; the programmes rarely preach political solidarity.

We all want to 'gaze' and documentary gives us the opportunity to do that without embarrassment. Yet exposure is only useful if it tells us something about ourselves, in a way which makes it possible to move on and not to experience the next documentary on these lines in precisely the same way. More disabled people on television is one thing, more exposure in this impairment-based, disability showcase context is quite another.

Power is rarely ceded, nor can it be taken away. However, it can be challenged by the establishment of an alternative 'cinema', and it is this which makes the training and employment issues in broadcasting so important. But radical approaches to disability (which may be artistic, journalistic, fictive or combinations of these) do not follow just because a producer has an impairment, and to some extent 'identifies' with others. For instance, pressures to deny must influence one's approach to others with impairments. Desmond Wilcox experienced eleven months' blindness, when, as a young reporter, he was hit by a criminal. Now he admits to being virtually totally deaf and dependent on lip-reading. Under a *Mail on Sunday* headline, we read of 'The disability that Desmond Wilcox fought to keep secret for 30 years':

When I was at the BBC I would never have confessed to being deaf. It is a competitive industry where ruthlessness and ambition are encouraged. In those days when the BBC was not as politically correct as it is now, I feared that my disability would have been considered a handicap to promotion... In those days [they] didn't have management policies concerning the employment of disabled people, or minorities or ethnic groups. I felt they wanted fully fledged, fully able, fully competent people, so I covered up my disability.[20]

He is now an 'active supporter of charities for the deaf' and is 'stridently passionate in trying to change attitudes towards the deaf ...', believing that attitudes towards 'the deaf' are worse than towards people who are blind. As an independent producer, however, he does not offer comment on the implications today for deaf and disabled people in the continuing 'competitive industry, where ruthlessness and ambition' are still the name of the game.

Media products are not 'widgets' but cultural artefacts that can maintain or undermine cultural oppression. In the case of disability the internalisation of this oppression – colluding in those tragic images with which we are presented, or denying them in unrealistic supercripdom – is as important as the external oppression (such as lack of rights of 'access' at every level), making disabled people's non-participation in society the norm that is ignored, and participation, the media-attractive, 'extraordinary' exception.

Notes

1. Laurie E. Klobas, *Disability Drama in Television and Film* (McFarland, 1988), p. xi.

2. David Hevey, *The Creatures Time Forgot: Photography and Disability Imagery* (London, Routledge, 1992).

3. Alison French with Veronica Groocock, *I, Alison: Reaching for a Life of My Own* (London: Pan, 1991), p. 71.

4. Charles Rose, *One Step at a Time: Emmett – My Son's Battle to Walk* (London: Bloomsbury, 1991).

5. In *One Step at a Time* (p. 104), Rose describes how Emmett's trip to the US to undergo a new technique of gait analysis and subsequent surgery was paid for by 'One Small Step', Guy's Hospital cerebral palsy appeal, 'in exchange for our support for the Appeal', which had the aim of establishing a Gait Analysis Laboratory in London and was publicising the trip in the hope that it would be newsworthy enough to be picked up by newspapers. The family were thus accompanied to the US by a six-member film crew, four journalists, a professor of neurology and a PR person.

6. Desmond Wilcox emphasises the 'partnership' he developed with subjects of *The Visit* in *Return Visit* (London: BBC Books, 1991).

7. Philip Rosen, 'Document and Documentary', in Michael Renov (ed.), *Theorizing Documentary* (London: Routledge, 1993), p. 72.

8. Renov, *Theorizing Documentary*, p. 26.

9. Ibid., p. 3.

10. Transformation is at the heart of the ubiquitous 'cure' story. See David Hevey, 'The Tragedy Principle: Strategies for Change in the Representation of Disabled People', in J. Swain, V. Finkelstein, S. French and M. Oliver (eds), *Disabling Barriers: Enabling Environments* (London: Sage Publications/Open University, 1993).

11. John Naughton, TV Review, the *Observer*, 24 June 1990.

12. Vanessa Perkins and Maureen Owen, *Sorry, Vessa* (London: Chapmans, 1991).

13. QED: On His Own Two Feet (1991, BBC)

14. Wilcox, *Return Visit*.

15. Ibid.

16. 'Mum's the Word', in the Channel Four series *People First* (transmitted 9 June 1994).

17. French, *I, Alison*, p. 70.

18. Sandy Smithies, 'Watching Brief', the *Guardian*, 10 March 1988.

19. Suggested by a participant as a title, from the rhyming slang for 'thalids'.

20. Kim Willsher, 'I am now so deaf I have to lip-read to my wife Esther', *Mail on Sunday*, 14 January 1996.

A Family at war
Angela Carmichael

ANGELA ('Angie') CARMICHAEL was educated away from home at two boarding special schools, which has helped to make her a keen advocate of integrated education. Her first job was with BT, and she subsequently spent several years living and working in several locations in the UK and the former West Germany, returning to her home town of Bath when her son reached primary-school age.

From 1988 to 1992 she worked for the Same Production Company as a researcher, and later assistant producer, on Channel Four's disability series *Same Difference*, and then with the same production team as assistant producer on *Seeds of Protest*, a two-part documentary for the series *People First* (C4), which charted the rise of the Disability Movement in the US and in Britain. Since then she has pursued her commitment to the empowerment of disabled people by working as an advocate, while also collaborating with Hummingbird Films as Associate Producer for two *People First* programmes: 'Breaking the Silence' which investigated the abuse of people with learning difficulties; and 'Dirty Tricks, Angry Voices', an analysis of the disability civil rights campaign and political opposition to it. She has also produced reports for ITN and the BBC and recently formed her own production company, Sparring Partners.

This piece by Angie Carmichael arises in part from some of the work she did in researching and covering the campaign supporting the Civil Rights Bill for disabled people (a Labour private member's bill which in effect was passed as a baton from Alf Morris to Roger Berry and finally Harry Barnes). Disability as headline news is a novelty, unless it involves a particularly tragic or famous disabled individual. Carmichael charts the reactions of television current affairs and news programmes reactions to a saga that unfolded in a way that even disability activists had not predicted.

On Wednesday 11 May 1994, *Channel Four News* devoted fifteen minutes to an item placed first on its running order, provoked by Nicholas Scott's admission that he had misled Parliament in denying that his officials had drafted wrecking amendments to the Civil Rights (Disabled Persons) Bill, then at the Report Stage. To add to his discomfort, the daughter of the Minister for Disabled People had criticised the government and her father for 'denying 6.5 million disabled people their civil rights'. After twelve years of pressure inside and outside Parliament, Disability rights were 'on the agenda'. But was this a triumph for a long, hard-fought campaign or were disabled people being dragged into the media spotlight on the coat-tails of a minor political scandal?

The civil rights movement in the UK was born in 1981 in the shape of the British Council of Organizations of Disabled People (BCODP), an association of local and national groups which worked hard to establish itself as the authentic voice of disabled people against an establishment more comfortable with consulting non-disabled charity chairmen on disability issues. Particularly on a local level, member organisations pushed forward initiatives in areas like access, employment and the arts. Some disabled people became councillors or local government officers and so raised the profile of disability rights and gained political and presentational skills. But all this made little impact on the national scene: by early 1994 the great mass of the population was still unaware that disabled people routinely experienced discrimination with no redress under the law.

Over the previous twelve years, fourteen attempts, in the form of private members bills, had been made to bring in legislation establishing the civil rights of disabled people, and every one of these had failed, with barely a whimper from the media. Special interest groups that pursue their aims through the democratic system in this way do not attract the sort of attention that will move public support and so embarrass a government sufficiently to produce action.

Why had the disability rights movement in the US, where legislation was enacted in 1990, been more successful? It seemed to some British activists that exploitation of the American media had been crucial: the US rights movement had conducted a skilful campaign dominated by high-profile demonstrations, culminating in a mass crawl up the steps of the Capitol Building in full view of a phalanx of news cameras. The power of this image, transmitted throughout the States and picked up by international news services, was widely believed to have been a deciding factor in winning the congressional vote.

In the UK, a group called Direct Action Network came together in 1993, aiming to draw the attention of the media to the campaign for disability rights. Its first act was to picket the Christchurch by-election, which was being contested for the Conservatives by Rob Hayward. The previous year, Mr Hayward had talked out the 1992 Disabled Persons (Civil Rights) Bill, before losing his Bristol seat at the general election. This background was put before the voters of Christchurch by activists picketing an election press conference, attracting considerable local news coverage: the seat was lost by the Conservatives.

Actions like these certainly attracted more media attention than the quieter efforts to move legislation. Whereas in 1988 a study by the Broadcasting Research Unit[1] had shown that news broadcasts involving disability were largely concerned with medical breakthrough and 'achievements', by 1994 the picture had begun to change, and disabled protesters were entering the public consciousness, largely through sporadic television news items, both local and national. Alan Holdsworth of Direct Action Network believes that protest has changed perceptions: 'Civil disobedience has brought disability issues to the public's attention, and reports of direct action in the media provoke public debate. Disability has now moved from the health agenda to become a political issue.'

If direct action had achieved a profile, where was analysis of the issues? Did news editors have a grasp of the focus of the campaign? In March 1994 I was involved in a proposal put to ITN/Channel Four News for a news report on the forthcoming Second Reading of the Civil Rights (Disabled Persons) Bill. The item was accepted, in the context of growing disagreement between the Minister for Disabled People (Nicholas Scott) and the Commons' All Party Disablement Group, and also in the knowledge that a demonstration involving hundreds of disabled people was due to be staged outside Parliament. Political controversy and public protest provided just enough bait for the news editor's hook, and we were able to produce a report which we believed covered the issues and, very unusually, was presented from the point of view of a disabled person.

On the day (9 March), the report was scheduled as second item, but was swiftly pushed down the order as news came in of the transit van bomb-attack on Downing Street. This was probably one of the best news slots allocated to disability rights legislation up until that time: however, the 1994 bill was potentially major legislation likely to affect millions of people, and it had all-party support. In this context, why had the other major news programmes not tackled the subject?

In general, coverage of disability as a civil rights issue before May 1994 had been limited to specialist programmes. In 1988 See Hear (BBC) reported on the sit-in by deaf students at Gallaudet University in the US, which forced the removal of the hearing Principal in favour of a deaf candidate: surely an event worthy of 'mainstream' coverage? This was followed by documentaries and reports from Channel Four's People First (C4) and From the Edge (BBC), highlighting the adoption of equal rights legislation in the US and its likely arrival in the UK, but still current affairs departments avoided the issue. Why?

On one side, the news broadcasters at BBC and ITN had appeared largely oblivious to the political dimension of disability, and it was not until the early 90s that broadcasters and outside organisations started compiling written guidelines on the portrayal of disabled people and the use of images of disability.[2] At this time the BBC set up its

Disability Programmes Unit, while ITV's disability slot Link was already being made by an independent company controlled by disabled people.[3] The pitifully small number of disabled people working in the media was exposed, and as a result some bursaries and media training-schemes were established. All the major broadcasters displayed increased awareness of the need for equal opportunities policies to extend to disabled people. However, at the core of broadcasting activity, these organisations continued to churn out programmes that were much criticised by many disabled people. While Children in Need and The Visit (among many others) still occupied prime slots, and while even the basic terminology of newsreaders displayed complete unawareness of the disability agenda, it was obvious that there was a very long way to go before disability would be seen as an equal rights issue analogous to race.

On the other side, the disability rights movement had not set out to harness the power of the media as effectively as some other pressure groups. Whereas, for example, environmental campaigners had from the outset combined direct action with publications, research and media training for its spokespeople, the disability movement had tended to use political channels while building up its organisational base. As we have seen, by 1994 the anger of disabled people was beginning to spill onto the streets, but the intellectual case for disability rights and the reality of discrimination were not being articulated via the media.

On 10 May 1994 the two sides – the media establishment and the disability rights movement – were forced together when Nicholas Scott apologised for misleading Parliament with his previous statement that 'nobody in my department has been involved in drafting amendments' designed to wreck the

Disabled Persons Bill. For better or worse, the mainstream news organisations would now have to cover disability as a rights issue: after all, what was all the fuss about?

The next day, when the Opposition set upon Nicholas Scott with calls for his resignation, all the news organisations carried reports. The following analysis concentrates on the Channel Four News item, precisely because it was in many respects a step forward, but still illustrates some of the shortcomings of mainstream reporting of disability issues.

The item comprised two reports: first, Elinor Goodman on the political controversy (6 mins); second, Lindsay Taylor on the background to the legislation (7 mins).

Elinor Goodman's report was a straightforward political correspondent's report on the parliamentary controversy. There was no attempt to explain the substance of the bill: its importance was emphasised by the politicians interviewed, but no disability spokesperson was included. The language used was outdated, i.e. 'the disabled', and the only image of disabled people was that of a lone protester outside Richmond House who conveyed lonely pathos rather than the cutting edge of a protest movement.

The report from Lindsay Taylor that followed examined the background to the controversy. It contained many elements that displayed sensitivity to the issues involved. Five disabled people stated their views, including two comments from Rachel Hurst of BCODP, who refuted the government's claim that the bill had enormous cost implications. The reporter's terminology was appropriate, and he also emphasised the concern disabled people felt that the need for civil rights would be submerged in political controversy.

However, some of the images used tended to negate the message. The report began with a sequence shot in a day-centre; the views aired by disabled people there were strong, but the cut-away sequences focused on assistance, with people being lifted, pushed and wheeled around the centre. To illustrate employment rights, the reporter visited a binding workshop employing visually impaired people, and a manager was interviewed. It may be that the intention was to show that employment opportunities for disabled people are largely limited to such establishments, but the impression gained was that this was the type of workplace which the bill would support, whereas disability groups have been working towards integration in employment and it is in this arena that anti-discrimination legislation is vital. It might have been more relevant to show a disabled worker in an integrated work environment, illustrating that such situations are positive for both employed and employer, but are rare without the backing of legislation. Lindsay Taylor nevertheless avoided the temptation to focus on the disagreement between Nicholas Scott and his daughter Victoria, Parliamentary lobbyist for RADAR, only including one comment from Ms Scott. This is in contrast with other news broadcasts that day: for example, disabled commentators were completely absent in the News at Ten report, when the campaigners' point of view was put by Victoria Scott alone, no doubt because this offered the additional opportunity of focusing on a family dispute .

The 'Nick and Vick' circus raises a number of questions surrounding news coverage of disability. On one hand, it brought an unprecedented degree of publicity to the civil rights campaign; on the other, it reinforced the perception that disabled people cannot speak for themselves and need to have their

Disabled civil rights demonstrators, 1995
courtesy of GLAD

campaigning done by professional non-disabled charity workers such as Ms Scott. If coverage is to contribute to the emancipation of disabled people, this type of treatment must become as unacceptable as reporting on the demise of apartheid in South Africa and interviewing the white Bishop Trevor Huddleston as the sole voice of Black liberation. For its part, the disability movement must also be ready with its own skilled spokespeople and achieve greater control over the news media by creating news opportunities. The cascade of publicity last May illustrates the need for a hook to hang the story on: if as disabled people we can create our own hooks using, for example, civil disobedience, research findings or individual cases of discrimination, we shall be in a better position to control the coverage of the issues involved. Richard Wood of BCODP comments: 'Media coverage is generally abysmal, only arising in response to demonstrations or at key times . . . the media form part of a range of contacts which disabled people need to make to progress their cause.'

While disabled people are making progress within the broadcast media, both as independent producers and as employees, it would be unrealistic to expect every news item touching on disability to have a disabled producer. It is therefore extremely important for the future that those who portray disability on television are informed and aware of the principles involved: the careless choice of a shot can reinforce an image that disabled people have been attempting to discard for years.

In campaigning for equal rights legislation, the disability movement has constantly drawn parallels with racial equality and its position in the legal framework. It is now some time since television awoke to its power to affect racial stereotypes and the need to reinforce equality throughout its output and workforce. The realisation that disability equality is directly comparable and demands similar treatment must follow, and soon.

Notes
1. G. Cumberbatch and R. Negrine, *Images of Disability on Television* (London: Routledge, 1992).
2. These include: Channel Four's *Disability and Television: Guidelines on Representation for Producers* (1992); guidelines issued by BBC Directorates (Radio, Television, World Service, etc.); the Employers' Forum on Disability's *Disability Etiquette: A Guide for Programme-Makers on the Portrayal in the Media of People with Disabilities* (1992), issued for the Telethon Trust; the RNIB's *Interviewing VIPs: Hints for Journalists* (1992); and RADAR's *Guidance on the Language of Disability* (1992).
3. Coffers Bare Productions.

2.7

The signs for deaf TV

(an interview with Terry Riley)

Chris Davies

For biographical notes see Part 2, Chapter 1.

In this article, based on an interview with Terry Riley, a Deaf producer who has worked for some years on *See Hear* (the BBC's weekly programme for Deaf people), Chris Davies discusses television output for Deaf viewers on the BBC and other channels, and with Terry Riley speculates on the future for the Deaf audience.

It is an arguable case that Deaf people, particularly those whose first language is British Sign Language, are doubly disabled by television and film. While, in common with the rest of the disability community, they find themselves rarely represented on screen (and when they are, the portrayal is hardly accurate), they also find the medium of television itself largely inaccessible. There have been improvements: more programmes are now subtitled – though, since most of these are on teletext and not on screen, this is at additional cost to the Deaf viewer – and the early-morning news summary from Monday to Friday on BBC2 and some regional news programmes have both sign language and subtitles. But few mainstream programmes have the total access provided by a combination of on-screen subtitling and sign language interpretation. Given all this, any programmes that not only have these facilities but also look at issues that particularly concern Deaf and hard-of-hearing people are probably gold dust to those otherwise so badly served.

Although Channel Four followed suit with, initially, *Listening Eye* and, latterly, *Sign On* (both produced by Tyne Tees television), the BBC was the first to produce a dedicated programme for Deaf and hard-of-hearing viewers. *See Hear* was born out of a combination of lobbying and identification through personal experience. The Community Programmes Unit were approached by a group of Deaf people to make a programme for the *Open Door* series in which viewers made programmes with the technical assistance and professional advice of BBC staff. As the programme concerned was entirely about the absence of Deaf people and their issues, the Community Programmes Unit took a proposal for six programmes to the controller of BBC television. Legend has it that since the controller had a profoundly Deaf relative, he immediately identified with the argument and gave permission for twenty-six programmes! The result, *See Hear*, began in 1981.

At that time Terry Riley was working for the Gas Board, inspecting meters. In 1987 he replied to the only advertisement ever placed by *See Hear* to recruit outsiders as production staff. With his appointment, he became one of the few Deaf people working behind the camera – previously, the contribution from the Deaf community had mainly come from the other side of the camera. In 1993 he was promoted from Assistant Producer to Producer. As both consumer and provider of Deaf television, he is therefore in a good position to judge what, if any, progress has been made. He is not optimistic:

Job opportunities are very few and far between. However, more and more Deaf people are now involved. For instance, *Sign On* have got three. There is an awareness, although progress being made now is stagnant. I doubt whether Deaf programmes would be made now – if we were just starting. We were originally on the bandwagon of the Year of Disabled People [1981] when we first started, but I feel now that there is an element of marginalisation.

I asked him whether he could be more specific about 'marginalisation':

***See Hear* is the only BBC Deaf programme. We have BBC signed news at 8 p.m. and *Sign On*, but that's it. You never see a Deaf person in soaps. When we originally went out at 12 p.m. on Sundays and built our audience up to 1.5 million, they moved it to 10 a.m. and the figures just crashed. In the last twelve months we trebled our audience, which was great, but now [1995] it goes out at 10 a.m. it is more difficult to watch because of other commitments.**

Since he appeared not to place much importance on interpreted news, the obvious question was 'Surely such a service constitutes progress?'

That's a media access programme. I think we have to distinguish between access programmes and programmes for the Deaf community. The whole language and culture is different. When you talk about access, most hearing people can get the news every hour; on TV, radio, etc.

We just get it once. Also, I think Deaf people need a news programme of our own; our own style. The news programmes exclusively use hearing interpreters and therefore emancipation for Deaf people isn't helped – interpreters are getting full-time jobs, but Deaf people aren't.

Although I am a hearing viewer, I have watched a great deal of *See Hear*. Not surprisingly, given its long history, the programme has gone through many changes over the years. These days it is no longer studio based and has a whole team of presenters – rather than just one main one. It has also broadened its target audience, as Terry explains:

Over the last two years it's really gone to a wider aspect of the Deaf community which is so diverse; sign language users, oral users, hard-of-hearing, and then you've got social workers, professionals, etc. It has such a diverse target audience – probably more so than any other programme. There is a discussion whether we should do things for the Deaf that they know, or whether we should do items as part of information education – we are trying to get the right balance.

While Terry did go on to define the main target audience as being Deaf, some Deaf people have complained that the broadening of outlook has been in fact a dilution. Does he agree?

You can stay in the ghetto so long. We have broadened it, we've created seven new reporters. There is a group who think we've gone too far, but you could equally argue that other members/parts of the community are much greyer. Ninety per cent of Deaf parents have hearing children. We give information about hearing schools as well as Deaf schools. *See Hear* is the only programme from

Maggie Woolley, *See Hear*'s first deaf producer, 1987, courtesy of Stephen Iliffe

which they get their information.
Could it be broadened even further to include disability?

I don't think *See Hear* should cover disability in general because you've got *From the Edge* and other programmes like that. If you start going too broad then you lose the emphasis of Deaf issues. We have tried to re-balance Deaf/blind issues and Deaf people with other disabilities, but to cover the area of disability in general is really not our remit.

The problem with a programme that has run as long as *See Hear* is that it has to re-invent itself continuously. So where does it go from here? The future, according to Terry, is by no means assured:

The BBC is going through change at the moment; some say for the better and others for the worse. I desperately hope that *See Hear* will remain, because there is such a need for it. So many people get their information from *See Hear* or *Sign On*. The two programmes complement each other and that has to continue. To stop themselves losing audiences, ITV are now putting on blockbuster films and this pulls money away from minority programmes. *Sign On* (C4) has been cut from twenty-four programmes to nineteen. *See Hear* at the moment is OK, but who knows what will happen in another two years. My worry is that Deaf people have become too complacent; the programme is always there!

Terry's reference to Channel Four's *Sign On* points to my next question. The Tyne Tees programme has always, in my opinion as a hearing viewer, had a harder edge than its BBC equivalent. So did Terry think that *See Hear* has possibly got a little soft with age and needs to take more chances?

I think it depends on who you ask. Some say we are too superficial while others say we have actually developed a style that's quite hard-hitting. I think one of the problems is that the Deaf community never ask questions. They accept what they are told very easily, without challenging anything. I

think there are a lot of films that we've made that are superficial, but then we've made a lot where we go deeply into the subject. We do go into controversial issues, but probably not enough. We have had so many ideas but we are limited by the number of programmes we can make. It's also a bit of a catch-22 situation. When you go in hard-hitting you assume that the audience knows your starting point, but they don't. I think that we have proved ourselves over the years, asking more questions and being more challenging.

Just as with disability specialist programmes, the hope is that Deaf programming's strong example can be followed through into the mainstream. So which area of other programming would Terry target first?

Children's TV. It has to be children's. There's nothing at the moment for Deaf children. It has to be the first issue.

And drama?

I think the problem is that of the whole philosophy of disability in TV. Disabled people are always portrayed negatively. You never see a disabled person oozing with confidence do you? You need to change attitudes and to have a very good storyline in order to have Deaf people playing important roles in TV drama. We need a forum like the National Theatre of the Deaf to be able to push for Deaf integration in TV.

How did Terry envisage the future of Deaf and disabled people in TV? Perhaps unsurprisingly, given the background of the commercial market in which even the BBC is now forced to compete, he does not see it as being rosy:

I think it's quite bleak. The whole ethos of TV is changing. I'm a bit worried that programmes like See

Terry Riley – producer *See Hear,* courtesy of BBC

Hear may not be around in two years time. Having said that, there are a lot of people within the BBC who would like things to continue, but it's a question of finance! People have to be aware that it's not as easy as they think. We have to try and stimulate discussion, make our community more aware and able to argue the point clearly and logically. It's a change of philosophy that's needed.

If the future lies in the hands of those now emerging from media schools, how would Terry advise them about Deaf issues and who to consult?

When making a programme with Deaf people, don't patronise. Don't be afraid if you see anybody signing. It doesn't matter if you're Deaf or have a disability – we're just the same as anybody else – and we can make films just as well, perhaps because we think in a visual mode and our films don't depend as much on sound. Also, challenge in a good and constructive way. There is a difference between the two cultures in that a Deaf person may seem to be very blunt; in fact they're not, it's just their way. Once you get to know the different cultures and can bridge that gap, we are just the same as anyone else. Go to Deaf clubs, socialise and learn the language from a social perspective.

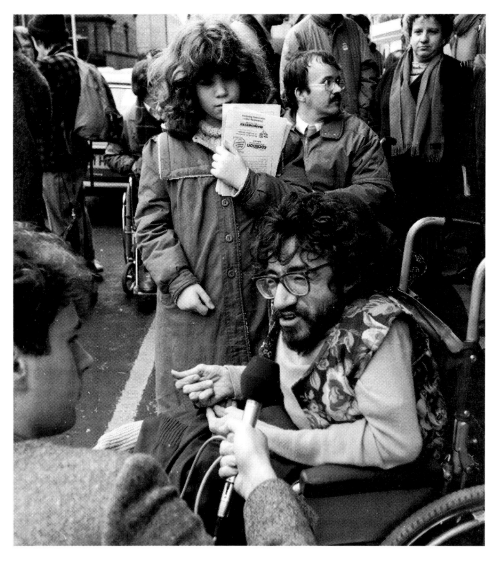

Nabil Shaban and supporters challenge Granada's decision to not cast him in *Micror*

'Would this man frighten your children?' (text taken from poster)

Part Three

Opening Doors Performance, Production and Training

Introduction

In accessing moving visual forms like film and television we are firmly in the hands of the film-maker or television director. Most commonly, disabled people are represented by non-disabled people either seeking the 'inner eye' on what is generally deemed a 'tragic' experience or using impairment as a direct threat, whether of violence or dependency, to other characters.

It has been possible to move from festivals of 'women's films' to festivals of 'women film-makers', and 'black' film seasons assume mainly black directors. Not so for disability, in which control of the product by disabled people is not assumed, and where criticism and analysis are still in relative infancy.

Any disability film festival will be an opportunity for disabled people to deconstruct the film, not an opportunity for them to celebrate the work of disabled film-makers or even disabled performers. Documentary work (or 'shorts') offer more in terms of potential expression of the authentic voice of disabled people. However, documentary works of any kind by disabled practitioners, let alone works of distinction, are still few in number, particularly when compared with the large numbers of films and videos of doubtful parentage but of technical and prize-winning merit, made by non-disabled directors on aspects of the 'plight', 'courage' and 'inspiration' of 'the disabled'.

Barriers to employment in film, television, theatre, the press and advertising are still significant, and with the inclusion of disabled people in the production process at such an embryonic stage, it is of limited usefulness at this stage to look at employment in these areas of the media in isolation from each other. Nevertheless, Part Three concentrates mainly on television, with some reference to film, theatre and the arts. It links the experiences of disabled people who have come into television or film in unconventional ways and looks at where the barriers exist in the structure of the broadcasting industry. 'Broadcasting' is used in its widest sense, and comments around employment and training opportunities will include radio, although it may not be specifically cited.

DOORS TO PERFORMANCE AND PRODUCTION

Doors which until recently have been closed are even now scarcely 'ajar', and practitioners, whether actors or producers, who have worked for many years in theatre, television or film and then acquire an impairment may suddenly see their industry in a new light. **Paddy Masefield**, a theatre practitioner, conveys the sense of shock he experienced at the time he became disabled, and **Ann Pointon** links the educational experiences of disabled people to the disadvantages they encounter in seeking employment in film, theatre and radio.

Unless famous enough to be in demand, actors and other workers in the film and television industry who have become disabled have tended to expect and accept unemployment. On the other hand, young disabled people who want to work in 'the media' have become less accepting of the barriers, but discover that appropriate training is very hard to get. Schools can be decisively negative, or helpful in nurturing ambition and talent. Disabled actors **Nabil Shaban** and **Julie Fernandez** talk about their experiences.

The debate about access for disabled people as performers and art-form practitioners has been more public than the debate about access for disabled people as part of the film and television production process. In particular, the film *My Left Foot* drew attention to a debate disabled people were already having about disabled people playing disabled roles, and **Yvonne Lynch** raises some of the issues in the debate.

In television the only open doors to new entrants have been in the specialist disability programmes, and **Kevin Mulhern**, producer of the longest-running of these, *Link*, tells how this particular programme was set up and how opportunities for training have arguably become more rather than less restricted for disabled people.

Those disabled people successful in getting into film and television have often entered these industries through initial low-level 'training' in community-centred arts activities. This is particularly true of disabled people working in specialist disability programmes, where an understanding of the disability world and a developing disability culture is a necessary competence. Producer and Director **Sian Vasey** describes how she is most comfortable in the world of specialist disability television.

Disabled people will differ in the type and amount of assistance they need, and some may need virtually none. They will also differ along all the other parameters of gender, race, etc. and in their disability experience, in terms of whether they acquired their condition at birth or in childhood, or whether they are established workers who have suddenly become 'disabled'.

Black disabled media workers like **Pamela Roberts** describe additional barriers she encountered in getting training, and **Paddy Ladd** talks about the educational disadvantage faced by Deaf people, the importance of television to the Deaf community, and of training to enable them to use the medium to their advantage.

The funding of arts-based initiatives, both large and small has been critical to the small inroads into employment made so far by disabled people. **Wendy Harpe** links funding in the wider television industry to the funding that has been available to disabled people at community level.

I could do your job
Paddy Masefield

Adapted from a speech made for the Arts Council of Great Britain's 'Initiative to Increase the Employment of Disabled People in the Arts', on 11 February 1992. First published in *DAIL* (Disability Arts in London) Magazine, May 1992.

Paddy Masefield is a member of the Arts Council of England's National Lottery Board, and serves on a number of influential committees, including Central Television's Regional Advisory Council and the BFI National Forum. He became the first honorary life member of the Directors Guild of Great Britain in acknowledgment of a distinguished career in the theatre. His contribution to the theatre includes the author and co-authorship of some thirty performed plays, mainly for young people. He has also directed seventy-five professional productions in repertory, touring and Theatre in Education, and has published consultancy reports for a number of regional theatre and arts developments.

In this contribution, Paddy Masefield conveys part of that experience of suddenly finding himself 'disabled' in the middle of an active working life, a not unusual one for adults in mid-career. But, what he brought to this experience was a swift recognition of his own past lack of awareness about disability, and a natural curiosity which led him to seek contact with others working in the arts sphere who identified as 'disabled'. This exploration led him to shift his personal perspective away from the medical model and towards the social model of disability. He has used this not only to help make sense of his own experience but to relate its implications for all disabled people who have his own dedication to and fascination for 'the arts'.

Colleagues, you see before you a person in a wheelchair. Many of you see the wheelchair more than the person, so you may assume not only disability on my part, but that I am an expert on disability issues.

In fact, what I am is an arts expert who only became a disabled person five and a half years ago. So perhaps I was asked to make this address because for twenty-one years I worked as a theatre director, administrator, playwright and consultant: in other words, frequently as an employer.

Yet somehow, although I worked for a whole panoply of highly motivated and ideologically OK institutions, I have no personal recall of ever plugging into the needs, issues or creative potential of disabled people.

So the first and biggest hurdle I had to face was the shock of my conscience, my ignorance and, most importantly, my lack of creative dialogue with a very large sector of the community that I had allegedly been trying to write, direct and communicate with, and for, for so long.

DOORS

From this sombre perspective of lost opportunities, I had to open some doors.

Now as arts workers, you're all used to proceeding through rather special doors: stage doors, recording studio doors,

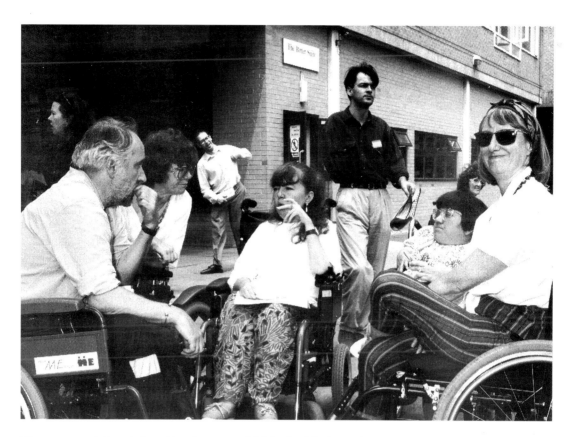

Theatre and Disability Conference, 1992, Paddy Masefield (left)

dressing-room doors, front-of-house doors, even office doors. Well, in my lifetime I've become aware of three historic doors that seem to dominate all others.

The first door had 'Men Only' written in bold lettering, and in my time in the arts industry, I've seen that door dented, the sign removed, and the door hung on one hinge waiting for final demolition.

The second door said 'Whites Only' all over its antique facade, and in my working life I've seen an alternative entrance blasted beside it that recognised the strength of cultural diversity and the richness of black and Asian arts in our society.

The interesting thing is, the third door had no need of a sign. It merely had huge steps in front of it, high handles, impossibly heavy hinges, no raised lettering, narrow lifts inside, more stairs, sudden drops, cluttered corridors that

led to inaccessible inner sanctums of power – because this was the door that was built by non-disabled workers, to disable those who occupy wheelchairs, or are vision impaired, or are shorter in stature, or have different muscular co-ordination to those proud builders.

And that door explains why most of you who are arts employers are totally unused to working alongside disabled people. It is not we who are in truth disabled, but society which disables us. And as a result, you have allowed yourselves to be disadvantaged creatively by shutting out our voice, our vision, our movement (just as certainly as contemporary society is ridiculously impoverished if it uses only male and white resources!)

A DIFFERENT CHAIR
If I look back at twenty-one years of my own life and career as a theatre director,

I ask myself if there is any reason why I should not aspire to the directorship of a major regional company, just because I choose to sit on a mobile metal chair rather than a collapsible canvas one with my name written on it. I think not!

But if I had been in this chair all my life, I raise the question, could I have been guaranteed a job as a director today at a senior level? I think probably not, because almost certainly, I would have been discouraged from drama at school, perhaps even banned; certainly have been denied entry to the drama schools; probably have given up on youth theatres because they met in upper rooms on Sundays with no accessible public transport; told I couldn't take a bursary in a repertory theatre because the technical, rehearsal and administrative areas had been made inaccessible, denied a schools touring job because schools had steps, hurdles and high jumps to keep me out; which seems to be where I started this cycle.

In my own life, I happen to have started five theatre companies, been present at the inception of Theatre in Education, the birth of the Standing Conference of Young People's Theatre, the creation of the Directors Guild of Great Britain. I have broadcast on the first local radio station in Britain; and I've been to the USA and Holland to represent my country.

What a tragedy, what a total waste of life, if all that had been denied me because of apathy, ignorance, fear and prejudice, if society had so disabled me!

Strong words? Too strong? Do you have a feeling that you're being got at? That you have come in here in good faith and that you are being attacked?

I hope I'm only using images and emotions to make you receptive to facts, and the facts show we do have a real, historic problem.

A DISAPPEARING TRICK

Let me demonstrate it through a simple conjuring trick, a disappearing act! On the one hand, let me present society, the employers, the conjurors. On the other hand you have the conjuror's assistants, us, the 6.2 million disabled people in the UK who will now disappear before your very eyes.

We start then with a figure of over 10 per cent of society being disabled, but in fact this 6.2 million may be a very conservative estimate if we also bear in mind that there are some 8 million people who self-define as having hearing-loss alone. So we who are disabled are already a very sizeable chunk of the arts audience, the arts market, the arts consumers, and of course should be part of the arts workforce. And there are over 2 million of us who are of working age.

But watch closely, because we are already starting to fade away before your very eyes. Because 'Abracadabra', the 1944 Disabled Persons (Employment) Act[1] only makes it obligatory for employers of more than twenty people to employ a disabled person if less than 3 per cent of their workforce is made up of disabled people who are registered. But even this 3 per cent obligation is not met because in 1990 only 24 per cent of employers met the terms of the 3 per cent quota, and since then the percentage of conscientious employers has dropped even further. So the disappearing act is accelerating.

But 'hold on!' shouts the audience of arts administrators. 'Surely the Attenborough reports, and the Arts Council's Arts and Disability Action Plan must have done something to make disabled people more visible recently!'

'Sorry, friends', says the conjuror. In your region (the West Midlands), only two companies in receipt of regional arts funding responded to that Action Plan, so it really is a pretty complete disappearing trick. After all, how many disabled people do *you* know who work full-time in the arts? (In 1992 Lord Rix estimated that in a subsidised arts workforce of around 500,000 people, less than 100 were disabled people.)

But don't be tearful. In case you've been upset by our disappearing act, I'll make us all reappear – because something like 70 per cent of those of us of working age are unemployed. And here we are, back before you, demanding the sort of recognition you would demand if 70 per cent of *you* were unemployed.

Now, you will tell me that most of the employers present are committed to the pursuit of an equal opportunities policy. That is tremendous, and I applaud you! I genuinely applaud the ramps, the adapted toilets, the induction loops you installed for your customers in the 80s.

Now, in the 90s, let us tackle the issue of access to employment. Let us ensure the boardroom, the administrative offices, the box-office, the dressing-rooms, the stage, the studios, the galleries are accessible. If you want to change public response, then we need a profile not only of disabled people as artists, as actors, as dancers, as photographers, as poets, as musicians: we also need a profile of disabled people as ticket-sellers, as front-of-house staff, in security, in marketing, in publicity, in catering.

WHY NOT HAMLET?

Perhaps that is one of our most urgent priorities – that you use your power as employers to change public stereotypes and make visible the hidden community. To be simplistic, we are not only saying 'Why not Hamlet?' to the theatre directors, 'Why not portraiture of disabled people?' to the television producers and casting agencies, but, 'Why not a hearing-impaired person in a police office, why not a managing director in a wheelchair, in a background shot of a working office in a TV series?' Why not? I don't know. After all the managing director of my local airport works from a wheelchair.

But most of all there is that 70 per cent of unemployed disabled workers waiting to do what you do, as well as you or better than you. That's a pretty potent force for you to tap into over the next decade; and maybe that tapping will ensure that the arts of the 21st century are made even more relevant to the whole of society by our successors then we have been able to make them so far in this century.

Note

1. Since this was written most of this act has been repealed by the Disability Discrimination Act 1995, including the 3 per cent quota provision.

Doors to performance and production

Ann Pointon

Ann Pointon started 'real' school, a secondary modern, at the age of eleven, following some years in hospital, with undemanding ward schooling. After a shorthand-typing course at a college for disabled students, she became a medical secretary, later followed by a move to the BBC, where she started in radio and then moved to television as a production assistant. She followed a typical 'late start' pattern for disabled people in becoming a full time university student at the age of twenty-nine, with O and A levels obtained via evening classes and correspondence courses. A return to the BBC led eventually to producing Open University programmes in Social Science and Continuing Education for some ten years.

She is now a freelance producer, disability equality trainer and consultant, and from 1991 to 1995 was Co-ordinator, Deaf and Disability, at Channel Four, for whom she compiled *Disability and Television: Guidelines on Representation for Producers.*

For disabled young people wishing to work, education is the key, but barriers to progress from primary, into middle and secondary school, and from there to further and higher education are still very strong. This reluctance to accept that disability is an equal opportunities issue at school, college and university level inevitably leads to disabled people being disadvantaged in trying to access employment in every sector. Film and broadcasting have particular barriers that are, however, also common to other areas of media employment such as the press and advertising.

Access for disabled people to 'the arts' has until recently been about access as audience, whether to theatres, concert halls or museums. In fact, a good deal of work has been done around facilitating access for people with physical and sensory impairments. As well as environmental changes, such as accessible entrances, there has been an acknowledgment of other access needs, such as admission for guide dogs, sign-interpreted performances for Deaf people, induction loops for hearing-aid users, and most recently audio description in some theatres and cinemas. In television, subtitling has increased, and at the BBC there is daily sign interpretation of news. For the benefit of people with visual impairments there has been a research project to investigate audiodescription for television,[1] although this is a more costly undertaking than audiodescription in the cinema.

Notably, cinema chains have been far less interested than theatres, galleries and museums in improving audience access, as evidenced by their slowness to take up ADAPT grants[2] to improve audience access to their premises. Acceptance of the idea of equal opportunities and access to disabled people wanting employment has, however, lagged behind, and the Arts Council's Employment Initiative was set up in 1992 to highlight this and to investigate why disabled people were not naturally coming into the arts arena as employees.[3] A key finding was that disabled people were not encouraged by teachers and career advisors at school to 'think arts' as employment. Disablement advisors in the government employment services usually had no contact or knowledge of employment opportunities, and conversely, arts employers did not easily think 'equal opportunities' for disability, and themselves had no knowledge of the specialist services and support available from the Employment Service via the Job Centres. Traditional recruitment networks in the arts also did not inform or attract disabled applicants. The same problems were observable in relation to film and television, with the exception of the largest broadcasters.

Of course, employment has always been a problem for disabled people, and two Scope studies[4] demonstrated the prejudice that bars disabled people who admit to having cerebral palsy from being given interviews compared with others similarly qualified who do not divulge this information. Although for some disabled people architectural or transport barriers are strong elements in the difficulties they face, far greater barriers are those of the fear and uncertainty of having disabled people in the workplace.

Historically, literature, film, television and other media have propagated misleading or distorted pictures of disability in our culture. And the lack of opportunity of contact with 'real' disabled people means that images of disability in popular culture are often not corrected.

In mainstream schools there is little opportunity of contact with disabled children, segregated by 'special' provision, and progress in mainstreaming has been disappointingly patchy and slow with considerable regional differences and little overall statistical change in the seventeen years since the Warnock Report recommended integration.

At secondary and higher education levels there is also little satisfaction to be gleaned if the evidence of a Skill (National Bureau for Students with Disabilities) survey in 1992 is typical.[5] This was the first stage of a project to find out what provision was available and what attitudes prevail. Of the forty colleges and departments in England providing fine art courses, and surveyed by Skill, four were physically accessible, and only seven had induction loops in lecture theatres for people with hearing impairments. That these were diagnostic of a more fundamental neglect was evidenced by the fact that some colleges were unable to provide equal opportunity statements with regard to disability; some demonstrated no procedure to implement the policies they had; and some of those without procedures also had no contact-person for on-going support of disabled students.

DOORS TO DRAMA

The beginnings of the access to employment debate started with 'performance', that is, should disabled roles be played by disabled actors? However, it was obvious that a key to any 'progress' (defined here as more disabled and non-disabled roles for actors) was the need to open up opportunities for training and for getting experience.

The barriers experienced by Nabil Shaban in the 70s in getting any drama school or institution to even interview him are still strong. In the end Shaban was only able to get the necessary training and experience by co-founding Graeae, a company for disabled actors. Two decades later, Julie Fernandez, after being plucked from her college for disabled students to play the disabled character Nessa in the soap *Eldorado*, is facing similar difficulties in getting more experience.

One of more powerful arguments

made for the *My Left Foot* producers was the need to have a 'name' in order to finance the film and, as both disabled and non-disabled people agreed, there were in any case few experienced disabled actors in the pool for selection. But lessons from the latter fact (i.e. the non-availability of experienced disabled actors) have not been learnt. The young Christy Brown, for instance, was not played by a commercial 'name' but by a young actor, whose performance many disabled people found unwatchable owing to its lack of realism. It is difficult to believe that there was no young ambitious person with cerebral palsy in some 'special' school who was yearning to act and who could have performed the role more acceptably, and got some experience.

Resources to gain experience and support disabled people in roles are hard to get. Producers do not automatically build access needs for disabled people into their budgets. Meanwhile, resources to help non-disabled people 'experience' and portray disability are ungrudgingly made available. It is hard not to appreciate the irony of non-disabled actor Anthony McPartlin's preparation for the part of the blind PJ in *Byker Grove*. In this instance the part started off as a 'sighted' part and so was played by a sighted actor, but the description of learning to be blind is not dissimilar from other descriptions of the lengths to which actors go to portray 'disability':

I was given my own Mobility Officer, who taught me how to use a cane, how to sit, how to cross roads – basically how to cope with not being able to see. She made me wear a blindfold and spent several days leading me round. It was vital research, but very stressful and exhausting.[6]

While such 'homework' to experience the 'alien' state of disability has been admiringly recognised in film by the amount of non-disabled actor nominations for Oscars, a second irony is the existence at the same time of discomfort at the sight of *real* disabled people on television. Nabil Shaban was turned down for a role in a Granada Television seven-part children's series *Microman*, because they judged that he might frighten the children. The acceptable face of disabled people on television is a very different one from those Oscar-winning roles, despite occasional television film dramas such as *Raspberry Ripple, Deptford Graffiti* and *Scallagrigg*, which cast a number of disabled people with varying levels of experience. Whether opportunities exist for some of them to move on from those roles is another question.

This scarcity of 'real' disabled people as role models, whether on television, in drama, or in schools as teachers, inevitably affects adversely the young disabled person's identity and his/her reaction to the discouragement that all young people (disabled and non-disabled) are exposed to when contemplating a career in this most precarious of professions.

ACCESS TO TELEVISION
Disabled people in front of and behind camera have become acceptable in specialist disability programmes such as *Link, From the Edge, Sign On*, etc., but as with drama the doors to college-based production training and mainstream programming are few. New entrants to television have tended to enter via these specialist programmes or from a handful of supported trainee schemes. However, because these opportunities are not widespread, the impact and influence of Deaf and disabled programme-makers has so far been limited.

The long running Deaf and disability programmes and established production units such as the BBC's Disability

Media studies at the National Star Centre

Programmes Unit have seen it as essential to organise appropriate support to enable disabled staff to operate effectively. It is, however, much harder for disabled people to get such support in the mainstream.

Perhaps as importantly, the new generation of disabled people wanting production careers will still find it difficult to get onto media studies courses, let alone be confident that, once there, they will have adequate support and access to teaching, to libraries and to course materials.

INFORMAL TRAINING

The arts sector and local authorities have played a key if unintended role in funding non-vocational 'training' activities such as video work for disabled people. Broadcasters, meanwhile, have lagged behind, and those who now wish to open their doors to talented disabled people have more recently been obliged to think in terms of targeted training. However, as training becomes less easily available within a deregulated broadcasting sector, and greater emphasis is placed on college-based work, little real progress

will be made until the further and higher education sector systematically tackles poor access, whether of buildings, printed materials or barriers in the enrolment process.

Less work-based training affects all workers but the difficulties are compounded for those disabled people seeking work in film and television, where the apparent 'glamour' of the business attracts unlimited numbers of recruits and companies can take their pick. The film industry in Britain is notorious for its periodic unemployment slumps, and the theatre has always been an uncertain prospect, but broadcasting in the shape of the BBC and the independent television companies, which once offered a very stable, albeit highly competitive, work environment, now exhibit more instability than in the past, as well as more intensive competition.

Ironically, as 'disability' has belatedly been recognised as 'an equal opportunities issue', deregulation of the industry has now offset the efforts that broadcasters had started to make to address training and employment for disabled people. The established television companies have shed labour and put more people on contract, and it is contract staff who lose out on training. The 1990 Broadcasting Act, which insisted that at least 25 per cent of production is farmed out to independent production companies, has led to a proliferation of new companies but most of these are very small. A business employing less than twenty people has no responsibilities to employ a 3 per cent quota of disabled people, and under the proposed Disability Discrimination Bill not only will this quota be axed but anti-discrimination laws will not apply to these smaller business.[7] Even the largest of the new independents will tend not to have a personnel section to deal with the

Ronnie West in the hot seat at TV-am, courtesy of Hugh Graham/Rex Features

equal opportunities aspects of their business.

The solution, of course, is for disabled people to run and staff their own companies, but with poor opportunities offered in the past, together with difficulties in entry to media schools, film schools and television training, there is not yet a critical mass of qualified disabled people available to make this happen. The handful of essentially 'disabled' companies (run by disabled producers) still find it necessary to employ qualified non-disabled staff and to crew with non-disabled people. More unfortunately, most non-disabled companies making mainstream disability programmes have not yet recognised any need or value in having disabled people directly involved in their productions.

'STRUCK DOWN'
People who are fully qualified and develop some impairment during their working life may continue to get work, but are actually more likely to experience a completely different status, in which work is much harder, or even impossible, to find. Some may not want or need to work because they have a pension; others may be unable to work in their old grade and need retraining. But many, particularly the under fifties will find unemployment an unhappy state both financially and in terms of wasted talents.

The process of rediscovering self-confidence, and a self-identity perhaps bruised by the experience of disability, may also subtly and disadvantageously affect efforts to find work. But the advantages that the 'qualified disabled' have is they do know their own talents and strengths, and they will probably have had uninterrupted schooling, a college-based or on-the-job training, and a CV.

For the young disabled person the objective and subjective situation is likely to be very different. Subjectively, although young disabled people seem very much more confident than they were twenty or thirty years ago, they will still have absorbed our culture's negative messages about disability. Successful disabled people 'overcome' their disability; this often means denial and pressures to pass for so-called 'normal'. 'I don't think of you as disabled' is a remark many of us have had to deal with. It is intended as a compliment, but its meaning is subversive and its effect a major challenge. It is not a comment that translates approvingly into 'I don't think of you as a "woman", "black" or "gay"'. But people do not make such connections because disabled people are still not expected to like themselves as they are. Finding ways of negating the existence of the impairment is seen as the problem, and not dealing with unemployment, inaccessible buildings and transport, and prejudice.

It is not surprising that many young disabled people leave school with low expectations. Some of these may well be justified if they have experienced a limited non-demanding education stemming from teachers' own low expectations, and until challenged there is a danger that they will be comfortable with a level of achievement well below a potential of which they may be unaware. While everyone needs positive encouragement, there is also a place for making demands of a pupil and giving constructive criticism. There is a tendency, however, when regarding the work of disabled children (and indeed adults) to perceive uncritically any level of achievement as 'wonderful'.

At secondary and college level some establishments for disabled students have developed a more media-oriented curriculum. These are residential colleges, however, and disabled people have to leave home to take advantage of them. Eventually, Shaban and Fernandez had

positive experiences, at Hereward College and Lord Mayor Treloar College respectively. However, the mere provision of 'media' on the curriculum may not be enough to counteract the deep-seated problem of low expectations, as I realised when visiting another residential college for disabled students to shoot their prize-winning multi-media drama for a television programme. It was apparent that the college had generous media provision for students, and the corridors were abuzz with activity and energy. Nevertheless, the college's educational psychologist proffered his view that 'of course most of these children will never work'.

And indeed many young students go straight home with their 'life skills' to helpful social workers whose highest expectations of them may be perhaps living independently of their parents (more life skills to learn) and a place at a day-centre or sheltered workshop. If they do get advice from the Disablement Employment Advisor, it is more likely to be of prospects in industry or retailing, not television, film, theatre or the arts.

The constantly recurring phrase of employers in all sectors is that they 'don't have jobs suitable for disabled people'. Such is the overriding power of the 'confining' wheelchair image that they usually mean sedentary, clerical and office based, and such is the overriding power of the 'helpless and vulnerable' image, that they also mean 'quiet', 'non-stressful' (interpreted as non-media with no deadlines and no demands for quick work) and of course 'junior' and well 'supervised', not professional, senior and supervising.

The misleading notion of 'suitable' in film and television also leads people unthinkingly to rule out swathes of jobs, like stage-hands or riggers; with the ubiquitous image of the wheelchair and white stick winning out over images of physically strong deaf people, or vigorous, sensible people with learning difficulties, the latter including people who might also be well suited to work such as that of darkroom technicians for which they are never considered.

When Raina Haig, who is visually impaired, started work at the BBC's Disability Programmes Unit in the early 90s, she described how a television training instructor 'threw a wobbly' when she was put on his production course.[8] That blind people 'cannot' work in television is, however, belied by the fact that the two most senior producer figures working in disability programmes in ITV and the BBC are blind, and that Deaf people 'cannot' produce video is belied by the Deaf graduates from the European Media School (previously the North East Media Training Centre) and the Deaf producers working in television.

There is certainly a lack of recognition of the very modifiable nature of so-called 'disability'. While 'impairment' (the bodily condition) might be a fixed thing, 'disability' is a very changeable condition in employment and other terms, and its degree is dependent on not only on attitudes but on external access factors such as technology and the workplace environment. Stephen Hawking, the renowned astrophysicist, has multiple impairments but is not disabled from earning a living full-time as a scientist. He was fortunate in not acquiring his condition in early childhood, when his genius would almost undoubtedly have gone unrecognised or unexploited in a 'special school', and his future set at its most ambitious in a day-centre.

The modern workplace is a generally artificial construction designed to meet the needs of a limited range of people with so-called 'normal' physical attributes. It has design and other barriers which can be tackled, and it is worthwhile doing so, since disabled people can only enrich the culture if they are allowed to contribute. The process of change may in fact be an easier process in the arts, broadcasting and film industries, which attract people who are innovative and delight in creatively breaking boundaries.

Notes

1. The Audetel Project's partners include the ITC, the BBC and the ITV Association, and is sponsored by TIDE (Technology Initiative for Disabled and Elderly Persons).
2. The ADAPT (Access for Disabled People to Arts Premises Today) fund raises money from government, trusts, industries and trade unions, and gives grants for work that makes arts venues more accessible to disabled people.
3. See Arts Council Employment Initiative Report (London: The Arts Council of Great Britain, 1993).
4. E. Fry, An Equal Chance for Disabled People? A Study of Discrimination in Employment, Occasional paper no. 4 (London: The Spastics Society [now Scope], 1986). This study was repeated four years later, when little improvement was demonstrated. See P. Graham, A. Jordan and B. Lamb, An Equal Chance? Or No Chance? A Study of Discrimination against Disabled People in the Labour Market.
5. See DAM vol. 3 no. 3 (Autumn 1993).
6. Report by Alison Peachey, Daily Mirror, 9 November 1993.
7. The Disability Discrimination Bill with these provisions was passed in November 1995.
8. Focus Conference Report, Focus: Access to Training in Film and Video for Disabled People (BBC Equal Opportunities Department, 1990).

3.3

Pandora's box
Nabil Shaban

From an interview with Ann Pointon, May 1995.

Actor Nabil Shaban is Jordanian but came to Britain as a young child. He has appeared in numerous television dramas and documentaries, including *Deptford Graffiti, Raspberry Ripple* and the documentary *The Skin Horse*. His work in the theatre has included the title role in Jonathan Miller's Royal Court production of *The Emperor*. He co-founded the Graeae Theatre Company, the first all-disabled theatre company in Britain.

In edited extracts from an interview Shaban talks about his school days and his attempts to get training as an actor. All traditional routes were closed, and it was only with the start of Graeae[1] that he was able to build up experience.

Graeae was established at a time when the disability scene was becoming very political and very active both nationally and internationally. As a new company Graeae performed *Side Show*, a work based on disability, at a World Congress on disability in Winnipeg, Canada, in 1979. The congress was organised by Rehabilitation International and was attended mainly by medical and associated professionals, and disability charity workers. It turned out to be a historic event for disabled people because it was here that they had their bid for 50 per cent representation on the RI board turned down. Fringe protest gatherings sprang up, and a decision was made by the disabled people there to start an international organisation of disabled people. A year later, Disabled People's International, the international umbrella for national groups *of* rather than *for* disabled people, was born.

There are now other theatre groups with disabled only or mixed non-disabled and disabled actors, but Graeae is still Britain's only full-time professional company of disabled performers. It has grants which are project rather than revenue based and still has to raise additional funding. It also acts as an unofficial advice and casting agency, a time consuming function for which it is not funded, and despite the passage of years since Shaban's struggle, it is forced into a training role because colleges and schools are still not taking the responsibility.[2] Its contribution therefore continues to be enormous.

I've always been interested in acting. Before I went to school I was fascinated by it, and I was always fascinated by television and used to wonder how this box contained these extraordinary adventures and people. I was always wanting to know how I could be in that box, and escape from the prison of the hospital and the cot, and find adventure and fantasy.

SCHOOL DAYS
When I was nine I went to a special school. It was residential so it had a home with a separate school but it was all part

of the same premises, and the curriculum was totally independent of anything else that was going on outside. The schooling was extremely poor because their emphasis was on the social, moral and physical well-being of the children as opposed to their academic well-being, because their expectations of you after leaving school were very low. They presumably didn't feel that it was worth investing a lot of time and effort, so there was only myself and another colleague who were literally the first pupils there to undertake any kind of external or national exam, which was the CSE and they decided that we would only do two subjects. Drama was not on the curriculum at all, although we did have a school hall with a stage.

As for career advice, there was nothing really. They had already decided what was going to happen to me as they decided with most of the kids. They would make a decision two years before you left and it filtered down to you bit by bit. What I did let on about was my desire to be a writer and an artist – a painter of some sort. But they rammed it down your throat that these were two very precarious professions and that really one should have something which is a lot more secure. Art, they said, was a hobby and very few people would be able to make a living out of it even if one managed to get to art school.

NOT ON TELEVISION
SO WHERE WERE THEY?
I'd already experienced some ridicule with respect to some of my more outlandish ideas about what would happen to me when I left school. This happened when a teacher read out to a class an essay I'd written in which I said I

Nabil Shaban in *Flesh Fly*, Graeae Theatre Co. courtesy of Patrick Baldwin

was going to be either a secret agent or a veterinary surgeon or a big game keeper, and he basically said, 'grow up, you're going to be disabled for the rest of your life, there's just no way you'll be able to do any of those things.'

And I hadn't thought of that. I'd just assumed that this disability was just something that you had for a period of time and that when you were sixteen it would be taken away from you and you could carry on like everybody else, because the fact of the matter was that you didn't see disabled people on television, or apparently in films, therefore where were they? They must disappear. I'm not saying I consciously thought that, but subconsciously I must have thought this could only be something that you had for a short period of time and then it would be taken away from you, particularly because they were always going on about Jesus curing and it seemed obvious that this must be what happens – at the age of sixteen, Jesus comes along and cures you and then you go out and you do all the things that you see on television.

PROMISED LANDS
AND DISAPPOINTMENTS
Before I went to the Derwen College (then a sheltered workshop and training centre), I did a PHAB[3] drama workshop at the Star Centre for disabled students at Cheltenham, and it was one of the happiest weeks of my school days because I was in a mixed company of able-bodied and disabled people. Everybody was young, enthusiastic, idealistic – there was fun all the time – and at the end of that week I really felt that this was what I wanted to do, to be an actor, to be in the theatre in some way. And when I got back to school, of course, the depression was even greater because I'd tasted of the forbidden fruit, I'd seen the

promised land and I wasn't going to get any of it.

Then, a younger member of staff who was a bit of a radical and who had introduced me to lots of music, literature and ideas, knowing how depressed I was about going to the sheltered workshop, asked me what I really wanted to do. At first I wouldn't tell him but he kept pushing until I said, I want to be an actor, and he said, why don't you try. I, of course, said I hadn't got a hope, that I had to get training; I was in a wheelchair and no one would have me. He persisted against all my arguments, encouraging me to write to all the drama schools in the country. So I wrote, telling them I was in a wheelchair and asking if I could come for an audition. He was disappointed when the replies came, but I wasn't because I knew what would happen; every single reply had turned me down and wouldn't even consider me for an interview or an audition. A couple of places suggested that I take it up as a hobby and join the local amateur dramatics and a couple suggested that I did some tape recordings – write plays or perform them and just do them on tape. One or two suggested that I enter into some sort of correspondence with Michael Flanders, for advice, which I did – and we did have quite an interesting correspondence up until the time he died in 1972 or '73.

In many ways his advice was possibly the best advice, which was to create a demand for yourself because you are not going to get the opportunity to act. They won't have you because you're in a wheelchair, you've got no experience, you can't get training. What you've got to do is write something which people want. You also write yourself a part in it and if they want the material enough, they'll have to have you as part of the package and then you stand a chance of getting in.

It was that piece of advice which fired me and provided us with the ideas for the creation of Graeae. He said, just keep writing, it doesn't matter what you write. You've got a unique life, there's no one else who's got a life like yours.

I was also later turned down by the British Drama League advertising for amateurs for two-week summer schools, who returned my money after accepting me when I wrote with the cheque to say, by the way I'm in a wheelchair but I don't think there'll be any problem, you've got lots of able-bodied people there and I'm sure we can sort out any access problems. After an exchange of letters, my last one being very abusive, they complained to the Principal, who threatened me with expulsion and insisted I write a letter of apology.

I had other ideas about getting in through the film industry, maybe being an editor after a BBC producer came to our school and I overheard them talking about me, saying I'd be a very good film editor. Later I got a book out of the library, found out what editing was and thought, great, that's what I'll do. So I wrote to a number of film companies and they all got back and said well, you can't just start as a film editor, you have to start as a runner, for which you have to be physically fit.

HEREWARD COLLEGE

Eventually I managed to get to Hereward College for disabled students to do business studies, where Richard Tomlinson was a lecturer and was doing drama workshops. He was developing a show about disability called *Never Mind You'll Soon Get Better*, and I became stage manager, because I arrived half a term late when he had already assembled the cast. The following year we took it on tour and changed the title to *Ready Salted Crips* and it was a great success.

By then I had applied to go to university because I'd got grades which were beyond my imaginings and he was leaving Hereward to go to Illinois University for a year. But we were both convinced that the idea of a theatre company of disabled people was a viable idea, so we kept in touch. He pursued *Ready Salted Crips* in the States but called it *Side Show* and again it took on another evolutionary form.

At university in Guildford, I was very much involved with the student drama group and was in *Macbeth*, *As You Like It*, the *Caucasian Chalk Circle*, the *Insect Play*. I was also involved in the TV society which actually produced in-house television programmes. I was amazed that I didn't have a struggle to get in. In fact, I'd gone for an audition to be in *Macbeth* fully expecting them to say no after my other experiences, but the guy who was directing the show had already seen me in something that I'd done and he offered me a part.

THE FOUNDING OF GRAEAE

When Richard got back from the States round about 1976 or 1977, he told me that 1981 was going to be the International Year of Disabled People (IYDP) and that he reckoned that would be the time to establish this theatre company which at that time didn't have a name. Also there was going to be a World Congress on disability in Winnipeg, Canada, in 1980 and we should try to get this theatre going for that. He then wrote to the Winnipeg organisers, told them a lie, namely that we had the theatre company, a show, and a cast of disabled actors, and asked them to invite us to perform. They said yes, and so from 1977 through to 1980 we were piece by piece, bit by bit, assembling this Graeae project.

There were nine in the company: six actors including myself, two stage managers and Richard; and we had no funding apart from whatever money Winnipeg were prepared to give us and whatever money Richard could raise from rich friends of his. We tried the Arts Council but they said no because we were not a professional theatre.

THE BOX OPENS

We went to Illinois University, who paid our accommodation, travelling and food, before we went to Winnipeg and we did twenty-seven shows in twenty-three days in a whole variety of venues, and for lots of different types of people ranging from an entire audience of children to an entire audience of Baptist ministers; from medical people to Rotarian businessmen, to theatregoers. So we did a complete range and that was my training, having to work so hard and so intensively in lots of different conditions. It also brought us face to face with the world of critics, and radio and television because we were a very exciting idea to people even in the States who consider themselves to be at the forefront of anything. We were feted and got lots of TV interviews, all before we even got to Winnipeg, which was great because by the time we got there we were honed down, we were sharp, and we also had a body of reviews and a lot of confidence to take back with us to England. I certainly felt very confident afterwards, as did Richard, and we knew that when we got back we were going to have to take things further. A Pandora's Box had been opened.

When we got back to Britain, we basically begged, borrowed and stole whatever money we could get just for travelling because the cast was widely dispersed. We had people in Devon, Cornwall and London, and we could only perform at weekends because some of the cast had full-time jobs and families. I was responsible for setting up the British

Working Hearts, Graeae 1986, courtesy of Paul Armstrong

tour after we'd got back, and I was determined that we had as wide a geographical spread as possible and that we made sure people knew we existed. So, because we only had three days a week in which to perform, when I picked a location I would then try and set up three different venues in that location.

We were amateur then, of course, and we weren't getting paid – I was running up massive phone bills and was on the dole – and I remember my amazement when we started to hit some of the important theatres in London, on the fringe. I was a complete novice about the theatre scene. The Soho Poly Theatre was one of our greatest allies, and at first I just told the guy there, a good old Marxist, that all the cast was disabled – I was really selling the freak element for all it was worth because I knew that was what would grab them – and he was really fascinated by it all. I made excuses when he asked to see a script because I felt that if he saw the script alone, it wouldn't work. In the end he just accepted what I had to say and he booked us in for four or five nights, which

was very important because, although I didn't know it, it was a prestigious fringe venue. So people from publications like the *Times Literary Supplement*, the *Observer*, the *Guardian*, and regional TV people all came and from that point on, we started to get national coverage and interest.

Notes

1.   Pronounced 'gray-eye' and named after three women in Greek mythology who shared a single eye and one tooth.
2.   Comment by Artistic Director Ewan Marshall, *DAIL* vol. 5 no. 6.
3.   Physically Handicapped and Able-Bodied, a youth organisation associated with the National Association of Youth Clubs to help disabled and able-bodied young people to mix together socially.

To Eldorado and back

Julie Fernandez

From an interview with Ann Pointon, June 1995.

Julie Fernandez is a television presenter and actress who played the part of the wheelchair-using teenager, Nessa, in the BBC soap *Eldorado*. Since then she has done some presentation work on disability programmes for the BBC, and, while not giving up trying to establish herself as an actress, she is planning to study law part-time.

In edited extracts from an interview, Julie Fernandez talks about her school experience and the opportunity she had to move into a television soap.

While the Arts Council's Employment Initiative did seem to indicate that schools generally, both special and mainstream, did not 'think arts' (or media) for disabled pupils, some colleges for older disabled students, have made considerable changes to their curricula.

But these changes have been recent. In 1992 Taylor and Seville[1] of Hereward College could write that only seven years previously their students' experience of the visual arts at the college was 'perilously close to "independence through basket weaving"'. Since then curriculum developments have included Televison, Teletext, Graphic Design, Animation, Photography and Drama.

Julie Fernandez, in her experience at Lord Mayor Treloar College, was one beneficiary of a changing climate.

SCHOOL DAYS

I first went to a disabled day school in England and I felt that it was 'pathetic'. At the age of seven we were still at the level of 'Jack and Jill', and how to add two and two. I then went to school in Germany for a short time and they were very positive; you worked hard and did everything that everyone else did and they did not think children should have an easy time just because they were disabled. I then came back to England and from the age of twelve I went to the same day school I had been at earlier.

At eighteen I went to Lord Mayor Treloar College for disabled students. We did huge musicals there, including *West Side Story* and *Bugsy Mallone*, and we went the whole hog – we had twenty wheelchair dancers on stage, choreographed it ourselves, played our instruments ourselves, and for me it was fantastic.

We were the first ever disabled group in the whole of England to do drama GCSE and we all got Bs. Our teacher felt we should all have got As because she thought we had done it really well, but she also thought the examiner didn't know how to handle and mark a disabled group.

A lot of people ask whether I wish I could have gone to an able-bodied school and I can quite honestly say Treloars opened so many doors for me and I was so happy there. But I think if I'd stayed at the other disabled school I would probably have been a vegetating nothing.

As for ambitions, to be honest, at twelve I was a typical little girl who wanted to be famous, and of course my

Eldorado, (BBC)

mother said, 'Don't be so silly, for God's sake there's no chance, it will be hard enough to get to university.'

When I went to Treloars I was very behind with my schooling because I'd had something like fifty operations, but within two years I had caught up seven years of school. At the beginning they seemed to me to be saying, very politely of course, that I was too thick to do GCSEs, but I did them and I also got through my A levels.

When I first applied to university I was going to do business studies and German, but the ones I applied to said at first, 'yes we're accessible', then when I rang later they told me that the buildings I would need to get into were not. So I went from business studies and German, to business studies alone, to hotel management and then to law. And it got to the point where I must have contacted about twenty universities and polytechnics and they all said the same sort of thing which was 'sorry, the buildings that these classes are in are non-accessible, and tough luck'.

I then started to panic about what I was going to do until completely out of the blue, a casting agent contacted Treloars, because it is the largest boarding school for disabled people in Britain, in a desperate search for someone to take the role of Nessa Lockhead in *Eldorado.* After talking to my GCSE drama and English teacher she asked if I was interested and although I was doing my A levels, I said yes, I'd love to, and I'll do the audition. A couple of weeks later I met Julia Smith in London and she told me then and there that I could have the job and did I want the part, so it kind of landed on me.

ACCESS SUPPORT

We let them know politely what I needed as a disabled person, and although this wasn't a lot there were certain things that were necessary. And things were promised, some of which unfortunately I never got, because I think they then viewed the situation as me being a stroppy actress, which I wasn't; it was just that I needed certain things as a disabled person.

For instance, most of the crew got cars, which were on contract with a car hire company, but none of the actors got cars. We got picked up to go back and forth from work, but out of working hours we didn't get them and I said, 'Look, I really need a car'. The only place that I could find to live was up a mountain in the middle of nowhere with a dirt track road, and I pointed out that they had got three or four cars constantly sitting around waiting to be used. But they still wouldn't give me one because I was an actress not a crew member, so I then had to spend a fortune every month on the little wage I had really trying to hire out a car.

I think I'm very different from some other disabled people my age, because I've always had to grow up quite quickly, and I've always felt older than I really am. It's just sense, really, for me to ask for a car, but they really thought that I was being an obnoxious pain in the neck when I felt I was not asking for special preferential treatment; I needed a car, otherwise, I was stuck.

They paid a certain amount of money every week for a 'chaperone' who would go to work with me because the studio site in Spain was completely inaccessible. It was on the side of a mountain, and because there was no concrete on the floor every time it rained it was just mud. So I had someone living with me permanently, which was great, and I suppose she was an 'access worker' really.

AGENTS

Throughout *Eldorado* I didn't have an agent, although I did find someone who helped me negotiate the deals in the beginning. However, she was a theatrical agent so she really didn't want to have anything to do with it after the first two or three months. Then it was a problem because without an agent I was fighting all the battles on my own as an eighteen-year-old who hadn't a clue about what was going on in the TV world. I argued points that to me seemed sensible and logical but clearly weren't so to them.

After that I wrote to some forty to forty-five agents and sent a CV off with some pictures. Out of the forty, twenty-six replied, twenty-five of them saying no and just one saying yes, and that was purely because she was one of the other actress's agents. So then I went with her but as she'd never had a disabled person on her books before, she wasn't at all positive and so I left her after about six months. Now I am with another agent and it is a battle to get work, an incredible battle.

DISABLED ROLES

I'm in the ordinary Equity Spotlights but not on the separate disabled actors register. I just don't think it will make any difference to whether I get jobs or not, because there are actually hardly any disabled roles. Those disabled roles that do exist are usually taken up by able-bodied people 99.99 per cent of the time. Also the disabled roles that do come up are very rarely auditioned; they seem to be already cast before you even know they're looking for people. There is also the problem of how many casting agents know about the register, and I'm not criticising it, but a lot of people just don't know it exists.

I'm going to contact Graeae, and I recently noticed another company which wants to do a production of *Hamlet* with a mixed able-bodied and disabled cast, so I'm going to get my agent to contact them as well, but to be honest with you, and this sounds a bit nasty, I haven't wanted to categorise myself quite yet. What I've been trying to do is to make it in the able-bodied world and I didn't want to categorise myself and go into a disabled theatre company straight away. Now that I feel I'm on my way to getting there, I will get involved, but I think if I'd slotted myself straight into disabled theatre, I would have probably thought, this is where I'm going to stay. That's not a negative view, it is just that I wanted to fight the other side first.

Note
1. M. Taylor and R. Seville, Hereward College in *DAM* vol. 2 no. 1, Spring 1992.

3.5

All the world's a stage
Yvonne Lynch

From *Disability Arts Magazine* vol. 4 no. 1, Spring 1994

Yvonne Lynch is a freelance writer, playwright and drama teacher. With Geoff Armstrong she co-authored *Why?*, a play written for Graeae Theatre in Education, and in 1995 she was commissioned by the New Playwrights Trust to write an introduction to their *Guide for Disabled Writers Writing for Stage, Screen and Radio*.

The issue of disabled actors for disabled roles is no longer in essence a controversial one, with more and more debates with producers and directors tending towards a discussion of practicalities. Many of the 'practical difficulties' can be seen as excuses, which some producers are prepared to use and others not. Compare part of a quote from one producer, cited in Cumberbatch and Negrine:
Had the setting been different it would have been easier to rehearse but the rehearsal rooms had inadequate facilities and it was not clear whether I would get clearance to use a disabled actor, to provide extra transport and so on . . .
with a children's drama producer who said:
absolute balls . . . just bullshit. We rehearse where we want to and all the studios have double doors for moving sets. We have no problems at all. No problems with acting as such and I have no problems getting actors.[1]
The debate among disabled people reflects both a recognition of the complexity of casting decisions, where there is a shortage of disabled actors and a diversity of impairments. Here, Yvonne Lynch tackles some of the thorny questions in the debate.

All the world's a stage, but unfortunately not all the men and women get the opportunity to be players or actors on it. This seems especially true if you happen to be disabled. The number of well-known disabled actors can be counted on one hand. But why is this, when there is, after all, no shortage of disabled characters? Our plays, films and literature abound with central characters who are disabled: *Richard III, The Elephant-Man, Rain Man, The Hunchback of Notre Dame*, to name but a few. While some of these characters may well be questionable negative stereotypes, what is even more negative is that disabled actors seldom get the opportunity to play them.

So why are such roles usually played by non-disabled actors? When Daniel Day-Lewis was chosen to play the part of disabled writer Christy Brown, there was a storm of protest from the disabled community; but the reasons behind the casting were clear: Day-Lewis was a star with a name and no movie-backers were likely to invest millions in casting a complete unknown in such a central role.

However, no amount of method acting can disguise the fact that Day-Lewis (as with the other non-disabled actors playing these roles) is imitating a situation, a way of life, of which he has no personal experience. This is not to say that in order to play a murderer you need actually to kill someone. What it does mean, however, is that the audience concentrates on watching the 'marvellous' actor at work. The audience knows that Day-Lewis is a handsome, athletic, good-looking man, which gives them even more reason to admire his technique when they see him transform himself into role as crippled Christy Brown.

Now, I don't mean to imply that the role of Christy Brown should only have been played by an actor with the same degree of cerebral palsy. We don't do ourselves any favours by becoming too specific: you could wait your whole life for a part to come up that fits your exact individual experience of disability. What I do mean is that, in the case of *My Left Foot*, a wheelchair-using actor could have played the part. Obviously it would have to have been an actor who could have realistically taken on the role but, that said, he would have shared with the character a common experience of disability which would have given the role an added weight of truth, rather than an underlying acknowledgment of make-believe.

It seems to me that being aware of the actor at work detracts from what the character is really saying. It may well be a technique that Brecht with his theories of alienation would have admired: the idea of acknowledging the actor while absorbing the character being played – but I don't think it is appropriate to modern, naturalistic theatre, film or TV. We no longer accept – nor should we – white actors blacking up to play Othello, so why are we still accepting non-disabled actors playing disabled characters? Sometimes it is inevitable that the part goes to a non-disabled actor; for instance where a character acquires a disability within the story. A blind or visually impaired actor should not necessarily play the part of Gloucester in *King Lear* – it would certainly add a different dimension to the play, though it might be an irrelevant one with regard to understanding Shakespeare's symbolic intentions.

Unfortunately for disabled performers, directors and writers get a lot of dramatic mileage out of the 'before and after' scenario. This, by definition, excludes those of us who cannot possibly 'act' the before (i.e. unimpaired) scenes. This, in turn, begs the question of why is there such concentration on that transition – it isn't the only dramatic thing that ever happens in a disabled person's life.

Even those characters who are disabled from birth, like Richard III, get played by non-disabled performers. There really shouldn't be anything inevitable about that. While most disabled actors might aspire to these classic roles, many would be happy to start off with smaller, bit parts. And they are everywhere. Television is full of them; with all these emergency services dramas, there are dozens of impaired characters walking or wheeling about; in *Casualty, The Bill, Blue Watch, Nurses, Health and Efficiency*. Not to mention our 'full of social issues' soaps – even *Coronation Street* has three disabled characters but only one disabled performer.

This isn't counting those TV programmes that are merely vehicles for their stars, for example Richard Briars' appalling show *Tell God I'm Waiting*, where even the practicalities are ignored. How many electric wheelchair users do you know who can transfer, unaided, to an old-fashioned invalid carriage, and manage to take their chair with them? And why was Sue Johnson using a wheelchair

Anthony Sher as *Richard III*. Shakespeare Centre Library, Joe Cocks Studio Collection

Tim Barlow and Jim Gibbins rehearsing Frankenstein, Graeae Theatre, 1984

in her recent show about a taxi company? Because of her success as a disabled character in *Goodbye Cruel World*? If programme-makers want characters with disabilities, why aren't they employing disabled people?

Why not? Because where are all the disabled actors? Equity does have a list of performers, but none are yet household names. I know that many are out there struggling to get on, to get parts, trying to penetrate our national theatre companies, but there are barriers all the way. Not just physical barriers (though plenty of these exist) but more often attitudinal. I teach on Jackson's Lane Theatre Training Scheme for disabled people and when I tell people this, some immediately think that the scheme is some sort of therapy. Or they say (not realising that they are speaking to a disabled person), 'Why? What's the point? Who's going to give them a job?' My point exactly. Who is?

If disabled actors are not even getting the opportunity to be cast as hospital patients (unless of course it's a BBC or Channel Four drama set in an institution), never mind *Richard III*, how long will it take before disabled characters become an everyday aspect of films and plays? People who just happen to be disabled; where their impairment is incidental and not imbued with some deep metaphorical meaning?

I remember when I was touring with a play called *Why?* (a love story) for Graeae Theatre Company, a radio interviewer compared the scenario to *Romeo and Juliet*, but maintained that disabled performers couldn't take on the title roles in Shakespeare's play. Why not?, I replied, there wasn't anything in the text that said explicitly that they weren't disabled. Disabled people are lovers, and parents, and workers and any other role you care to name, and there should be no reason why they can't play those parts.

It seems that nothing can change effectively until more appropriate accessible training exists. The course at Jackson's Lane is a foundation level City and Guilds course, but after completion students really need to move on to the next level before they are in a position to apply for professional work. Four students from last year's course did go on to do pre-degree Access courses at Tower Hamlets college (it does have limited access), but for students who don't want to follow an academic route, the way into established accredited drama colleges is incredibly difficult.

That is true for anyone who wants to attend, disabled or not; both because of over-subscription and the outrageous cost, with little or no possibility of grants. For disabled students it is even more difficult, because of physical barriers, attitudes and the poverty trap: the twenty-one hour rule[2] that makes full-time education almost an impossibility for many disabled people.

Until we have more trained disabled actors it is almost impossible to change things, to challenge the Day-Lewises and Robert De Niros of this world when they take on disabled roles. There has to be better access to drama colleges for disabled students and a rejection of the financial penalisation when they choose to take up full-time courses. Disabled people need to demand their rightful place on this world's stage, to become players themselves.

Notes
1. G. Cumberbatch and R. Negrine, *Images of Disability on Television* (London: Routledge, 1992).
2. The rule under which over twenty-one hours of educational activity can result in loss of benefits.

'The only cripple in the room'
Kevin Mulhern

From an edited interview with Ann Pointon, May 1995.

Kevin Mulhern, who went to Worcester College for the Blind (now New College Worcester), started as a freelance journalist, working on a range of papers including *The Times*, and also in radio on programmes that included *Start the Week* as well as *In Touch*, the long-running radio series for blind and visually impaired listeners. He joined the *Link* programme in 1981 and now runs Coffers Bare, the independent production company that produces the programme weekly for Central/Carlton Television. His journalistic values are paramount, and in the area of disability it is rare for any other television programme to tackle a topic that hasn't already had at least a preliminary airing on *Link*.

The odds against disabled people getting into television production are long, and as Kevin Mulhern explains, the existence of specialist programme strands like *Link* is only a very limited answer to the problem of lack of poor training opportunities. He argues that they may even be disadvantageous.

There are one or two targeted training schemes, but there are so few places that a disabled person would be fortunate to gain entry in this way. For instance, the Channel Four scheme 'Fourthought', shortly to be replaced,[1] was able to take on only four people every two years; at the BBC's Disability Programmes Unit they have had two trainees each year, and in BBC radio there have been a number of short training placements. The popular journalistic way into television is boosted by the RADAR[2] bursaries for journalism courses.

Like many non-disabled entrants, a number of disabled people now established in television, entered via the presenter route – on specialist programmes, however, and not *News at Ten*! – but companies are much less prepared to take on inexperienced disabled people as production trainees. At basic grades there is real difficulty, with disabled secretaries, production assistants and other support staff particularly difficult to find. Even producers at the 'coalface' of disability production have blocks about disabled staffing at this level, as Kevin Mulhern was surprised to find when one BBC producer and colleague stated that she thought 'we couldn't have a disabled secretary because you really need somebody who's capable in that job. Anybody could do my job, but the secretary is too important to be a disabled person.'

In a business that is not making 'widgets' but reflecting powerful ideas and images, it is particularly important that disabled people are fully included in the production process. Mulhern, however, believes the main problem to be solved is that of getting disabled people in at every level in the workplace, rather than that of simply getting disabled people into the production unit.

'DISABLED PEOPLE DON'T WANT ANOTHER DOCUMENTARY, THEY'VE HAD ENOUGH'

In 1975 Charles Denton, who was then Head of Documentary Features for ATV, told Richard Creasey, who was a researcher at that time, that he wanted to do a documentary programme on disability. Richard went out, met a lot of disabled people and came back saying that disabled people didn't want another documentary, that they had had enough. What they really wanted was a programme that aired disability issues which they saw as important. This was at a time when there was very little tradition of consumer-based programmes, but Charles Denton was totally sympathetic and thought it a good idea. ATV initially made just six half-hours to be broadcast only in the Midlands. Now, in television, if you get ten viewers' letters after a programme, that is pretty good, but this triggered a huge postbag. Hundreds of letters were coming in: 'I need more information', 'I need ideas'. This coincided roughly with the development of the political side of disability and *Link* became a half-hour programme going out every other week, alternating with a programme called *Getting On*, for elderly people. The only disabled person involved at that time was Rosalie Wilkins, as a presenter.

THE AMERICAN INFLUENCE

I joined in 1981 during IYDP (the International Year of Disabled People), when Rosalie and Pat Ingram, who was then the producer/director, went off to America to make a one-hour special programme, as a *Link* spin-off, called *We Won't Go Away*. It was while they were in the States that they got very much into the disability movement and I think came back with the realisation that they had to involve more disabled people.

In 1982 I was 'floating' and was doing *Start the Week* for the BBC, so when I was asked if I wanted to work on *Link*, I said yes but not really full-time. I then became the second disabled person visible on it, but there were still no disabled directors or producers, just presenters who were very much the front people plucked out of somewhere else and dropped in. Rosalie came from a tradition of disability, and I came from journalism with *The Times* and other newspapers, to radio, and then to TV. So there I was as a presenter, suddenly thinking, God, this is very tokenistic.

FROM 1.5 TO 2.5 DISABLED PEOPLE

Eventually I took over as producer, and in 1986 my avowed aim was to put more disabled people in – but we failed, we failed! Structurally, Central – as it then became after ATV – just wasn't geared to having disabled people coming in as secretaries, as PAs, at these entry levels, so we had to keep importing disabled people at a higher level than their training granted, but these were still presenters, reporters, and never directors.

By the beginning of 1988 I went to Central and said, 'I can't do it, here I am, I've had another two years, and all I have managed is to get the number of disabled people up from 1.5 to 2.5; it's useless, I'm off.'

COFFERS BARE: AN INDEPENDENT

By then the industry was changing and the independents were coming in, so they suggested I would get a better shot at getting more disabled people involved as an independent. And that's what happened. By this point *Link* was a weekly fifteen-minute programme, and we started producing it in the middle of 1988, as Coffers Bare, an independent production company.

We have had more success in getting

131

more disabled people in, but it has still really been at the level of presenters, directors, producers. And what people have tended to do is to get experience and move on, so at this level I think we became an unofficial training ground. To a certain extent people just learnt as they went along, because on weekly programmes you don't have time to say, let's have an in-house training course.

I've got my first ever disabled production manager now, and she's a wheelchair user, so we are faced with access problems. We have to have a rule that we never go anywhere to shoot where we can't get access from a wheelchair. In the old days we would have gone if it wasn't a wheelchair-using disabled person doing the interview and it was, say, a minister we were interviewing who was up a flight of stairs. Now we just let them know that we don't. But it's a nightmare; Britain is just accessible.

On the programme side, I think we have changed enormously. We're now in our twentieth year and in ITV I think we're second only to *Coronation Street* for duration. That first decade of *Link* was full of social workers – the professionals telling people how to do it – but when I took the programme out of house, I do remember saying to myself that unless it's a *disabled* social worker or occupational therapist, or a professional who has been criticised, we are not putting them on the programme; they are not going to be there just because they are professionals.

In terms of training for production, because of the industry move away from producer-broadcasters and towards independents providing programmes for publisher-broadcasters, training on the job is now much harder than it was when I first started.

Training people when you are operating as a small independent rather than a large company is not as easy, because a person could sit in the *Link* office now for a month or more and not see the full range of television, whereas at Central when we were an in-house production I could say 'Right, we've got nothing happening in studio or editing this week, so go to another studio or cutting room or to somebody else's dub in the building'. There are also other disability-related problems in the smaller companies. Many, for instance, are up three flights of steps in a back room, whereas if I take a disabled person to a studio in LWT, I can get that person into the studio and into the edit suite because LWT is fully accessible. On the other hand, they are not training disabled people.

In the long term, the media courses may make up the shortfall, particularly for reporters and presenters, although in the production area I think it is difficult even for the non-disabled person. But if you don't go to a media school who is going to train you? The BBC? ITV? It is much less likely than it was.

TRAINING ON SPECIALIST DISABILITY AND DEAF PROGRAMME

I think the very existence of specialist programmes is a real problem. It tells most programme-makers that this is the place to train blind, deaf and disabled people, that it is a more comfortable area in which they can be trained. Certainly the advent of the BBC's Disability Programmes Unit (which I'm not criticising at all) actually formalised what was really happening throughout television. The attitude is: if you've got someone in a wheelchair, put them on the disability programme because they will have taken the problem of access on board. So really what's happened is that other programmes have not done that much training, and the specialist programmes have done it simply because

Rosalie Wilkins – Early days on the *Link* programme

they were there.

Perhaps if we had we sat down ten years ago and had this conversation, I would have said let us have a moratorium on disability programmes training disabled people; let us get the companies to do it themselves, then send them back to us after they're trained. But now, of course, the companies are just not doing as much training overall, and we are now in a very difficult situation. If one asks the question 'where would you like to start from?', well, the answer is not from here. Unfortunately, I would guess that, technically speaking, there are now less disabled people being trained than there were, but this is probably not because we cannot break down a lot of the barriers of television, but to do with these other factors.

TRAINING IN THE USA

In terms of media courses, I think the USA is probably twenty years further down the road, with its two-stage educational system. In Britain the whole concept of higher education has been that you go and read a subject like history or religion or whatever and then you give the benefit of this to a profession. In the States now the graduate schools are turning out a lot of people in media studies right across the board, all the way through from film-making to reporting, and there are a lot more disabled people employed in media studies.

Also, the growth of stations there gives more opportunities. There are so many small cable stations which start very small and can grow very quickly, and they are not seen as second rate to be in, but as a way of getting into media. In Britain I think if you said you wanted to work in television and then went to work for, say, Coventry Cable, people wouldn't be impressed. Whereas there is no shame there of going to a tiny station on leaving media school, and again, there is a plethora of disabled people involved in those kind of companies.

There are a lot more disabled people getting there – there's John Hockenberry, now at ABC News, who started with PBS Radio, and Bree Walker of Philadelphia; there are people there who are very visible. People go on to cable, satellite, and then on to the networks. However, it has to be said that I don't know what percentage of disabled people are coming through as directors or producers, but my suspicion is that it is still not significantly high yet. But there is a structure there, and it may well be that things will get better as the years go on. Also, they have staffing levels in America that we have lost here – probably 200 per cent more than we have. The days are gone here when you had enough crew to go out with, and this has implications for training.

THROUGH THE 'DISABLED' DOOR

As for disabled people not wanting to work on disability programmes, I'm very mixed about this, but I don't think you can separate this out from the disability lobby. The fact is that we live in a society which is very prejudicial against disabled people, but it's not unusual or unexpected that disabled people pick up those values and repeat them. If one looks at the black experience, in the 30s the movies are full of stories of black, mainly black women it has to be said, born light-skinned, who wanted to pass themselves off as a white. In the disability field there's no real difference because there is a stigma attached to being disabled and therefore somehow if you're working on

a programme that deals with disability, it is undoubtedly stigmatic.

All I can say to them, to be honest, is that there is no shortage of non-disabled people who are wanting to work on disability programmes, so if it is going to get you a training, why worry? In fact, I don't think they're worried as much about starting on a disability programme, as about the likelihood that if they start on one, then they'll never move on to anything else. But it is just not a realistic attitude. By and large, at the moment you take a job in television anywhere you can because you need the training and you need the experience. You can always become proud and unemployed after you've been trained, as opposed to before.

'THE ONLY CRIPPLE IN THE ROOM'

As for the future, I'm forty-four years old and I've still not gone into a room and met a commissioning editor who has a disability. I still go to meetings of the networks, sit down and think 'Oh, God, I'm the only cripple in the room again'. If you are from a racial minority you must know what this is about, not only are you the advocate but the representative, and it is so tiring. I have been boring people for fifteen years by saying at the end of the day, it isn't about programmes but about the inclusion of disabled people in the industry.

Notes
1. By a bursary scheme planned for 1996.
2. Royal Association for Disability and Rehabilitation

'Sorry, I can't make the tea!'
Sian Vasey

Sian Vasey of Circle Pictures is an independent television producer, currently working at the BBC in the Disability Programmes Unit.

She attended three special schools, none deemed particularly praiseworthy, and on leaving spent an enjoyable three years as a clerical officer at the DHSS. Then came a degree course at college, coinciding with a 22-month long marriage which Sian describes as 'a bit of a nightmare'.[1] After a spell at IBM and a second bout of working for the civil service, she joined Artsline, the London arts and disability information service. While there she was one of the prime movers in the setting up of the London Disability Arts Forum (LDAF). From Artsline she moved to television journalism, joining the *Link* programme as a presenter/reporter. She temporarily disappeared from the screen in 1991 to take up the editorship of the well-received but now defunct *Link* magazine, a national disability publication.

A brief period acting with the Graeae theatre company was not, she says, because she actually wanted to be an actress; it was more a case of mixing fun, with political aspirations. Having just joined the Union of Physically Impaired Against Segregation (UPIAS) she had some 'half-baked' notions of applying some sort of political principle to what Graeae was doing.

Sian has directed and presented many *Link* programmes, and as an independent producer made *Mum's the Word* and *We Have the Technology* in Channel Four's *People First* series. At the BBC she is involved in producing the series *From the Edge* and *Over the Edge*.

As a wheelchair user who needs personal assistance, Sian Vasey describes her work in television and the kind of facilities that she, along with some other disabled people, need in order to work effectively. In 'specialist' television it is easier to get the necessary support.

There is a temptation, and indeed a pressure, for disabled people to deny their needs ('I am not disabled, I can do the job just like anyone else') but although a popular strategy with some disabled people, the denial syndrome may be counterproductive if the lack of useful aids prevents one from doing a job competently. Many disabled people struggle on regardless, preferring to try and make their way in mainstream programmes, and some have been very successful. Martin Duffy is a wheelchair user who now runs the Ideas Factory, a production company specialising in disability with bias towards adventure activities and sports, but he first did a long stint as a freelance radio reporter and then a television reporter with Granada's early-evening regional news. For some the direction is reversed, with disabled presenters like Andrew Miller moving from Channel Four's children's programme Boom, aimed at a mixed disabled and non-disabled audience, to the BBC's programme Advice Shop.

In the USA there are high-profile wheelchair-using location journalists such as Donna Kline and John Hockenberry, who has extensive experience as a reporter in danger zones in the Middle East.[2]

Sian Vasey has always been clear about her preference for work in specialist disability programmes and not simply because of better disability access. As she said in an interview with Chris Davies

I don't think that the mainstream is a superior place to be. That's what a lot of disabled people do think – that somehow there is something intrinsically inferior about working on disability. Why should there be?

As to claims that disabled people who want to work in television should first learn the necessary technical skills in the mainstream, before capitalising on their particular expertise in disability:

Some people would rather do it, and ignore the alienation. They want to be mainstream more than they want to feel comfortable, but that tension is an issue for them. Personally, I want to feel comfortable, I really can't hang around for any length of time in places where I know I'm not being regarded as a member of the same species.

DOING A RUNNER

In television and film production, 'the bottom' can mean the humble glories of being a 'runner', which might literally involve running up and down Wardour Street with polystyrene cups of coffee. It could also be secretarial work; or assisting a camera crew; or any number of jobs broadly requiring a degree of able-bodiedness. Yet it is only after doing jobs of this kind that the majority of people move on to jobs which are more cerebral and creative, and which can more feasibly be performed by disabled people.

Even after training when the individual enters the world of work, this problem, which we might call the 'sorry, I can't make the tea' problem, still exists and makes it less likely that disabled people would undertake the types of training that could lead to work in the media.

For someone like me, significantly disabled from birth, this inability to start at the bottom was a major difficulty, and I have arrived in television as an independent producer via a curious route. When I left school in 1975, I was attracted to journalism as a way of getting directly on to the media path, but I grasped that, after training, a first step might be that of 'cub' reporter – a mobile job which involves running around the neighbourhood reporting funerals, local mishaps and garden fêtes. Although a number of disabled people have made successful careers as newspaper, radio and television reporters, this work is remarkably unsuitable for someone such as myself who not only uses a wheelchair, but who because of limited arm movement cannot transfer themselves into a mini-cab, drive an adapted car, or use public transport. In those days there were no accessible black cabs or Dial-a-Ride, which today make things marginally better.

The question of training was also complicated by the fact that journalism courses took place at colleges rather than universities, and while it seemed just about possible to go to university because they had more organised systems of halls of residence, colleges seemed more difficult to access, because of the lack of accommodation on site. Even with accommodation provided, there would still have been the personal

Sian Vasey (left) and friends courtesy of David Hevey

assistance problem to solve.

Not surprisingly, I dispensed with the idea of going away to study, abandoned media ambitions and joined the DHSS, working in a benefit office situated about a hundred yards from where I lived with my parents.

My sideline as an actress with Graeae, and activities in the disability arts movement, led later to my becoming a presenter, then reporter on the ITV disability programme *Link*, and I have gradually learned the skills of production and direction on the job.

WORKING IN 'DISABILITY-VISION'
Of course it makes sense to employ disabled people on disability programmes, both on screen and off, although many disabled would-be programme makers feel strongly that they want to work on general not disability programmes. But my own personal experience of working for *Link*, Channel Four's *People First*,

BBC Radio 4's *Does He Take Sugar?* and, most recently, the BBC's Disability Programmes Unit has been that this is where I am useful and relevant.

A person can only really do the job if they are interested and in some way involved. At the most cynical level, as the disability movement has grown, a disabled person working in the area really needs to know the field well in order to navigate the factions and make the programmes unscathed. However, I think overall most of the disabled people who work for any length of time in the area are genuinely motivated by wanting to make some sort of difference through their work and got their jobs as a result of being involved in the disability movement in the first place. As in other areas of television people are often picked up from community or fringe arts groups, but in disability it is the disability arts community that has most notably proven to be a reliable source of television personnel and has fed a substantial number of people into the arena.

There are many disabled people who work in the media who avowedly deny that the fact of their being disabled has anything at all to do with the fact that they are doing the job they are doing. In the case of disabled people who are not working in disability programming they may well be right, but even then I would argue that equal opportunities will have had a hand in their career at some stage.

I would also argue that the only real route to a job in television is through politicisation at least to a level where an impaired individual identifies as a disabled person. There are no statistics on where the disabled people who have managed to find work in TV are employed, but my suspicion is that the majority of those who do creative work, that is, re-searching, directing or producing, are working within disability-specific pro-gramming or at least got started there. These specialist strands of Deaf and disability programming, which, with few exceptions, have off-peak transmission hours, are often labelled ghetto-vision.

Most of the programmes came about (some more directly than others) because the disability movement shaped disability into an issue which was poten-tially controversial, and made broad-casters aware that this issue needed and deserved attention. Disabled activists were then central to the creation of a field of opportunity for disabled people to get access to work in television.

THE ACCESS WORKER

There are some obvious advantages to positive recognition as a disabled person, by oneself and by others. I have consider-able access needs and find that working in disability programming brings some automatic recognition of and assistance with those needs. Over the last few years

I have been supplied with what is known as an access worker who facilitates me with going to the loo and assists in all sorts of other ways. I have had this paid for from Channel Four budgets for independent productions, and by the *Link* programme which is funded by Central Television.

If, however, one were working in mainstream television, in Current Affairs, Features and Drama, I find it hard to believe that the presence of such a worker would be understood or even tolerated. While I have no proof that a programme team would not welcome me and my access worker with open arms, people in the mainstream media still have a lot to learn about disabled people and it is hard to imagine producers behaving in an entirely enlightened way towards disabled colleagues, particularly when one considers the way the subject is often treated in programmes.

For the last year I have been working on contract at the the BBC's Disability Programmes Unit (DPU), which currently produces the series *From the Edge* and *Over the Edge* and where serious efforts have been made to crack the facilitation aspect of the access issue. To this end the DPU has a team of five workers employed solely to facilitate disabled workers with whatever they need. The access team also facilitates disabled workers who have been seconded to other BBC departments. The editor of the DPU, Ian Macrae, who is blind, writes: **Traditionally, the impediments for disabled people getting into television have been the belief, by those able-bodied people who control the industry, that we can't do the jobs, together with access-related difficulties.**

In using facilitators to crack the second set of problems, we can

begin to argue strongly against the attitudes that have kept us out. There's no doubt for example that with my impairment logging rushes is a time-consuming process. Now, I am perfectly willing to spend the time it takes me, but sometimes for operational reasons it has to be done quickly. When there's a facilitator around to be whistled up, the problem (which is purely to do with access) is solved. It works too. I once logged six 30-minute rolls of Hi-8 transfers in just over three hours working with a facilitator to race-read the numbers and pictures. That's actually faster than some of my colleagues at Video Diaries and Video Nation could work.

What facilitators enable us to do is to work efficiently and effectively thereby giving us access to the legendary level playing field. All we have to do then is overcome the prejudice and ignorance which still, by and large, keeps us out of the game.

At the DPU, access workers have their own room and are available when required for facilitation purposes. They go out on all shoots, sometimes to facilitate the contributors as well as staff and also to satisfy the BBC safety requirements. At the moment there is nobody currently working at the DPU who needs constant facilitation and when one is working with a number of different people it seems to me that the workers do not necessarily have the most satisfying of jobs.

There may also be a tension in the worker's necessary involvement in the work of production while simultaneously maintaining their role of disinterested support workers with their first loyalty being to disabled workers. This is a problem with which the DPU is still grappling. Will Davidson, the access manager, writes:

Facilitators are employed at the DPU to meet the access requirements of the disabled people who work on the production team and for disabled *contributors* involved in the production process. As in other environments, they work as directed by the disabled person, but they are sometimes expected to anticipate access requirements using initiative and demonstrating an understanding of television production.

The access support seems to work well when the facilitator is calm and competent, and able to work with people, especially trainees and contributors, in a way that allows those people to feel completely comfortable in making access requests. It is the facilitator's job: it is what they are paid to do. Access work is not doing someone a favour, it is providing a professional resource that is being paid for.

In the past when I have had an access worker either at Coffers Bare, which produces *Link*, or at my own company Circle Pictures, the job has been combined with other production work, and although I have only worked with one individual in this way, it has worked well.

Indeed the availability of such assistance is a key to being able to work, not only in the media but anywhere, for many disabled people.

ON LOCATION

And there are other advantages to working in 'disability-vision'. Not least, it means there is usually more than one disabled person in the team, so one doesn't have to fight to get the basics, like an accessible loo. Also there is a fair chance that some contributors' homes will be accessible as they will often have access requirements too. This makes life much easier when planning shooting days which are often a minefield of access logistics, and which can dictate a degree of compromise. It may well happen that contributors will be chosen with access considerations in mind; in other words, don't expect to be interviewed by me if you live at the top of a spiral staircase – although a programme I recently made for Channel Four involved someone who actually did. In this case I managed to make a feature of adversity in the programme by showing a crew tramping up the stairs while I interviewed her over the telephone.

LIFE AS AN 'INDIE'

As a disabled person working as an independent producer I do somehow feel doomed to be quite isolated. It is hard to imagine a future full of collaborations with other independent production companies, simply because of access. Independent production companies are usually located in trendy inaccessible premises, as indeed are facilities houses. Finding somewhere accessible to edit is a big headache. While the concept of 'producer choice' in selecting resources and personnel may be fine in principle, its practicality is severely limited for disabled producers. Top of their list are not the places offering good bargains, fast editors and efficient engineers, but those offering an accessible loo.

With its long hours and filming days, working in television is more physically demanding than, for example, working in the civil service. Perhaps it is for this reason that this industry is the only one that I know of which is putting resources into these practical solutions for disabled people.

Compared to some industries,

broadcasting is thus very welcoming for disabled people in some areas although very excluding in others. In order to work within it I have found that you have to find the furrow you want to plough and take it seriously. But if I wished to plough something other than the disability furrow, I doubt that I would have found such an accessible niche in the industry.

Notes

1. See interview with Chris Davies, 'Meeting Sian Vasey', DAM vol. 2 no. 4, Winter 1992.
2. See John Hockenberry, *Declarations of Independence* (London: Viking, 1996).
3. Davies, 'Meeting Sian Vasey'.

Television training for deaf people

Paddy Ladd

From an unpublished report (1992) for Channel Four Television, 'Training of Six Deaf Students in Television, Film and Video, NEMTC, 1989–1991'.

Paddy Ladd is a leading activist in the Deaf community. He was a founder member of the National Union of the Deaf, and was a co-presenter, researcher and director on *See Hear* (BBC) in its early days. Frustrated by the slow rate of change, and the continuing infantilisation of Deaf people and their issues on-screen, he left to found the London Deaf Video Access Project. He is a former development worker for the British Deaf Association and was a team member of the Open University's course on 'Issues in Deafness'. He has held the Visiting Chair of Deaf Studies, researching Deaf culture at Gallaudet University in the USA, and on his return in 1993, began a Ph.D. and part-time lectureship at the University of Bristol's Centre for Deaf Studies.

The British Deaf community, identified as those using British Sign Language as their first language, is small (some 50,000 to 100,000) relative to the very large numbers of people in the population, mainly elderly, who have some hearing impairment. People who have become deafened later in life may not wish to use sign language and will feel their 'community' to be mainly with the hearing community.

The Deaf community,[1] recognises its own distinctive culture and identifies itself as a linguistic minority, using a capital 'D' in Deaf to denote the parallels with, for example, French or German people, culture or communities. The reluctance of many Deaf people to identify as 'disabled' and their wish instead to describe themselves as members of a linguistic minority, is a matter of continuing debate with the disability movement. Nevertheless, the Deaf community has always supported the disability movement in the push for anti-discrimination legislation and became an extremely effective lobby at the time the first Broadcasting Act (1990) was going through parliament.

Access for Deaf people can be about interpreters, or induction loops, or information technologies, without which their situation is similar to the blind person denied information in braille, or the wheelchair user who cannot get into the library because of the steps, so that particularly in terms of the social model, disabled people see no contradiction in including them.

Television is a key medium of information and expression in the lives of Deaf and deafened people, and broadcasting organisations have to a limited extent recognised this in the provision of such specialist programmes as the BBC's See Hear and Channel Four's Sign On.

As in disability programming, the early days of programmes for Deaf people did not assume that producers would be Deaf, and people like Maggie Woolley, the first Deaf producer in television, had to struggle to get adequate interpreter support in the office and studio. Today, more Deaf production staff are working on programmes for Deaf people and there have been two two-year training courses at the North East Media Training Centre (renamed the European Media School) for Deaf students.

The following piece by Paddy Ladd is part of his report on the completion of the first course, which received funding from the European Community's Horizon project, together with support from Channel Four and Tyne Tees Television, which produces Sign On for Channel Four. Six Deaf people graduated from that course in 1991 and twelve from the second course. The first graduates got some work on the Sign On programme and banded together to form a company called Deaf Owl. Since then they have been exposed to the employment difficulties that all media graduates face and have dispersed to work separately. The second group, whose comments are positive and ambitious, face an even more difficult market. But the demand for videos and programmes utilising sign language, and the existence of mainstream programmes that would benefit from the production skills of Deaf people is likely to rise. Clearly, a systematic approach to employing Deaf people after training is a necessary part of any future schemes, but Paddy Ladd is in no doubt that such training is necessary.

For some people outside the Deaf community, a course is a course, is a course. To those in the community, however, this course is a vital part of Deaf people's history. Everyone involved with setting it up should take comfort from knowing that future generations of Deaf people will thank them for their efforts.

Why is television so important? The reasons fall into three categories.

The first is that the Deaf community's first language, British Sign Language (BSL), is a visual language, one which cannot be written down. English speakers have been able to communicate across the nation for the last seventy years via written media, by auditory media such as radio and telephone, and visual media such as film and television. These communication channels have proved essential to the development of the British nation.

The 'Deaf nation', by contrast, has as its only means of communication, the visual medium. It is only in the last ten years that these have been explored for and by the Deaf community. By that criteria alone, the Deaf world has been held back from easeful development for sixty years.

We now approach the second category – the Deaf education system. Some readers may have wondered why the Deaf community has not used English to communicate across the nation. Apart from the fact that this is the community's second language, there is a question of English literacy.

The British Deaf Community, as a linguistic minority community in Britain, has been under systematic attack for the last 120 or so years. That attack has been focused on the language of the community, British Sign Language and has been carried out primarily in the education system. Such an attack has not been confined to BSL. Other indigenous British languages, such as Welsh, Cornish and Gaelic, have also been proscribed, again primarily within the education system.

There is one crucial difference, however (for a variety of reasons, too lengthy to describe here), and that is the banning of BSL and its 'carriers', Deaf teachers, causing damage to the community far in excess of that done to Welsh and Scottish communities. The main example is the English literacy rate of the deaf school-leaver, which has commonly been assessed as a reading age averaging eight-and-a-half years. In the 116 years since BSL was first proscribed in deaf education, successive generations of Deaf people throughout the whole country have been cast adrift into society without the basic rudiments of an education, of a positively valued self-image. When this is combined with an almost total lack of access to radio, television, cinema, theatre, affairs of the workplace and the local community, and even to their own parents and siblings, perhaps one can begin to realise the extent of the 'holocaust' that has taken place. As has been often said, the really remarkable fact is that the Deaf community and its language have survived at all.

Nevertheless, it *has* survived. But there is still no recognition amongst broadcasting authorities that the Deaf community needs an increase in the amount of Deaf programming to compensate for the lack of access to other radio and TV programmes.

RECOGNITION OF BSL

In the 70s and 80s the first changes in the education system began, and BSL became recognised as a language by a significant few. Since then, there has been a resurgence in all things Deaf, whether TV programmes, Deaf poetry and theatre, or the great upsurge in the numbers of hearing people learning BSL.

The third category is one of power relationships. Although Deaf people have started to work in television, two things are still lacking. One is control over the amount and type of output. The other is the making of films from a Deaf viewpoint. Only those to whom BSL is a first language, who see and interpret the world in an entirely visual way, can find the appropriate styles in which to create programmes that make maximum contact with the Deaf community.

It is therefore a task of maximum importance to train Deaf people to become film-makers, and to support them in reaching inside themselves to find the styles and the Deaf TV grammar that the world is waging so anxiously for.

Nor is it only television that requires Deaf film-makers. The whole world of video lies out there waiting for those Deaf directors to make information videos that compensate for Deaf people's almost total lack of access to society's information. Deaf culture, Deaf art forms, Sign storytelling, Deaf old people's memoirs, Deaf minority groups and political activities, all urgently require the use of the video medium to kick start the community into the 21st century.

Note
1. The history of the Deaf community is well documented in Harlan Lane's *When the Mind Hears: A History of the Deaf* (Harmondsworth: Penguin, 1988) and (USA: Random House, 1984).

3.9

Getting into video

Pam Roberts

From 'Pam Roberts, Videomaker', FAN (*Feminist Arts News*) vol. 2 no. 10. Also reproduced in R. Rieser and M. Mason *Disability Equality in the Classroom* (London: ILEA, 1990); 2nd edn (London: Disability Equality in Education, 1992).

Pam Roberts is a freelance producer, equality trainer and consultant. When trying to break into film and television she sought out appropriate courses for herself and became particularly interested in the technical side of production, after which she set up and ran courses and training sessions for disabled people, including one for black disabled women. She worked at the BBC's Disability Programme Unit for over two years. She now lives outside London and is studying an M.A. in media management part-time alongside her other freelance activities.

This piece was written in the late 80s before Pam Roberts moved into television. However, the barriers still exist for disabled women, and particularly for black disabled women. WAVES (Women's Audio Visual Education Service) is one agency which is still committed to providing courses for disabled women as well as general courses, but new funding has to be found each time. However, there has (to our knowledge) been no video or film course targeting black disabled people since July 1989.[1]

Both the BFI and the Arts Council have made moves to see that some of their production fund monies are targeted at disabled people, and that general schemes such as New Directors (BFI) do not exclude them. However, Andy Kimpton-Nye in an article on the New Directors scheme reported that only 1 per cent of all applicants were disabled in 1994/5 and notes that funding at this level and Arts Council funding tend not to be aimed at people who are without experience.[2] Even the Disability and Perception initiative launched by the BFI in 1995, which sought proposals from disabled directors, writers and producers, assumed a level of prior experience.

I have sickle-cell anaemia, a hereditary blood disorder. When I was growing up, sickle cell was not classified as a disability, but as social leprosy, owing to the ignorance and lack of information that surrounded the disorder.

Having left school, I worked on various community projects and was involved in women's issues. In 1983 I co-founded an educational and resource project for girls and young women in the London Borough of Waltham Forest. The building we acquired for the project was 'the pits'. It was while renovating the premises that I picked up an infection which developed into pneumonia leading to both my lungs collapsing.

I was hospitalised for three months and came out barely more than a skeleton. The months that followed I was constantly in and out of hospital with repeated crisis: blood clotting in the joints. It got to the stage where a friend commented, you only come out to get

Image and Action – an introductory video course for black women, courtesy of Pam Roberts

your hair done just in time to go back in again. The constant 'sickling', the clumping together of blood cells, led to the deterioration of my hips, now leaving me walking with the aid of crutches for short distances and using a wheelchair for long distances.

To take my mind off my now visible disability, I was introduced to video as a form of therapy. However, my interest developed beyond shooting friends' party videos and I shot my first professional video, *Is It a Bed of Roses?*, a thirty-minute documentary looking at the social prejudices faced by a young unmarried mother.

January 1988, the Girls' Project folded and I decided to focus my energies on developing a career in the media, aiming to become a director. I realised, with just one video to my name, I wasn't going to get far and needed specialised training. By chance I came across an advertisement from the British Film Institute offering production awards for 'New Directors' to make a twenty-minute film. This seemed ideal.

After managing to book an appointment to see the contact person, I was told in a sickly-sweet way, that 'it's not meant for the likes of you'. Unperturbed, I set off for the heart of the British film industry, Wardour Street, Soho. As I didn't know where to go and what to ask for, I just walked into Warner Bros. and told them what I wanted to do. When the doorman told me to go to Walt Disney I thought he was taking the piss, until he pointed me in the direction of Golden Square.

It soon became apparent that what I was doing was totally unheard of: the industry was being confronted by a black disabled woman; producers would gasp in astonishment, mop their foreheads fervently and adjust their glasses to make sure they saw right.

After constant knock-backs and insults I set out on a one-woman crusade to train myself. Hurdle number two: training courses were expensive and definitely not designed for people with disabilities, but a certain amount of letter-writing and grovelling to sponsors resulted in obtaining a couple of courses.

In the last year I have gained training in every aspect of production from script development to computer graphics. I was awarded 'Newcomers' for first time film-makers to attend the Edinburgh Television Festival. *Is It a Bed of Roses?* has become a success, distributed by the British Film Institute; offers of purchase have come from the Health Education Council, with international recognition from the New Zealand Health Authority who've also requested a copy; but the cherry on top of my cake is a trainee directorship with a production company.

My observations and experiences over the past two years have not been put to one side as a bitter memory. In my capacity as a freelance course organiser, I have initiated and am now co-ordinating a video production training course for black disabled women. I hope that the course will provide a vehicle for black women who want to develop a career within the media and address a serious issue.

Notes
1. 'Image and Action: Video Training for Black Disabled Women' was run in July 1989 by Pam Roberts, sponsored by the Women's Training Link and MAAS (Minority Arts Advisory Service). The latter organisation no longer exists.
2. Andy Kimpton-Nye, 'The New Directors Scheme', *DAM* vol. 4 no. 2, Summer 1994. However, more recently, the first set of grants under the Arts Council Film, Video and Broadcasting Department's Disability Video Project went to people who had not previously made videos. See also Part 3, Chapter 10.

Funding the starters
Wendy Harpe

Wendy Harpe has been an arts administrator since 1964 and with her husband Bill bought the 'Blackie' (the Great George's Community Cultural Project, based in a black church from which Liverpudlians gave it its name), giving birth not only to the centre but to the community arts movement in Britain. She took over as Joint Head of the Access Unit at the Arts Council in 1990, with special responsibility for disability and became Head of Arts and Disability in 1992, a new post which she held until the Disability Unit was closed in 1995. She was a true ally of disabled people during this time and with drive and effectiveness encouraged, funded and nurtured a number of key disability arts projects, including the Arts Council's Employment Initiative, a report on *Creativity in Black Disabled Communities*, and disability-led revenue funded clients, the *Disability Arts Magazine (DAM)* and the National Disability Arts Forum (NDAF).

A limited survey in 1990 for the Focus Conference on the provision of film and video training for disabled people revealed that little training for them was being offered in broadcasting and higher education sectors and that disabled people interested in arts/media subjects were getting some of their first 'hands-on' experience in projects funded by local authorities and arts organisations. Wendy, as head of the Arts Council's Disability Unit (now closed), was at the sharp end of arts funding for disability projects or disabled individuals.[1]

Given the instant celebrity status conferred on anyone appearing on television and the high visibility of the media, whatever the reality, jobs in film and television are seen as glamorous, important and influential. As a consequence, these are areas in which people want to work and will fight to get into. Both film and television are industries able to choose from what society only too often defines as the 'brightest and the best', that is, talented, educated, trained, articulate, self-motivated, confident young people who are often already able to demonstrate their commitment and abilities with concrete achievements.

In training terms, media courses are oversubscribed and applications for graduate traineeships in television run into the thousands. At the same time the industry itself provides limited training .

During the late 80s and 90s, factors such as government and market-led changes at the BBC, international competition and the deregulation of the television industry have led to a growth in small independent production companies. However, it has also led to less in-house training by the large television companies, the largest provider of which is the BBC, which in the past operated almost as a trainer to the industry, as staff moved out into independent television.

Meanwhile the British film industry continues to struggle with a lack of infrastructure and funding, with talented film-makers fighting for scarce resources borrowing from family and friends, and working for nothing just to get their vision on celluloid.

TRAINING OUTSIDE THE INDUSTRY

The new way to acquire skills, in addition to those provided through the higher education system, is through modular courses. These are delivered by numerous agencies and co-ordinated through the Industry Training Organisation, Skillset, and these respond to demand. But these courses have to be paid for and are therefore less accessible to individuals who lack money (this certainly includes the majority of disabled people) and to small production companies who often cannot either afford the course or spare the staff to go on them.

While some providers are themselves commercial concerns, others receive public funding. There are therefore courses aimed at women wanting to re-enter the workforce (European money); courses aimed at those who are unemployed (European and local authority money); and there are also a number of European programmes funding work with disabled people, and some training agencies who are beginning to access this money. To date, however, this would not seem to have produced anything substantial in the way of vocational training for disabled people, apart from the training of Deaf people in film and video by the European Media School (originally called the North East Media Training Centre). This course received EC Horizon Project funding, with additional support from Channel Four and Tyne Tees Television. Nevertheless, non-vocational training may operate as an important access point for disabled people in the community.

The reality is that while corporations such as the BBC with public responsibilities, or even commercial stations concerned to meet their employment obligations, can (and sometimes have) set out to both train and employ disabled people, the present system with its emphasis on short courses, its inability to employ people when trained, and its need to find funding, and in some cases make a profit, is less likely to do this.

This is not specific to the media — there are already long reports on how the Training and Enterprise Councils (TECs) have failed to meet the needs of disabled people across all fields. However, if the education system is inaccessible and the alternative has not to date delivered, where are the trained disabled people going to come from?

ALTERNATIVES

Within the media, as within the arts, initial involvement often comes from a chance contact that is then followed by more serious involvement: it can start at school or through contact with a community arts organisation, it can include working at open studios, in amateur societies, with community video workshops and so on. But given the inaccessibility of most public buildings (including arts and community venues); the lack of accessible public transport; the segregated education still offered to too many young disabled people; and the often low expectations of young disabled people, the chances of disabled people following any of these paths are remote.

It has to be recognised that one needs to *actively* include disabled people if they are not to be excluded, and it is perhaps not surprising that where disabled people have become involved in media (video, film-making and photography) it has often been in the first instance through arts groups which work in the field of disability rather than through media groups *per se*.

For instance, the Shape organisations — the first of which was started in London in 1976 and which by the late 70s were established throughout the country – were set up to produce art for and with disabled people. Although they worked with a number of other 'disadvantaged groups', a commitment to arts access for disabled people remained a central part of their remit. At a time when disabled people's access to arts activity was largely limited to therapeutic provision within a medical or community care context, Shape provided one of the few points of contact with professional artists. Not surprisingly a number of Shape organisations, plus some community arts groups, established video and photographic projects specifically with disabled people. On this basis, however, most media groups at present exclude disabled people, despite their often vaunted open access policies and their ideological history.

COMMUNITY VIDEO

Community video was no exception in its early omission of disabled people's voices, but the philosophy behind it was important.

It started in the 60s and 70s, as people became aware of the impact of television, and a number of projects emerged that were mainly concerned with video as a tool for change. Often run by community artists, these groups contrasted the passivity of watching television with the active nature of making it.

The Canadian experience of the Change and Challenge Programme, whereby isolated communities made videos of their lives as a way of communicating with central government, was translated into community video in a British context. Community groups were encouraged to use television to explore their own lives and neighbourhoods so as to learn about themselves and communicate with other groups.

Many of these groups focused on particular communities, such as women, black youth, working class communities, or on specific issues such as health, and forms of community action. Those involved, from TVX in London to the Great George's Project on Merseyside, were generally more concerned with encouraging people to explore, understand and use video than with vocational training. Funding came not from the industry but through local authorities, regional arts boards, health councils, and so on.

Additional funding in the system from the Arts Council and the British Film Institute was also given to visual artists and film-makers who in parallel, and often entwined, developments began to explore video as an art medium.

Video is now commonplace – it is used in the home and as a basic tool within education and business. There are a whole range of secondary industries – including corporate videos, pop videos and educational videos – and a whole network of media groups, some of which specialise in vocational training for work in the industry. Video artists are now shown in art galleries and have festivals devoted to their work; and the medium itself has developed, with artists working with interactive video and on the internet. It is still the case, however, that many groups are still primarily concerned with allowing people the experience of using video for their own purposes.

DISABILITY CULTURE

Nevertheless, it was mainly through community organisations arts organisations like Shape and other publicly funded film and video workshops that disabled people began to get some hands-on experience.

As with the early media groups, much of the work has been concerned with self-image, encouraging people to

become familiar with new technologies, building confidence, etc., and some have evolved into more structured training courses. They do not necessarily provide a professional training, but they can and do provide a point of access.

However, the field of disability has changed almost as fast as the media industries. Over the past ten years disabled people have not only analysed the representation of disability within the media, and found it unsatisfactory, but they have begun to establish their own cultural organisations which focus on the work of disabled artists – artists who are concerned to explore in their work the experience of disability. This is the disability arts movement.

'Disability arts' is comparatively new as a 'movement' but its impact and relationship with the media is as likely to be as varied and complex as that between other cultural expressions and the media. Its finance is from that now familiar mix of Arts Council, BFI, regional arts boards, local authorities and charitable trusts.

BROADCASTING AND THE ARTS

Television and radio are both art forms in their own right and media that feed on other art forms. Not surprisingly, therefore, relationships between the subsidised arts and the broadcast media reflect this duality. They range from the recording and transmission of works by subsidised arts organisations (operas, classical music, dance) to the movement of performers and writers between the media and subsidised theatre. However, the interlocking nature of these areas are only recently being recognised by the funding bodies, and reflected for instance

Sue Smith and David O'Toole in CandoCo's *Back to Front with Sideshows* (1994) courtesy of Hugo Glendinning

Green Candle - Wheels in Action courtesy of Alice Dunhill

in the joint review of orchestral provision being carried out by the BBC and the Music Department of the Arts Council.

For disabled people these institutional relationships are beginning to bear fruit, with work made outside the broadcasting industry reaching a wider audience and funds to generate original work becoming available.

Although the Arts Council of England had been supporting film production since 1963, it was not until 1986 that the Film, Video and Broadcasting Department (FVB) was established — primarily to support arts programmes for television.

Within this activity, the FVB has funded productions that have shown the work of disabled artists, including *The Fall*, a dance piece choreographed by Celeste Dandekar, and *Behind the Eye*, a programme that explored the work of three visually impaired artists. However, the impact of the disability movement can be seen in the establishment by the FVB of a Disability Video Project which will fund work by disabled video-makers. The first set of grants all went to people who had not previously made videos.

The above is not to say that neither had previously funded disabled video- or film-makers (the BFI for instance funded much of the early work of Stephen Dwoskin) but that from now on there will be a pro-active effort to ensure that disabled film- and video-makers are targeted and that disability culture will be specifically funded.

It is perhaps through such initiatives that the funding system will most help to ensure that disabled people will gain access to the media – and this applies across all art forms. Disabled performers, who are largely ignored by inaccessible drama and dance schools, can get their experience through disabled theatre groups; thus, the funding of disabled companies such as Graeae, New Breed and Mockbeggar and integrated companies such as CandoCo will build up the pool of performers available for work on radio and television.

In disability – as in other areas – the subsidised arts can in fact provide the space for people to learn, to experiment and to fail in a way in which the larger and increasingly commercialised media industries cannot.

But while public subsidy may provide an effective and appropriate base for disability arts, and while it certainly can through community arts and media groups provide a first point of contact for disabled people, it cannot provide access to the media on the scale which is needed. This must be done by the media courses within colleges and universities and through the training courses either supported by or set up by the industry. Until this has been achieved the importance of such funding cannot be overestimated.

Note
1. The effect of the funding system on disability access is now changing with the injection of arts lottery money in capital projects. However, it is too early to assess its effect on the training infrastructure for disabled people.

Part 4

Culture and Identity

'Viva' – charcoal drawing by
Gioya Steinke

Introduction

THE NEW CULTURE

Given the structural barriers to disabled people's employment in the media, it is unsurprising that a disability movement has grown that is pressuring the system and finding informal ways of gaining experience prior to getting into the paid sections of the arts and media industry. Not only are disabled people becoming more vocal in their demands for example for anti-discrimination legislation, but many now contend that there is an identifiable and growing 'disability culture' that is feeding the politics and self-expressive arts of the 'movement'. The growth of this culture and movement is an essential element in the current appraisals and critiques of the tragedy-centred portrayals of disabled people that have not only underpinned a range of stereotypes of disabled people but by their reiteration have influenced the type of services and treatment disabled people receive in society. Progress both politically and artistically has been patchy. There are continuing lively and heated debates about the existence or non-existence of a 'culture', the difference between 'disability arts' and 'arts and disability'; and the questioning not only of the medical model of disability but the replacement social model.

DISABILITY ARTS

Disabled people can challenge the lack of status in society of people 'labelled disabled', by a positive acceptance of the body's impairment and an identification of the experience of being disabled by factors other than that impairment, that is society's attitudes, its environment and its institutions (the social model).

In an extract from an address on disability arts, **Allan Sutherland** states that he sees disability arts and disability politics as intimately connected, and in a longer piece **Elspeth Morrison** and **Vic Finkelstein** explore the role of culture in the empowerment of disabled people.

As other people who have been identifying themselves as 'non-normal' or owners of some 'shameful' condition have 'come out' and re-expressed that condition in different language ('black is beautiful'), so identification with disabled people's oppression is being made. **Jenny Corbett** draws attention to the parallels of identifying as 'disabled' and coming out as gay or lesbian.

Alison Silverwood finds connections in her search for disability arts and political analysis, while **Roland Humphrey** questions not only the notion of a common culture but the relevance of the social model.

No one would gainsay that there are not many rich strands in disability arts. Annie Delin suggests that for some Heart 'n' Soul, a popular group of performers with learning difficulties, represents the essence of disability arts. 'What for instance is Deaf Arts?' asks **John Wilson**. 'What can my camera tell me?' asks **Mary Duffy**, disabled artist and writer, while **Millee Hill**'s concern is the marginalisation of black disabled people's arts in the 'white disability movement'.

The link between political action and disability arts is nowhere more clear than in the approach of Survivors Speak Out, and its off-shoot Survivors Poetry – as **Peter Campbell** and artist **Mandy Holland** illustrate.

THE DISABLED AUDIENCE

Very little work has been done around the perception by disabled people of the 'disability product', particularly compared with the perceptions of non-disabled people. **Annie Delin** and **Elspeth Morrison** state in their useful guidelines on marketing to a disabled audience, that it is unhelpful and uninformative to use the names of their medical conditions in grouping people and offer a working definition from Artshare Avon.

While there is a developing culture and, if not a 'community' according to many definitions, at least a 'disability movement' with a voice, it is also true to say that most disabled people will not have had the opportunity to identify with this, and that many, if they have had that opportunity, may have dissociated themselves from this.

The language debate, for instance, highlights the relative importance or unimportance that different disabled people feel about disability language and confusions about use. The listener who called Nick Ross on Radio 4, protesting sincerely that she likes being called 'a cripple' and does not want an alternative term, is not using the word in the free but ironic and political sense that performers on the disability cabaret circuit do.

So how do audience researchers gather disabled people's views? The research commissioned by the **Broadcasting Standards Council** to survey disabled and non-disabled responses to the BBC drama *Scallagrigg* called the categories of responding disabled people (1) activist, (2) 'unhappily' disabled and (3) resisting disability.

Although one might disagree with some of the 'characteristic' views ascribed by the researchers to the three groups, the separation provided a somewhat crude but arguably useful way of looking at where the views of disabled people converged or diverged. Overall the study raised the question of whether the audience is actually ready to see more disability of an uncompromising kind on television and in film, and explored the problems that disabled and non-disabled people had with particular images and narratives.

Alan Holdsworth / 'Johnny Crescendo', courtesy of David Hevey

4.1

Disability Arts, Disability Politics

Allan Sutherland

From a speech to the London Disability Arts Forum Conference, 24 July 1989, reported in *DAIL Magazine*, September 1989.
For biographical notes, see Part 1, Chapter 2.

Some of the contributions in this section of the book are about the reclaiming and assertion of identity, with 'art' as central to this. But given the situation of disabled people, such assertions are seen by many as inevitably also being political acts, with disability arts and disability politics in a close and fruitful relationship.

I think disability arts and disability politics are extremely intimately connected. I also think that the development of a disability culture is the most important thing that is going on in the disability movement at the moment. [...] I don't think disability arts would have been possible without disability politics coming first. It's what makes a disability artist different from an artist with a disability. We don't see our disabilities as obstacles that we have to overcome before we try to make our way in the non-disabled cultural world. Our politics teach us that we are oppressed, not inferior. We may be second-class citizens, but that doesn't make us second-rate people. We have the right to celebrate who we are. And as we would not be us without our disabilities, we have the right to celebrate being disabled. Our politics have given us self-esteem. They have taught us, not simply to value ourselves but to value ourselves *as disabled people*. That's why we can have disability art; because we realise that our disabilities give us something important to make art about. And I'm not talking about tales of personal tragedy. Art has to be measured in terms of what it values.

And stories about how dreadful it is to be disabled value being able-bodied, not disability.

We have also learnt the importance of taking control of the things that affect our lives. Just as we must have organisations *of* rather than *for* disabled people, so we must have art that is *of* disabled people. That is why it is so important to distance ourselves from art therapy.

The term 'art therapy' is one of those phrases, like 'military intelligence', that contains an internal contradiction. Art therapy uses the forms of art for entirely unartistic ends. In particular, it leaves out communication, for it assumes we have nothing to communicate. We, of course, know better, but as in so much else, we have had to reclaim our very right to existence.

4.2

Broken Arts and Cultural Repair:

The role of culture in the empowerment of disabled people

Elspeth Morrison and Vic Finkelstein

From John Swain, Vic Finkelstein, Sally French and Mike Oliver (eds), *Disabling Barriers, Enabling Environments* (London: Sage Publications/Open University, 1993). Prepared from a paper published in S. Lees (ed.), *Disability Arts and Culture Papers: Transcripts of a Disability Arts and Culture Seminar* (London: Shape, 1992).

Elspeth Morrison is a producer in the BBC's Disability Programmes Unit. She was previously editor of *DAIL* magazine, and a performer on the disability arts circuit. She is also a disability consultant and equality trainer and has directed the Liverpool-based disabled 'fringe' group No Excuses.

Vic Finkelstein is a lecturer in disability studies at the Open University. He was a white anti-apartheid campaigner in his home country of South Africa, and as a wheelchair user served time in prison for his political activities. He married and settled in Britain after first coming to the Stoke Mandeville Spinal Injuries Unit for treatment. He has contributed papers on disability to numerous journals and conferences, together with developing and writing Open University course materials. The intellectual rigour of his work together with that of other analysts including Professor Michael Oliver and Jenny Morris have provided some of the linchpins of current disability theory.

The disability movement is a movement of social change. In this paper Morrison and Finkelstein look at what constitutes 'culture' and what the role of 'arts' might be for disabled people, arguing that 'the presence or absence of disability culture and involvement of disabled people in the arts is an indication of the general state of their success in reflecting upon and managing their own affairs.'

INTRODUCTION

In every society human beings come together in groups and subgroups so that their society and physical environment can be modified to improve the quality of life (in food, shelter and leisure). How these different groups actively engage in shaping the world they live in, the artefacts they produce and the mannerisms observed in their use, the different interpretations they make of their lives and the way they present and convey these views to each other, all form the sum total of a society's culture. In all, then, we can locate evidence of the real experiences and aspirations of different social subgroups by the level and way their culture is expressed, especially in its concrete form in the arts.

However, from time to time different subgroups can become dominant within a larger social structure, and the culture of this subgroup is then likely to become the dominant culture in the greater society. When any dominant group asserts its power by imposing its culture on others, or diverts wealth to its chosen art form, then the cultural expression of other groups in the arts will be suppressed. The output of these groups may fail to develop, or their culture may disintegrate or disappear. If culture and artistic developments are interpreted as integral aspects of the human social condition, a subgroup's lack of artistic development could be seen as the result of its failure to develop an active social life, or as a reflection of the dehumanisation and suppression of that group. The very limited opportunities for disabled people to take part in all forms of the arts as spectators, creators or participants raises questions about whether or not we are an oppressed and marginalised subgroup and what we might be trying to do about this.

It is arguable that while the most powerful groups in society have placed their cultural tastes at the top of a hierarchy of artistic forms not all people will be equally devoted to these fashions and traditions. The lower status of their own customs could then well lead to a general loss of interest in the arts and this could gradually spread throughout society. This could be expressed in encouraging schoolchildren to think that careers in science and maths are for the brightest pupils while arts and vocational training are for others. In this context it seems understandable why those active in promoting empowerment through self-help organisations might not see an equally important role for disability arts and culture in advancing the well-being of disabled people. Participating and enjoying disability arts could then be seen as only a sideshow in the drama of struggle for change, something to provide relief from the tensions of boring or stressful committee meetings. In this

paper we will argue that the presence or absence of disability culture and involvement of disabled people in the arts is an indication of the general state of their success in reflecting upon and managing their own affairs.

CULTURAL DEPENDENCY

In our society cultural custody has for the most part passed into the hands of a small elite who acquire fame and fortune through support and funding from the most powerful sections of the community. Through its support the white upper-middle and upper classes have come to dominate all arts and culture. Unsurprisingly, then, in this climate, disabled artists may look for self-esteem and financial gain in the non-disabled dominated arts and media.

After all, when the little information that does exist about disabled artists is often patronising, if not actually offensive, there will be a strong incentive to keep this side of one's life somewhat hidden. If disabled artists or musicians are recognised living or dead, all too often their lives are seen in terms of their medical condition and their imagined ability to overcome personal tragedy. Passivity and dependence are attributed to us and our only *collective* identity is as the disabled – as tragic *individuals* who to a varying degree are the recipients of care unlikely to be creative without the stimulation and assistance of others often in an institutional settling such as the day centre or rehabilitation unit.

It is very unusual for interpretations of their creative work to be analysed in relation to how (and if) the person's impairment informs their work. While we know that Stevie Wonder is blind there seems to be a lack of interest in how this might influence and enhance his music. Could insight about the music of one disabled artist have some particular

Photo courtesy of David Hevey

relevance to other disabled musicians? Isolation due to lack of information about other disabled artists could encourage an individual to develop their creativity no further than as a tool for assimilation into the dominant culture and access to their arts. They may then easily become culturally dependent on the dominant sections of society and miss the opportunity to experience the growth in self-confidence that can follow identification with others who see themselves as members of a distinctive social subgroup with a unique, but equal, identity to other groups. Many disabled people feel that there cannot be any such thing as a 'disability culture'. Even among the more informed, the idea that our shared experiences and perspectives might contribute to the birth of a culture can generate anxiety. There appear to be two general reasons for hostility towards the growth of a disability culture:

1. In Britain many people believe that

'culture' equals 'opera and art galleries', where the middle class go instead of watching football. Viewed this way, culture is seen as a possession of the elite and a pursuit of the rich. 'To be cultured', it is imagined, is to be rather like a pearl, understated, refined and in the best possible taste. It is often seen as having nothing to do with the 'real' world – that is, as a reflection of one's experiences and perceptions quite independent of those of the dominant group. Recognition of the importance of participation in the arts and culture of one's own group, as part of human development, is not something that is cultivated in the British character.

2. Many disabled people believe that encouraging a disability culture can only reinforce negative images of 'disability' – that is, they have not questioned the tragedy view of disability and when they think of a disability culture they assume that this must mean art forms which only

present the negative side of disabled living. They ask: Why should I give credence to a life that has imposed barriers on me? What is there to celebrate and explore when my life be so grim?

Both these reactions miss the point. Discrimination against people on the grounds of 'non-normal' bodies or intellectual capacity places them outside the mainstream of social life. In order to participate meaningfully within the community members of this group must actively engage in the issues that confront them. In doing this they provide the material for their own cultural development that is self-determining and self-governing. This activity is an affirmation of existence despite insistent illustrations all around us which portray what we will never be. For example, a deaf person goes to the theatre and experiences a hearing writer being translated; or a wheelchair user finds art gallery paintings endlessly drawn from the shoe-using artist's point of view. The struggle against disabling barriers, however, is an active and creative engagement. From this point of view, the struggle to remove barriers could be regarded as the seed bed for human arts. For us, the only difference is that the barriers which we have to address are dissimilar to those faced by able-bodied people.

PRESSURE FOR CHANGE

Of course, not all disabled people accept that they are incapable of functioning independently and equally with others in society. The discussion among organised and informed disabled people has always focused on finding new ways to integrate into the mainstream community but on their own terms. Thus the day-to-day experiences of disabled people can be characterised as involving a unique tension which, at one level, involves the passive experience of being prevented from controlling one's own life, and at the other, actively struggling to overturn this situation. Both the absence, and recent emergence, of disability arts and culture might be thought of as a mirror reflecting the current status of this tension between passive and active roles.

As long as traditional media imagery, and so on, represents disabled people as tragic individuals, with no collective voice and with little access to each other, we can expect the activities of disabled people to go no further than personal complaint. At an early stage in coming together in associations, then, the first choice is almost always to make a combined plea to those in power for greater access to resources. If joint action is undertaken, these associations often settle into the familiar pattern of pressure-group politics – that is, appealing to existing power structures to be relieved of their debilitating situation.

Arising out of the struggles of *individuals*, pressure-group politics encourages the development of an elite leadership which then negotiates with those who hold power. In pressure-group politics the struggle for civil rights is controlled by the active few, while the mass of disabled people remain in their traditional passive relationship to others. Only now the others are not able-bodied benefactors but other disabled people. For this elite, negotiating for an improved quality of life, there is unlikely to be sensitivity about the absence of disability arts. This is because they are concerned with clarifying and presenting their own perspective of the issues and an inactive membership has little to express when it is in a passive relationship to others.

THE CULTURAL RECORD

Pressure-group politics can be the natural first line of action when disabled people come together. However, organising a collective voice may perversely end up by only transferring the microphone to the voice of the elite. The presence or absence of a disability culture and the numbers of disabled people involved, frequency of performances and general social recognition for disability arts can provide important insights into the progress of disabled people moving from passivity to an active role in their own affairs.

If disabled political activists and disabled artists see little point in supporting each other we can be sure that progress towards equal rights has not yet moved beyond the efforts of individuals to escape their own personal restrictions. The disabled political activist is likely to be locked into pressure-group politics, escaping a passive disabled lifestyle by becoming the active spokesperson for others, who continue in their passive and dependent lives. Similarly, the disabled artist could be locked into expressing personal life events in the hope that fame will allow escape from the dependency role that society expects of disabled citizens.

On the other side, the spontaneous growth of a disability culture, in the absence of support from organisations of disabled people, can be regarded as a symptom of ordinary disabled people losing interest in the issues that an elite leadership regards as a priority. A developing disability culture can not only increase insight into the progress of disabled people becoming active in the area of civil rights, but can provide important opportunities for individuals to gain confidence by forming a new and independent social identity. From this point of view the formation of a distinctive and vibrant disability culture is a vital component in the construction of an accessible route to empowerment.

ACCOUNTABILITY

Many people are uncertain about accepting that disabled artists might also be accountable to a disabled constituency. Art involves personal creativity and some people may have difficulty in seeing the disabled artist as anything other than an independent and uncontrollable misfit. They may dismiss creative worries with 'Well, that is only their view', or confuse personal dislike of an art form with the observation that the person is generally no good. While the portrayal of disability issues in the arts arena should be viewed with the same critical eye as the presentation of issues in the political arena, we should also take care not to underestimate the role of the arts in assisting the processes of change.

While there is broad agreement among disabled people in the UK that the portrayal of the disability experience is generally both negative and inaccurate, it is participants in the arts who can breathe life into alternative images. This should mean that while we share a common understanding of disability we may express this in many different forms and in different arenas. Taking part in the arts should also be viewed as a tool for change as much as attending meetings about, say, orange badge provision.

ARTISTIC EFFECTS

Gaining access to new ideas or creating challenging alternatives when passivity predominates among the disabled community can be hard work. Charity imagery, tales of tragedy or outstanding courage in the media, fairy-tales and other children's books loaded with disabled villains can all combine to undermine a view of ourselves as valid human beings. If one of the creative activities of art is to present a mirror to society, what we generally see is a distorted reflection of ourselves.

Disability arts, on the other hand, where, for example, sculpture is designed to be touched as well as seen, and songs are written about the world as we see it, can redress the balance and engage a lot of people in questioning assumptions that their exclusion from society is a fact of life.

The arts can have a liberating effect on people encouraging them to change from being passive and dependent to being creative and active. We may not all want to be artists producing and performing work, but arts events can provide another accessible route for looking at the world in relation to disabled people. Meeting together at a disability arts event can also provide rare opportunities for disabled people to exchange ideas. Having someone on stage communicating ideas and feelings that an isolated disabled person never suspected were shared by others can be a turning-point for many.

However, unless there is a flowering of cultural activity new artists will not be inspired to develop more sensitive presentations of our place in society and to inform future generations. One of the ways of understanding long-gone societies is to look at their cultural artefacts. If historians only uncover images of disability in charity advertising and stories of helplessness or courage with no alternatives, what will that mean for a future population of disabled people? Evidence of pride in ourselves is also provided by the legacy we leave behind. Our cultural development will provide not only a record of an active journey, a passing view of ourselves as we are but also a perspective on the world for future generations to built on and develop.

CULTURAL INTERVENTIONS

Arts should provide disabled people with ways of confirming their own identity and, as a secondary gain, inform, educate and attract the non-disabled world. Until recently the arts have placed too much emphasis on educating non-disabled people rather than providing a medium for communication with each other. What is needed is that disability arts (and the disability movement) does not simply imitate the view of the world that pleases white middle-class males. The arts and the new cultural development can provide space for reflection on disability life from the rich variety of experiences of different groups of disabled people. Helping disabled people to ensure an integrated role for disability arts and culture in the nation's repertoire of cultural life can provide an opportunity to challenge narrow thinking, elitism and dependency on others. Introducing disabled people to the social role of artistic creativity and opening a debate about disability culture is a dynamic way of assisting disabled people to challenge their assumed dependency and place in mainstream society.

A Proud Label

Jenny Corbett

Extracts from 'A Proud Label', *Disability and Society* vol. 9 no. 3, 1994, pp. 347–51.

Jenny Corbett is a lecturer in the Department of Education and Community Studies, University of East London. She is a member of the Executive Editorial Board of *Disability and Society*, and Chair of the disability arts group Survivors' Poetry.

This extract from 'A Proud Label' is about the search for and expression of identity. However 'right-thinking', 'tolerant' or well intentioned non-disabled people are, or think themselves to be, they impose with disability a loss of status; a loss that makes it easier to be 'caring' of the 'unfortunates'. The measurement of how 'disabled' a person is, and thus how much status they have, is a measurement of how far they appear to be or can pass for 'normal'.

The pressures to deny disability are great, and it is easy for disabled people to collude in this. Of those disabled from birth or early childhood, Sally French says, 'we deny our disabilities for social, economic and emotional survival and we do so at considerable cost to our sense of self and our identities; it is not something we do because of flaws in our individual psyches.'[1]

However, the understandable strategies of denial may be sometimes be challenged by changes in people's circumstances that serve to emphasise a mismatch between experience and the denial game. Disabled people may then, quietly or noisily, 'come out', recognising that the emotional (and indeed intellectual) stress of this mismatch is too much for honesty, pride or healthy self-love to contain.

Corbett opens with a quote by Jenny Morris.

THE IMPETUS TO PASS

... Morris expresses a deep regret at the denial of personal experience of disability in the effort to pass. She insists that:

To experience disability is to experience the frailty of the human body. If we deny this we will find that our personal experience of disability will remain an isolated one; we will experience our differences as something peculiar to us as individuals – and we will commonly feel a sense of personal blame and responsibility.[2]

The denial of difference and impetus to assimilate at all costs carries a high price in terms of human suffering and frustration. As Abberley expressed it, in what has become a seminal paper on disability politics and oppression, to deny all differences is unacceptable:

similar to the assimilationist perspective in race relations and thus similarly devaluing and denying the authenticity of an impaired person's experience, dissolving real problems in the soup of 'attitude change'.[3]

Rieser supports Abberley's contention, adding moreover that he felt angry that he had been brought up to deny an important part of his real self:

This denial of difference is an understandable but serious mistake

that many people make. I now know this is a reaction to the prejudice against disabled and other 'different' people that permeates all parts of society.[4]

There are social problems for all of us who are outside the norm.

Assimilation is no answer. It denies our differences, our needs and our perspectives. It makes our identities invisible. Yet such is the power of the *status quo* that we are usually socially conditioned to hide our differences. When Edgerton referred to the 'cloak of competence'[5] as a means by which people with learning disabilities tried to pass for normal, the equation of 'competence' with concealment of difference suggests that we are rewarded for our skill at deviousness and are punished for open honesty. Part of 'social skills' training for people with learning disabilities is often an attempt to modify and change spontaneous behaviours that deviate from the norm. These may be as innocuous as lively laughter and hugs for greetings, when a handshake is the socially acceptable sign. Hiding our identities and presenting social masks is presented as an element of social decorum and an essential ingredient of social assimilation. Thus, we are encouraged to feel fear of exposure and to practice the art of concealment.

It is the confrontation of this fear, in ourselves and from others, which has helped us to become visible and to challenge prejudice. Dawson and Palmer boldly illustrate this challenge in their guide to self-advocacy for professionals who are working towards empowerment, by producing drawings of people saying they are:

**not apologising for being me
taking pride in who I am**[6]

The emphasis has moved from merely finding means of expression towards asserting identity and self-esteem. 'Coming out' includes taking responsibility for assuming ownership of our own needs.

COMING OUT

The term 'coming out' has most commonly been associated with gay and lesbian politics, rather than with disability politics. However, it is a term which Hevey, who refers to himself as a disabled photographer, uses to powerful effect:

Disabled people were coming out of the institutions and day centres in anger at their conditions. People were coming out of physical or psychic prisons into a powerful personal and political light.[7]

He goes on to describe what he terms:

the psychic journey of transforming my and others self-loathing into self-love (or, at least, self-respect).[8]

The journey into self-respect seems to me to be a critical element of coming out. For Hevey, whose epilepsy could have remained an invisible disability, it meant choosing to come out in solidarity with his fellow disabled activists. For many disabled people the choice to come out may seem irrelevant as their visible difference is undeniable. Yet, a move from self-oppression into self-respect can take place even when the nature of difference is evident.

In a discussion of lesbian and gay rights in education, Bradley notes that 'gayness' is much more than sexual preference:

it's identity, community, a source of pride, an asset not a handicap, a cause of happiness; with our problems coming not from our gayness but from the prejudices of others.[9]

Surely this applies also to disability rights? The 'personal tragedy' approach is one with which both young gay people and young disabled people have had to contend, with comments such as:

How sad for you.

What problems you have to cope with.

No wonder life is difficult.

What courage you show.

Thurlow, with reference to gay people, suggests that this individual tragedy model is paternalistic and that:

Our right to determine how we lead our own lives, decide who we want to spend our time with, and control our own bodies and what we do with them, is denied.[10]

Such sentiments could be expressed by any number of disability rights activists, similarly concerned with issues of freedom of expression and acceptance of responsibility.

DUAL OPPRESSION

The area of dual oppression (i.e. black and disabled; female and disabled; gay or lesbian and disabled; any combination of these experiences) is vexed and contentious and, as such, one which I feel able to explore in only the most tentative way. What is useful in examining dual oppression is that it demonstrates the obtuseness and profundity of identities and the danger of simplistic stereotyping.

Hearn insisted that 'no one took my sexuality seriously because I was blind'[11] and so her lesbianism was socially ignored because blindness apparently made her asexual. Finger notes that people living in institutions, who are dependent upon carers, could find that:

they may outlaw gay and lesbian relationships, while allowing heterosexual ones. Disabled lesbians and gays may also find that their sexual orientation is presumed to occur by default.[12]

While Hanna Rogovsky explores the issue of guilt in disabled women (1991) and Stuart suggests that the experience of being black and disabled varies according to cultural contexts,[13] Finger's implication that 'spoiled identities' are, by definition, deviant in the eyes of those who, professionally, label them, takes us right back to Goffman's imagery.[14] Mindful of the hostility levelled at Goffman's notions of stigma, I felt loath to make reference to his work in this paper. However, I feel that recent comments such as those which Finger has made,[15] indicate that Goffman's imagery still casts a shadow and that attitudes among care-givers can still be dangerously negative and informed by perceptions of deviant identities.

In his recent study of the Disability Civil Rights Movement, Shapiro illustrates the judgmental attitudes that influenced a decision upon whether a woman who was seriously disabled in a traffic accident could leave a nursing home to live with her lesbian lover. This issue compounded the obstacles placed in their way as both the judge and her parents tried to insist that she was incapable of making a sound choice.[16]

One of the key factors in dual oppression is that of presenting a level of complexity which many people find too challenging. Thus, charities like Mencap and the Spastics Society[17] offer images which show disabled people and sometimes black disabled people but, not yet, black and gay disabled people. There are too many variables which may conflict and create unease. Dragonsani Renteria (1993) expresses this in her poem 'Rejection'[18], opposite, when she says:

Often the experience of dual oppression means that, far from being accepted in all aspects of your identity, you end up being criticised by different groups as not sufficiently reflecting what they perceive as an appropriate identity. Tanis says:

At the disability conferences or

Claire and Geraldine in Love (Again) courtesy of David Hevey

Rejection

SOCIETY REJECTS ME for being Deaf.

The Deaf community reject me for being a Lesbian.

The Lesbian community reject me for not being able to hear them.

The Deaf-Lesbian community rejects me for being into S&M.

The S&M community reject me for being Deaf.

Society rejects me for being Chicana.

The Hispanic community reject me for being Lesbian.

The Gay Hispanic community rejects me for being Deaf.

Patriarchal society rejects me for being a woman.

I am rejected and oppressed,

Even by those who cry out readily

Against rejection, oppression, and discrimination.

When will it end?

Dragonsani Renteria

events: 'You are so obvious about being gay, Tanis. Why don't you try to tone down a bit?' Oh, sure. Why don't you try to hide your wheelchair or camouflage that white cane? When I try to be more moderate or more mainstream, I am accused by fellow lesbians and gay men of being 'in': 'Why aren't you out at these events? You should be proud to identify with us more. Where is your feminist support of our struggle?' I left it at the door when I had to climb steps to get into your club! Do I have an attitude problem? I can't please everyone all the time.[19]

Dual oppressions confront stereotyping and force a recognition that we are not neat types who can be itemised purposefully.

The issues highlighted in experiences of dual oppressions point to the similarities and differences between disability politics and gay pride. They are both influenced by changing conditions and cultural dimensions.

Perhaps a key difference is that, whereas sexuality is seen as a central issue in relation to gay and lesbian people (ignoring the complexity and diversity of our lives), it is often seen as peripheral or even non-existent in the lives of disabled people. Also, the built environment itself acts as a barrier to many physically disabled people, preventing their entry into full social participation at a level which most gay and lesbian people take for granted.

Notes

1. S. French, 'The Roots of Denial', in J. Swain, V. Finkelstein, S. French and M. Oliver (eds.), *Disabling Barriers – Enabling Environments* (London: Sage Publications with the Open University, 1993).

2. J. Morris, 'Personal and Political: A Feminist Perspective on Researching Physical Disability', *Disability, Handicap and Society* vol. 7 no. 2, 1992, p. 164.

3. P. Abberley, 'The Concept of Oppression and the Development of a Social Theory of Disability', *Disability, Handicap and Society* vol. 2, 1987, p. 16.

4. R. Rieser, 'The Way It Is', in Paul Barker and Derek Jones (eds), *Disabling World* (London: Channel Four Television Publications, 1992) p. 11.

5. R.B. Edgerton, *The Cloak of Competence* (Berkeley: University of California Press, 1967).

6. P. Dawson and W. Palmer, *Taking Self-Advocacy Seriously* (Nottingham, East Midlands Further Education Council, 1993), p. 10.

7. D. Hevey, *The Creatures Time Forgot: Photography and Disability Imagery* (London: Routledge, 1992), p. 79.

8. Ibid., p. 83.

9. P. Bradley, 'In and Out', in *School's Out* (London: The Gay Teachers' Group, 1987), p. 4.

10. P. Thurlow, 'It's Only a Phase . . .', in *School's Out* (London: The Gay Teachers' Group, 1987)

11. K. Hearn, 'Oi! What about Us?', in B. Cant and S. Hemmings (eds) *Radical Records: Thirty Years of Lesbian and Gay History* (London: Routledge, 1988), p. 121.

12. A. Finger, 'Forbidden Fruit', *New Internationalist* no. 233, 1992, p. 10.

13. O.W. Stuart, 'Race and Disability: Just a Double Oppression?' *Disability Handicap and Society* vol. 7 no. 2, 1992, pp. 177–88.

14. E. Goffman, *Stigma: Notes on the Management of Spoiled Identity* (Harmondsworth: Penguin, 1968).

15. A. Finger, 'Forbidden Fruit', *New Internationalist* no. 33, pp. 8–10.

16. J. Shapiro, *No pity: People with Disabilities Forging a New Civil Rights Movement* (New York: Times Books, 1993).

17. Spastics Society renamed Scope in 1995 (eds).

18. D. Renteria, 'Rejection', in R. Luczak (ed.), *Eyes of Desire: A Deaf Gay and Lesbian Reader* (Boston: Alyson Publications, 1993), p. 38.

19. Tanis, 'Who Are You?', in R. Luczak (ed.), *Eyes of Desire: A Deaf Gay and Lesbian Reader* (Boston: Alyson Publications, 1993), p. 69.

4.4

Searching for Disability Arts
Alison Silverwood

Extract from *DAM* vol. 4 no. 3, Autumn 1994.

ALISON SILVERWOOD is a contributor on disability, lesbian and feminist issues to a variety of publications in the UK and USA. She hopes 'we can encourage non-disabled people to find a cure for their often chronically negative attitudes towards disabled people'.

Disabled people who become 'political' discover 'disability' in different ways. Some are already political along other fronts, having consciously been part of a questioning counter-culture, and thus also having natural expectations about disability in terms of how it could be explored. This drive to locate disability, to inform oneself and to seek reflection and resonance may be very strong. And when one has already challenged 'common sense' views that equate the status quo with a natural state, then a challenge to other assumptions about 'normality' can be a relatively small step.

I was looking for disability arts. Coming from a socialist background and the feminist and gay liberation movements, I felt sure there'd be a political analysis of disability. Art can express politics in a powerful way.

I asked librarians, 'Where are your books about disability?' They looked puzzled. 'Do you mean about aids and things?' 'No. I mean about the way society treats disabled people, about people's attitudes'. They didn't know what I was talking about.

Then I found the Greater Manchester Coalition for Disabled People and my first item of disability arts, Ian Stanton's *Shrinking Man* tape. It was a good day. I love that mixture of humour, political clout and creativity in Ian's songs. 'Got a chip on your shoulder/ a real bad attitude/ is it any wonder people treat you the way they do? You really should be grateful for all we try and do for you/ and be a quiet little crip without a chip.' Well, is he good at sing-along, community-building ditties, or what? Guess it depends on whether you agree with him. I wrote a gushing fan letter; Ian was modest and warm in reply.

I scoured television and radio listings. I sent for everything possible about disability politics and disability art. I went to see David Hevey's *The Creatures Time Forgot* photographic exhibition in Bradford. I was very excited because so many issues were addressed by his work. I enjoyed the mixture of gender, race, sexuality, visible/invisible impairments. I was particularly overjoyed by a photograph of two lesbians. It was a great photograph; proud, joyful, relevant. I would love that picture on my wall. It adds to my feeling good about being a disabled lesbian.

Soon after this I had telephone contact with a couple of women in *No Excuses* theatre cabaret, which had a big effect on me. I was proud they were an all-woman team and whenever I saw them on TV. I felt elated. I love their way of getting serious political ideas across by taking the piss. I felt the way they worked collectively, co-operatively, supportively with each other showed on stage. I liked their decision to only perform at accessible venues.

I came into contact with Sue Napolitano's poetry in June 1991 and was impressed. She's strong, clear and funny. She rabble-rouses and tackles tender, intimate, personal experiences. She's positive, witty and acute. Sue is a powerful performer, who gently takes an audience by the scruff, gets them on her side and somehow gets us chanting 'Break the Rules'.

Sue uses experiences from her own life and analyses them. Take her monologue about the struggle to fulfil her 'latest wild idea' – to bath independently. A salesman 'dripping with sales patter' takes the bath (which won' t fit through the front door) into her back garden. She has to put up with 'ho-ho jokes' about people passing on a Number 11 bus and him saying he wants to be a guest at the party when she finally gets in. Sue remarks dryly, 'It is important to be polite when you're disabled, you know.'

The non-disabled salesman is rude and invasive, asking, like so many others, for an explanation of her life story. However, Sue needs his information because the woman who usually lifts her in and out of the bath is pregnant (and Sue doesn't want her to have a miscarriage!).

The bath Sue needs costs £2,000 (typical rip-off). She laments the age it takes to get an assessment by the social services and that if they decide it's not needed – 'after all, they're the experts' – Sue would be faced with trying to raise £2,000.

Sue delivers this monologue with so much irony and humour it is impossible for her audience not to be on her side.

Yet the political points are delivered with serious impact. As Sue concludes, 'This is the sort of thing you have to put up with if you're disabled and want to take a bath.' Disabled people can identify with her and non-disabled people (if they are open to it) learn a lot.

Sue's poetry is personal and political, a combination I find powerful. When a non-disabled person comments over her head, 'Hasn't she got a lovely smile?', Sue replies, 'I can curl my lip and snarl', throwing in for good measure that she 'has had hairy armpits for over twenty years' . The staccato rhythm in this poem is the craft which conveys her anger and distaste, her art is in direct accessible language which fits her theme.

'I hear you snigger when I say "Hump"', Sue begins another poem in a low, 'Gothic' voice. 'To be straight is to be good', she tells us, summing up with lovely irony a whole ethos of our society. In challenging this stricture Sue is courageously vulnerable. She states how long she kept her body hidden in swathes of clothes, how long it took her to wear a swimming costume in public and to say the word 'hump'. She now asserts, 'This body is where I live my life.'

4.5

Thoughts on Disability Arts
Roland Humphrey

From *DAM* vol. 4 no. 11, Spring 1994.
Originally published in *The Phoenix Artpaper*, Retford Disability Art Group.

Roland Humphrey founded DAM in 1990 and was its editor and creative force from the first issue (Spring 1991) to Spring 1995.[1] He came to the experience of disability later in his adult life and in this piece provocatively challenges whether he is thus regarded as a 'real disabled person'. But that he made *DAM* a rich source for the 'disabled voice' is evidenced by the blatant plundering of *DAM* by the editors of this book, particularly for Parts Four and Five with their themes of identity, culture and control.

Here in this piece, Roland Humphrey highlights some of the parameters of the debate around what might constitute art or 'disability art', written from the practical viewpoint of a magazine editor. It questions the limitations of the social model and challenges the assumption that disabled people have a common culture of oppression.[2] Ironically, the actual content of *DAM* could well be used in arguments against rather than in support of the challenge.

One of its founding editor's key concerns was to introduce new people in every issue, and usually a third of the contributing writers and/or artists were fresh to the world of disability arts, widening the field rather than, as he says, reinforcing the 'narrowness of the disability arts establishment'.

***DAM* has offered disabled people space for art itself, and coverage of those exhibitions which, even if reported in the mainstream press, would be unlikely to come from the perspective of disabled people themselves. It also pays them for commissioned work, a novelty for disabled people who have often spent their lives giving their work free to yet another exhibition on such themes as 'disability', 'empowerment', 'diversity' or 'community voices'. Although not a journal of 'protest', it has like *DAIL* provided a forum for debate and has not fought shy of controversy.**

The day the Winter issue of DAM was published I received a fax complaining that the cover images were not disability arts. I replied, somewhat testily, that as they were good quality art from people with learning difficulties their publication would do more to dispel prejudice than any number of treatises as to what was, or was not, disability arts. Around the same time I received a request for an article on disability arts and I accepted an invitation to talk on DAM at the Oriel Mostyn conference. Therefore I had to *write my own treatise on disability arts – ironic really. Anyhow I wrote the article. Here is the latest version. A personal view that I hope will encourage debate.*

The current thinking about disability goes something like this. 'Disabled people have physical and/or sensory impairments but these impairments are not what disables them. Society's attitude to the impairments is the disabling factor. The lack of facilities (e.g. inaccessible buildings) combined with lousy social attitudes (e.g. the reluctance of employers to employ disabled people) leads to us being oppressed. If society would change, and the oppression were removed, we would not be disabled, merely impaired.

This is the 'social' model of disability and it is preferable to the 'medical' model of disability where a person tends to become his or her impairment.

Disability arts is often defined as art that springs from the oppression of disabled people. This follows logically from the social model of disability. It is very neat but the very tidiness masks areas of confusion.

The social model of disability appears to have been constructed for healthy quadriplegics. The Social Model avoids mention of pain, medication or ill-health. For example, we, at the *DAM* office, have had Steve working with us. Steve has epilepsy. In order to control his seizures, his medication has been increased to a toxic level so Steve has had to give up work. Another example – a member of our board is now receiving dialysis three times a week. On Mondays, Wednesdays and Fridays she has to travel over 140 miles, have three hours' dialysis and then return home. The social model of disability does not cater for people in these sorts of situations because no matter how enlightened society's attitudes, such people are disabled by their physical condition.

Narrow, negative definitions are limiting. It is as if strictures have been handed down from the political movement to the artists. Recently, I was at the annual general meeting of the British Council of Organisations of Disabled People. Many delegates complained that the TV programme *Link* was not forceful enough in getting a political message across. But *Link* is a disability magazine programme not a party political broadcast. *Link* has to be good TV, first and foremost, otherwise it will be taken off air. Disability arts has to be good art, first and foremost, otherwise it will be ignored.

The definition of disability arts as art of oppression assumes that disabled people all have a common culture and this culture is one of oppression. It is akin to saying black art can only be about the oppression of black people; self-evidently black art is a celebration of the whole culture of black people. It is analogous to saying feminist art is only about the oppression of woman; clearly it includes a celebration of womankind. Black arts and feminist arts celebrate the cultural inheritance of being black or being a woman. How can disability art be seen as a celebration of disability? Nobody wishes to lose a sense or a faculty. Disability arts celebrates humanity – impairments do not disqualify us from that. The human condition is multifaceted and disability arts is a celebration of this difference.

Disabled people are assumed to be a homogenous mass united in the face of society's oppression; and with a culture of oppression. I am a middle-class, middle-aged male diagnosed as having multiple sclerosis fifteen years ago. I have little in common with a working-class, young woman blind from birth. When we include people with learning difficulties, mental disabilities and mental impairments with us, the differences in cultural identity become even greater; and this is setting aside the differences between people disabled from birth and those people who have become disabled. Our oppression is derived from our social and personal experiences – and our art is derived from these individual life experiences.

I am arguing that disabled people are

DAM cover, Double Self-Portrait
by Sandy Sham

people with vastly different and varied cultures ... of which the cultural implications of being disabled are perhaps a minor and variable pattern set within the major patterns of society, gender and class. But then I had the conventional route through school, university, work, marriage, children – all before I became disabled – so I'm not a proper, genuine disabled person!

This approach determines the way I do my job and *DAM* (once *Disability Arts Magazine*) is shaped by it. In 1990 the magazine was set up with three strands – disability arts, the arts of disabled people and access to the arts. Respectively: art based on the disability experience, art from disabled people but having no connection with disability (for example a landscape painting) and the whole panoply of access (physical and attitudinal). I would now, three years on, not attempt to separate these three strands. I would define them all, rather untidily, as constituting disability arts.

DAM is an unusual magazine because the message is so blatantly the medium. The implicit communication of both the print and the cassette versions of the magazine is to trumpet 'this high-quality magazine is produced by disabled people'. The implicit aim of *DAM* is to make society realise that its preconceptions about, and expectations of and for, disabled people are wrong. The key to remove prejudice is to communicate our common humanity.

In 1993 Johnny Crescendo released an album, *Pride*. Several of the tracks would fit the most rigorous definition of disability arts as they attacked Telethon and charities. The one that struck me as having the most potential for change in attitudes is not one of those – it is about his baby son. It has the most potential for changing attitudes because it touches a common nerve of the human condition. The song forces people to empathise with Johnny and see him, not as a disabled person, but as a real person.

DAM is an arts magazine. I hope it portrays disabled people as rounded, complete people. As such, *DAM* is the epitome of radical, disability arts.

Notes

1. *DAM* ceased publication in 1995.
2. There is a useful discussion around the social model and impairment by Liz Crow, 'Including All of Our Lives: Renewing the Social Model of Disability', in Jenny Morris (ed.), *Encounters with Strangers: Feminism and Disability* (London: The Women's Press, 1996).

Heart 'n' Soul

Annie Delin

From a feature in *DAM* vol. 4 no. 2, Summer 1994.

Annie Delin is a freelance writer and journalist who writes fiction, features and news for a wide variety of publications. She also works on public relations and press campaigns, and as a disability consultant and trainer. Her work ranges from civil rights campaigns to audience development in the arts.

Heart 'n' Soul is a rock band and performance group of people with learning difficulties which evolved from a workshop set up by guitarist Mark Williams with Shape in 1984. They started as The Mulberry Crew, and a number of the original members are still in the band, including lead performers Geoffrey Goodall and Pino Frumiento, who is also a songwriter. The music comes from Jan and Ricky Jodelko, who have also been in the company since the first show. It is probably the most experienced band of disabled musicians around, with a lot of exposure on television, and eight years of stage and touring experience in Europe. *Hearts on Fire* was their last full-length musical, and with Impulse Projects they devised a film called *Breaking the Rules* (transmitted on BBC2) which covered the build-up to its London premiere in 1994. The group is still based at the Albany, Deptford.

For a lot of people Heart 'n' Soul is disability arts. The ten-strong, funky musical, live loud and dangerous act is the most infectious demonstration yet that disabled people and performance do mix, and that when they do, everyone wants to listen. Yet for Heart 'n' Soul the climb up the ladder still proves harder than it should do. They've had better breaks than most – chances to tour, funding and support, enthusiastic audiences – but they're still struggling, eight years on, with perceptions about what their art really is, and how high it ranks against 'real' performance...

The culture of Deptford definitely influences their work, according to Mark [Williams, co-ordinator]:

It is definitely living on the frontline, but that does give us an edge. A lot of our funding comes from local councils and the majority of the members come from around here. They have a certain streetwise air, and in this community people with learning disabilities have good opportunities to integrate. Artistically, the area influences us because the music is street music – like the reggae and ragga music in the last show, a product of who our members are and where they come from.

...The keywords in the Heart 'n' Soul culture are power, respect, control – concepts lacking in the lives of too many disabled people. There's no doubt that what comes across on the stage has a powerful effect on disabled people in the audience, and Pino explains what that could lead to:

Some of the people watching us are disabled people and they'll be

Andy Bridle in Heart 'n' Soul's *The Power of Life,* courtesy of Leon Morris

thinking 'I wish I could do that'. We're teaching people how to be strong, and it's important for us to show other people that they can create their own stuff. They don't have to copy us but we show them how we do it and they can do it in their own way.

In between the glamorous high life, the company works hard devising their shows and in workshops where they brush up on technical and performance skills. Some of these are now targeted at new company members, coming into Heart 'n' Soul to take part in a training scheme which may, if the world of performance suits them, lead to full company membership in the future.

Three years' pilot funding was granted by Horizon, part of the European Social Fund, and matched by Lewisham Council and City Challenge, for a recognised training scheme which should eventually contribute towards getting an Equity Card, and towards City and Guild and NVQ qualifications. Twenty students have completed the course, and another twenty are now passing through, divided between technical and performance workshops . . .

The next big challenge for Heart 'n' Soul lies in convincing the 'establishment' that existing aesthetics and prejudices are not necessarily going to help in judging their work. On the plus side, reviewers for *The Stage*, *The Times* and the *Independent* have started turning out to see the previews.

... Nowadays, press coverage tends not to patronise Heart 'n' Soul too much – although the *Times* did say of *Hearts on Fire*, 'It's as if the local panto has been teleported to Mars.' Still, anything's an improvement on the 1988 headline which said of the Jodelko brothers, 'They're blind but blessed with talent.'

A problem now is the funding powers-that-be at the Arts Council, where Mark Williams feels that Heart 'n' Soul is 'not seen as performance first':

Its relationship to disability is always emphasised by other people. We've made a conscious decision in this show [Hearts on Fire] to work with artists of other disciplines, but to convince people that it has artistic worth is very difficult and frustrating. The Arts Council gives us project funding for administration but, although we have applied twice under the Collaborations Fund, which is for new art, we didn't get through. We were bringing in a new art form, crossing cultural boundaries, but we still didn't get through and no disability arts groups did.

Work happening in disability arts isn't being recognised as innovative or radical and collaboration between disabled artists and others isn't seen as exciting. That is both worrying and depressing. There's a glass ceiling created by the fact that people judging the application have no understanding of the new aesthetics of disability.

Meanwhile, back in the workshop, there's a definite consensus that whatever else the group is achieving – role models, new collaborators or not – it's bringing direct benefits to the people involved. Working as a company is one of them, according to Pino and Winston Green:

It's nice working with Alex and Mark – they know our feelings and our personalities. We work very hard with each other and I'm proud of all my mates. It gets me stronger and I feel like a different person when I'm on stage. I feel like a performer, like a normal worker – it feels good and different. You don't feel like you've got a disability at all, you feel like a free person.

Signs of Definitions
John Wilson

From excerpts in *DAIL* no. 84, November 1993, from an article appearing originally in *Mailout* magazine, Aug/Sept 1993.

John Wilson is Deaf and has been Deaf Arts Officer at Shape London since 1992. He is an actor and director and his theatre training has included study at the University of Reading (Theatre of the Deaf), Dario Fo's 'summer school' in Perugia and Augusto Boal's International Theatre of the Oppressed in Paris. He appeared in *Gary* (Edinburgh Fringe First winner 1990) and as Orin in *Children of a Lesser God* (Bolton Octagon, 1992). He has directed and co-directed several plays, including *Wild Child*, a signed opera based on the legend of the Wild Boy of Aveyron.

John has been Artistic Director of the National Youth Theatre of the Deaf, and more recently has been involved in a National Deaf Forum Theatre project with Shape and the London Bubble Theatre Company. He has acted as an advisor to Graeae, and does training workshops on a range of Deaf issues, including the use of Sign Language in theatre. He was also Sign Language adviser on *Four Weddings and a Funeral* (1994) and 'discovered' David Bower, who starred in the film.

For television, John has appeared as a presenter and contributor on a number of television programmes and series, including *See Hear* (BBC), *Sign On* (C4), *D'Art* (C4) and *Four Fingers and a Thumb* (C4).

It could be argued that the public profile of Deaf arts has been much higher than the profile of disability arts. This clearer perception of it as an 'entity' is aided by the easier recognition of the existence of a Deaf community, with a cultural inheritance based on a different language, i.e. sign language. In the media field, Deaf organisations have also been politically adept, arguing skilfully for recognition of sign language as their first language, and pressing for access via more provision of interpreters in performance and sub-titling in film and broadcasting. MOMI (Museum of the Moving Image), in association with Shape, regularly runs workshops and events which involve Deaf people, and the yearly Deaf Awareness Week organised by the British Deaf Association encourages arts organisations to put on additional activities. Performance art by Deaf people now includes Signed Song and Sign Dance, which, in the hands of practitioners like Colin Thomson (Signed Song), and Sarah Scott and Ray Harrison-Graham (Sign Dance), is usually irresistible to non-Deaf as well as Deaf audiences.

In this contribution, John Wilson attempts a definition of Deaf arts and identifies two central elements, i.e. control by Deaf people, and the use of authentic language.

Being a Deaf Arts Officer for Shape London can be confusing sometimes. I think I know what I'm about, of course, but the problem is that other people often want to define Deaf arts in quite a different way from me. We can sometimes end up working at cross-purposes.

Deaf arts are not just about making mainstream arts – the ones which use spoken language – accessible to Deaf people. I'm not knocking interpreted performances. I've seen interpreted shows which would have left me totally cold if I hadn't had the interpreter to watch, and I fully support and assist and advise theatres which want to develop expertise in signing their shows. SPIT (Signed Performance in Theatre) is an excellent project which is run by a consortium of London theatres and they are doing good work in co-ordinating and raising standards and targeting their publicity at the Deaf community. But going to a play in English and watching an interpreter all evening is a bit like having a shower with your coat on, and it isn't Deaf arts.

But it is not productive to argue negatively so I had better say what I think Deaf arts actually is. Like most things it's complicated and it's caught up in politics, power struggles and cultural identity and, above else, Deaf language.

The most important element of the definition of Deaf arts is that it is something which Deaf people control – and the upper case D throughout this piece is not a misprint, it's a statement of cultural identity. We've had a range of projects over the year – and they continue to be funded – where Deaf people have been recruited, with hearing people who usually can't sign, to be part of an 'integrated' company. Sometimes a Deaf person is taken on as an 'assistant' to the director but the reality is that the artistic direction and the process remains squarely with the hearing. The Deaf company members then teach the hearing members (and some of those I have worked with have become close friends over the years, so this is not a criticism of them) how to sign their bit of the script. The play, or whatever, is then duly performed and the Deaf members of the company end up being embarrassed both at the quality of the signing (could you become fluent in Russian in three weeks?) and because somewhere in the process the integrity of the language will have been compromised by the hearing director's view of what is artistic and what is not. Imagine changing the way words are pronounced to make them sound nicer!

So, language is also an important element of Deaf arts and its development reflects the struggle in the wider Deaf community to have the first language of Deaf people – British Sign Language – recognised as the authentic and official language. As that struggle advances, Deaf people become more confident in expressing themselves in the language with which they feel comfortable, and experimenting with it to produce art – creative signing which, being totally visual, conveys its meaning in space and time with an economy and an expressiveness which sets it apart from its spoken counterpart, poetry – not better, of course, but different. Watch a video of the late Dorothy Miles performing some of her vast repertoire of original work and I defy you not to be moved or amused or uplifted or saddened by it. Other Deaf people express themselves through signed songs or will weave visual language into dance or performance art, as in Deaf cabaret, in which comedy and satire (as performed for example, by the 'Deaf Comedians') are particularly important in the Deaf world.

Deaf arts is also about Deaf culture. It is hardly surprising that for many Deaf people the initial impulse is to create art which makes a statement about the integrity of the Deaf community – we live

Sarah Scott and Ray Harrison Graham in The Basic Theatre's *Signs of the Times,*
courtesy of Trish Morrissey

in a hearing society which is, not to mince words, oppressive — and like other cultural minorities art is a valuable tool in communicating ideas about the nature of that oppression and how to deal with it. But this is not the entire focus of Deaf arts, because there is a great deal more to Deaf culture than being angry. It's a way of saying, 'This is how Deaf people live their lives. This is what interests them. This is how Deaf people see the world.' It is essentially an exploration and a celebration of difference which runs as a theme through the work of Deaf painters, sculptors and photographers. I began to create my reality as a disabled

Photo courtesy of Mary Duffy

4.8

So you want to look?
Mary Duffy

'So You Want to Look? I'll Give You Something to Look At' was the original title of this piece taken from R. Collett et al., Val Green, Jude Thomlinson (eds), *Access to Image: Photo Work Book,* (Bradford: Valid, 1992).

Mary Duffy lives in Ireland and attended the National College of Art and Design, Dublin, studying photography in her final year. As a photographer and performance artist, she uses photography, text and her body to challenge notions of physical wholeness and disability. Her images and poetry speak not just of being 'disabled' but of being a disabled woman. She has exhibited and performed at the Diorama and the ICA.

This piece by Mary Duffy appeared with photographs as part of a book which arose out of the Access to Image Project organised by Valid (previously In-valid), a Bradford disability arts group. The project ran from 1991 as a series of workshops and an exhibition, which toured in venues all over the country. The 'Different Views' book contains many images from that exhibition and is also a very helpful and practical guide to disabled people wanting to get started in photography.

woman artist in response to a major life crisis when I was twenty-one. My major life crisis was that I was offered a job in a circus, the chance to travel the world and get paid for it. My job description involved shaving men from the audience with my feet. My whole world came tumbling down when two of those who were closest to me could not understand why I was upset. 'The most important thing for us about you is your attitude to your disability, that it doesn't matter. Now you can't let your attitude change, or, if you do, you'll have a nervous breakdown.'

What I heard in that response was that they were the ones who wouldn't be able to cope, and, for myself, I had never really considered the implications of my disability, the implications for my sense of well-being, my life chances, my sexuality and my relationship with those around me. When I did, my attitudes changed, and changed radically. My disability does matter and it's okay to ask for, and sometimes demand help. And no, I didn't have a nervous breakdown.

When I focused on my disability, I stopped painting and took up photography. 'The camera doesn't lie, they said to me, but they were wrong. The camera had been lying to me all my life. When I looked for my own identity as a disabled young woman to be reflected back to me from the myriad of images of disabled people photographed every day, only tragic, pathetic images of under-twelves, dripping with emotion, stared back at me, begging for pennies and blank cheques.

I began by creating my own images and in so doing, I had begun to create my own reality as a proud, disabled woman.

For ten years now, I have been looking at and exploring different aspects of how my disability affects my life. All of it is challenging for me and very difficult. That is, until it reaches the final print stage or

is delivered in the form of a performance. The delivery part I find easy. By then I've worked through the hard parts, all that soul-searching and raw honesty with myself that it takes to create the kind of stuff I do. I know that my work is also sometimes difficult for my audience, and at a recent performance in Leeds where I addressed the audience stark naked, the shock to most of those there was very palpable. Everyone who spoke to me afterwards, and some were still in shock, were 'gobsmacked' and wondered what it took to stand in front of a hoard of total strangers and tell them some of the most intimate details of my life, and, on top of all that, do it in my birthday suit.

My only defence is that I have been stared at all my life, and that by standing there stark naked and vulnerable, it feels like I am holding up a mirror to your voyeurism and saying, 'So you want to look, do you? I'll give you something to look at.'

Many of the disabled people in the audience in Leeds felt very vulnerable because my performance was then, at times, very close to the bone, in terms of our collective experience as disabled people, and how we have been treated by the medical profession, especially as children. I don't have any answers as to how to deal with these issues of re-stimulation, except to say that I hope the environment in which it takes place will always be sympathetic to discussion and sharing, after the event; that it won't happen in a vacuum. Also, I may consider giving it a disability pride warning:
This work can make you seriously consider your life as a disabled person and after a difficult readjustment period, to come out and be proud.

Black and Disabled in the Arts
Millee Hill

Extracts from an article in *DAM*, vol. 2 no. 1, Spring 1992.

Millee Hill was born in Bermuda and was brought up in Canada. She has a degree in law and is a freelance writer and journalist. She is active with Hammersmith and Fulham Action for Disability, and is keen to keep recruiting new disabled people to guard against the movement becoming too elitist.[1] She helped form the Black Disabled People's Group, of which she is Chair.

The disability world contains the same schisms, 'isms' and inequalities that exist in society generally, and the world of disability arts is no exception in reflecting institutionalised racism.

 Millee Hill looks at the lack of resources in the area of black arts and the kind of investment necessary to redress a history of neglect. Since the DAM article was written, the Arts Council of England has funded a 'Report on Creativity within Black Disabled Communities'. This unpublished report has formed the first pilot phase of the project 'Creativity within Black Disabled Communities', which has led to a second phase in which tenders are being invited to do continuing work.

. . . Despite the best efforts of black disabled people themselves, and those within the disability movement truly supportive of them, they have not yet become an integral and important part of the disability movement as it moves ever progressively forward. This is nowhere more evident or obvious than within the disability arts movement. In terms of the general mobilisation and politicisation of disabled people, clearly the white disability arts movement and disabled activists within it have done as much as anyone to raise the political and cultural awareness of grassroots disabled people. Perhaps this is because most people love music of some kind and are more easily moved by a message in a song than perhaps in any other medium. Having been to a number of disabled artists cabarets over the years, I can well remember being inspired by a message in a song and carried away with the sentiments of Johnny Crescendo, Mike Higgins and Ian Stanton.

But such feelings of inspiration, however heartfelt, do not begin to compare with the warm glow of mutual respect and admiration that swept over and enveloped me when first I heard a black disabled artist perform. I can honestly say that I was positively awestruck and filled with a sense of self-empowerment when Marvel sang 'to be gifted, disabled and black is where it's at'. I was able to identify totally with her when she sang about the oppression she had suffered not only because of her disability but also because of her race and gender. Sadly, such feelings of 'divine influence' are very few and far between for black disabled people, as the appearance of black disabled artists on the disability arts circuit are so rare.

Deborah Williams in *Sympathy for the Devil,* Graeae and Basic Theatre co-production

Here again, black disabled artists are grossly under-represented and marginalised within the arts movement just as their black disabled counterparts are largely unrepresented in the predominantly white disability movement and society as a whole. Martin Davis, a black disabled poet and writer, feels that there are numerous reasons why black disabled artists do not get a fair crack of the whip. Chief among these is the fact that black disabled people right across the board still encounter racism in all areas of their life. Indeed, many people both within and outside of the black communities acknowledge that however managed and defused, racism is still at the core of British society today. Though some seek to deny this, many reports (including a recent one by the Sickle Cell Anaemia Research Foundation) show that the problems common to all disabled people are compounded for black disabled

people by the dilemma of direct racial discrimination in crucial areas such as employment, housing and education.

Martin, who hails from Tottenham and has been giving public performances for a number of years, states 'it is about time that black disabled artists got some recognition. Racism is a big part of why we don't get offered the gigs or given the jobs or even receive the acknowledgment for work which we have already done.' Martin's poetry, infused with political and emotional sentiment, is written from a black man's perspective and suffering. He argues passionately that his race has shaped and determined his character just as much as his disability has. 'Yet white disabled people always want me to concentrate only on my disability and to ignore or forget the racial aspect of my character', he said. 'Black disabled people cannot do that because we are just as much black as we are disabled. Still, people just do not look at a black man and a white man in the same way,' he added...

At a recent seminar held by the Minority Arts Advisory Service[2] it was pointed out that 'the official validation of black arts expressions will be achieved only when the arts funding establishment creates space for black communities to lead the process of defining, accessing and evaluating the arts and cultural contexts in which they are located.' They question the Eurocentric notions of culture and the entrenchment of administrative enclaves. They emphasise the incapacitating effect of the lack of a black infrastructure as well as the government's responsibility to provide equal access to resources and services.

Reference was also made to the lack of investment by cultural providers which has blighted the black arts infrastructure for decades. Further they argue that black achievement cannot develop without the buildings in which to do so. At present there are few black-owned and controlled middle-scale centres and just one large-scale centre. Moreover, the Arts Council has failed to develop an adequate structure for training black professionals. They argue that the black arts sector requires investment public and private that is shaped to allow for self-help and community enterprise. They point out that the state has an obligation to provide for all its residents and citizens and affirm that there can be no substantial change for Britain's black arts organisations and groups without a fundamental alteration of funding practices.

Clearly then the situation is dire for all black people in the arts. It is even more so for black disabled people as they are to a very large extent marginalised even within their own black communities because of their disability. Black disabled people suffer exclusion on just about every front and are constantly grappling with double oppressions of racism and ableism. As many of them point out they are excluded from the predominantly white disability movement and society at large because of institutionalised racism; and marginalised within the black communities because of a lack of understanding about disability issues. Poet Peter McDonald writes:

Whenever the subject of race came up someone would remind me that as a black person who was also disabled my chances of achieving anything in life were probably less than zero. It was my destiny to suffer twice as much discrimination and to miss twice as many opportunities as the person who is 'only black' or 'only' disabled.[3]

No doubt there is a wealth of talent and artistry within the black disabled community. The recent Black Disabled People's Group Cabaret revealed just how many there are and how very underexposed and under-resourced it is. Many of the artists spoken to said that the onus is now on the disability arts movement in the first instance to make a break with the past neglect of black disabled artists and to create an environment in which they will be allowed to make a contribution to the disability movement, to the disabled community and to society at large. Until such an environment is fostered, future options for viability growth and development of black disabled art are limited and insecure.

Notes
1. 'Round Town', London Disability News, May 1993 (GLAD).
2. Since this article was written MAAS (Minority Arts Advisory Service) has closed down.
3. Peter McDonald, 'Double Discrimination Must Be Faced Now', Disability Now, March 1991.

4.10

Survivors
Peter Campbell and Mandy Holland

'Survivors Poetry' by Peter Campbell, from *DAM* vol. 1 no. 4, Winter 1991
'Out to Lunch' exhibition illustrations and narrative by Mandy Holland, with comment from
contributors to the *Link* programme, 9 October 1994, which featured the work.

Peter Campbell is a founder member of Survivors Speak Out, a campaigning and
support organisation for survivors of the mental health system, and a founder and co-
ordinator of the associated group Survivors' Poetry. He is a writer, performer and
campaigner and has featured in a number of television programmes concerned with
mental health issues.

**Members of the group Survivors Speak Out, who have been labelled as
'mentally ill', call themselves 'survivors' – a word which indicates survival of
the psychiatric system itself, also the process of surviving the negative
values and discrimination that surrounds any mental health condition, and
of the emotional and mental distress of the experience.**[1]

**As well as the difficulties encountered in the mental health system, there
is the problem of dramatic and lurid media treatment. The issue of lack of
resources in the community care system is more often than not subsumed
under horror headlines that give the impression of a constant threat posed
to the community by people deemed to be highly dangerous. Their own
'voice' is usually lost in the wind as more and more medical professionals
are brought in to confront the worries of family and the community as a
whole.**

**However, such are the physical associations with the word 'disability' that
people with mental health problems may not associate themselves with
other disabled people. Peter Campbell says, 'I have difficulty in thinking of
myself as a disabled person. I think this is partly because so much of my
fight against the oppression I have experienced in the mental health
system over the years was expressed in saying 'I am not disabled, I don't
feel that I am disabled. I think I started saying that before I had a very clear
understanding of the different meanings that being disabled could have.'**[2]

**But 'Survivors' now seem to be very much part of the disability arts
movement, and in this piece Campbell talks about the setting up of the off-
shoot group Survivors' Poetry.**

By the end of the 1970s I had already
been a regular recipient of mental health
services for a dozen years. At that point
at least two important things had
become clear for me: first, that my
relationship to my interior experiences

that were commonly characterised in
terms of 'mental illness was significantly
at odds with social responses, and
second, that most people had little or no
idea what it was like to spend substantial
periods of time in psychiatric institutions.

To explore and communicate these internal and external realities I began to write poetry again – something I had not done since childhood.

The reasons why people write poetry are individual. Nevertheless, it is clear that poetry is an important element of the language through which disadvantaged groups have sought to develop a stronger voice in society. Users of mental health services, despite being one of the most hidden of groups, are no different in this respect.

From the mid-70s magazines produced by the North American 'user movement' have consistently featured poetry. In Italy poetry performances have been part of international mental health conferences. In the UK, particularly in the last few years, national voluntary organisations in the mental health field have encouraged the output of poetry: MINDWAVES, the magazine of MINDLINK, the national 'consumer' network, has a regular poetry section; the National Schizophrenia Fellowship has sponsored poetry competitions. Independent groups of service users have also been active. The four poets who established Survivors' Poetry – Hilary Porter, Frank Bangay, Joe Bidder and myself – first met through poetry and music events organised by CAPO (Campaign Against Psychiatric Oppression), which have taken place regularly in London since the early 80s.

The aim of Survivors' Poetry is to promote the writing and performance of poetry by and for survivors of the mental health system (these include current and ex-psychiatric patients, users of tranquillisers and other medication-users of counselling and therapy services, etc.). It received grants from the Arts Council (of Great Britain) enabling it to organise series of fortnightly workshops and monthly performances in London [... and to produce] an anthology of poems.[3]

Survivors' Poetry also aims to bring poetry by users of mental health services to a wider audience – to audiences both within and outside the mental health system. Outreach work will be done to make contact with poets in psychiatric hospitals and day centres in the London area and to set up events in such settings, but it is also planned that poets from the group will be involved in other towns and cities in the United Kingdom.

Survivors' Poetry exists to encourage people who have been through or are still caught up in the mental health system to write poetry and to develop their writing skills. Regardless of the subject matter, regardless of whether they believe that system has saved or oppressed them, or both or neither. The creative arts have for too long displayed an extraordinary and ambiguous attitude towards 'madness'/'mental illness'. Perhaps through this there will be further chances to go beyond stereotypes and give the opportunity for individual voices and experiences to be heard and valued.

DECISION by Peter Campbell
I tell him I am Zeop the Centurion.
He writes it down into my case notes.
In the green room he plays with paper clips,
Talks to the girl from the Migraine Unit,
Decides he will sleep on it.
Next morning the staff team convenes.
Porcelain cups for psychiatrists,
Plastic for everyone else.
Decisions have to be reached.
I sit in a straight-backed chair.
'We don't think that you are Zeop the Centurion.'
He says.
'I know that.'
I say.
'Why else do you think I'm in here?'

Mandy Holland is an artist/photographer and is Director of Inter-Action, a community arts organisation based in Milton Keynes. She has produced a national touring exhibition, 'Out to Lunch', which was launched in 1994 at the Diorama Arts Centre, London, and was featured on *From the Edge* (BBC2) and *Link* (ITV) in Autumn 1994. 'Out to Lunch' has toured venues which so far have included the Watershed, Bristol, Castle Museum, Nottingham, Exhibition Gallery, Milton Keynes; and the (Piece) Centre Gallery, Halifax. 'Out to Lunch' continues to tour throughout 1996 and 1997, and Mandy Holland is currently seeking the funding to put the work into a book, together with additional writing.

Rooted in the artist's personal history 'Out to Lunch' offers a unique exploration of mental illness in our society.

In 1992 Mandy Holland found herself in a psychiatric hospital with her camera, and a compulsion to document the experience.

The thing I most enjoyed about the exhibition were the bits where she had extracts of official documents. There is something really eerie and grim when you set next to the human being – a person – her photographs as a human being growing and developing. They are the kind of very harsh and sterile and bureaucratic images that are the business of psychiatric institutions.
Peter Beresford[4]

If you have a psychiatric record, let's say, it's not like a criminal record where certain convictions are spent after five years. Your psychiatric record will follow you around for the rest of your life, which means that you may not be allowed to adopt; foster children; you may be refused life insurance in certain circumstances; you are certainly barred from certain professions and you will have trouble getting a visa for certain countries, so yes, we disable people as soon as we give them a psychiatric record.
Julie McNamara[5]

'Out to Lunch' includes snapshot images, diary writing and laser prints which illustrate the chaos breakdown.

When I was in hospital I created a visual diary using snapshot photographs of the environment in which I found myself and things that were important, and that was my way of taking control in a situation where I felt that I did have little say in what was happening to me.
Mandy Holland

Further images were constructed, upon revisiting the hospital, in an attempt to reclaim the space from the nightmarish to the everyday.

The corridors were very significant. They were places where people under medication spent a lot of time walking up and down. Restlessness was a terrible side-effect. When I was first offered weekend home leave, I

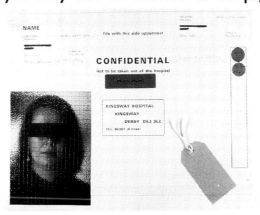

Mandy Holland © 1993

Mandy Holland © 1993

If only I'd been a criminal instead of someone who was ill my car insurance may not have doubled.

had to refuse it due to my small terrace house not offering me the space to keep walking.
Mandy Holland

Later pictures examine the long term effects that can result from experience of the psychiatric system and addresses issues of mental health currently at the forefront of public and political debate.
The final section about the lifelong implications of her experience show a drier wit and cooler eye. As she looks into an expansive country landscape, occupying space in the outside world again, she ponders the incredible truth: 'If only I'd been a criminal instead of someone who was ill, maybe my car insurance wouldn't have doubled.'
Claire Collinson.[6]

My experience of mental illness and my stay in a psychiatric hospital is something which is very central to who I am and I don't feel I need to hide that. There is a stigma attached by society to mental illness and this exhibition is one of the ways in which I am able to confront that stigma and to challenge people's fears and prejudices relating to mental illness.

For me it is also important to connect with people and in as many ways as possible, so not just through putting it on the walls in the gallery but have workshops that lead people into the work from a different perspective.
Mandy Holland[7]

Notes
1. Peter Beresford, *Link* programme, ITV, 9 October 1994.
2. *Link* programme, ITV, 9 October 1994.
3. From Dark to Light (London: Survivors' Press, 1992).
4. *Link* programme, ITV, 9 October 1994.
5. *Link* programme, ITV, 9 October 1994.
6. Ibid.
7. *Link* programme, ITV, 9 October 1994.

Defining Disabled People
Annie Delin and Elspeth Morrison

From *Guidelines for Marketing to a Disabled Audience* (The Arts Council of Great Britain, 1993).
For biographies see Part 4, Chapters 6 and 2 respectively.

On the disability arts circuit there is undoubtedly a sense of community, and that is probably also felt more widely in the disability rights movement. However, although the movement is a growing one it would be misleading to suggest that this is typical of disabled people in general. As well as a commonality of experience (whatever the impairment, all disabled people experience loss of status), there is enormous diversity within the disabled audience of which producers of film, television, theatre or 'events' need to take account. Delin and Morrison give a brief but useful overview.

DISABLED PEOPLE: WHAT ARE THEY LIKE AND WHAT DO THEY LIKE?

Definitions of disabled people are hard to agree and, in some respects, dangerous. Many now contend that people become disabled by their environment and the society they live in, and it's commonly accepted that the 'medical model', using names of conditions, is inappropriate and uninformative. A definition devised by Artshare Avon's Working Group and quoted by South West Arts in their Code of Practice is as follows:

Disabled people are excluded from full participation in society because of the organisation and design of the physical and social environment. Negative attitudes towards disabled people maintain the situation and ensure that disabled people are treated as less than equal to non-disabled people. The concept of disability embraces issues of mental health, learning difficulty and physical disability.

South West Arts goes on to suggest that their definition would include people with learning disabilities, people who are mentally ill, those with sensory disabilities such as blind or visually impaired people, deaf or hearing impaired people, people with hidden disabilities such as epilepsy and chest or heart conditions and those with disabilities linked to ageing. It is important to remember that disability is not necessarily apparent.

Disabled people come in all shapes, sizes and levels of ability. Their tastes vary from the classical to the zany by way of popular entertainment and highly specialist niche interests.

There is no value in making judgments on what disabled people, as a homogenous lump, might like. Sweeping generalisations such as 'deaf people like pantomime' are of no more use here than are statements like 'women like Mills and Boon' or 'kids prefer to see teenage mutant hero turtles'. Disability is caused in a number of ways and has far-reaching effects not just on the disabled person but on those who choose to share their lives and company. A percentage of people are born disabled, and in recent years many have developed a cultural identity as a disabled person.

A Good Read from the exhibition 'Louder than Words', courtesy of Stephen Millward

Other people become disabled through illness or accident. Feelings of isolation and trauma, and a desire not to identify disability as a definition may accompany their first years after this experience. At the same time, they will be learning which buildings they can no longer get into, and how public attitudes towards their tastes and needs have changed.

People who become disabled through ageing and its related complaints are particularly unlikely to want to be identified as disabled, yet to all intents and purposes they face the same obstacles. Expecting them to identify with specialised cultural experiences such as disabled theatre groups can be erroneous.

Many children become deaf 'post-lingually' (that is, after acquiring language) but some are pre-lingually deaf and as a result may have sign as a first or only language. Lip-reading may not be a skill their deaf parents encourage, because sign is a language in its own right. Other deaf people will prefer to communicate using English and a hearing aid or lip-reading, and many will have no knowledge of sign at all, particularly if they are becoming deaf as a result of ageing.

Some disabled people live in institutional settings such as longstay hospitals, or attend a day-centre, special school or college regularly. Others live at home with their parents, partner or children, or alone, and seldom or never attend a day-centre or 'club' for disabled people. Social services are in touch with many disabled people who need financial or domestic support, but many disabled people use the state support system infrequently, if at all.

These examples are given not as a definitive list of what causes and defines disability, but to highlight the complexity of the community labelled disabled.

The Disabled Audience: A Television Survey

Extracts from *Perspectives of Disability in Broadcasting*, Research Working Paper 11 (Broadcasting Standards Council, 1995).

This BSC Report was commissioned in order to 'aid the Council further in its task of considering complaints in relation to the depiction of disability issues and people with disabilities within broadcasting and television in particular'.[1]

A small-scale qualitative pilot project revealed a difficulty in getting respondents 'to talk about the way in which disability issues are presented in the media and the way in which people with disabilities are portrayed without discussing the questions surrounding the way in which people with disabilities are treated by society in general'.[2] Indeed the researchers 'had to force respondents to move on to a consideration of the media'. Because of this difficulty with the pilot, it was decided to look at audience reaction to a specific programme, and the BBC filmed drama *Scallagrigg* was chosen.

The survey included the responses of non-disabled and disabled viewers, and examined these in detail in relation to key scenes in the drama. However, the extract selected for the purpose of this book looks particularly at disabled people's views of the media and breaks down those disabled people into three categories: (1) activist; (2) 'reluctant' disabled; and (3) resisting disability. The sample was small, so it is perhaps inevitable that one might disagree with some of the views said to be 'characteristic' of these three categories, in particular those ascribed to the 'activists' who it was suggested wanted nothing but positive images on screen. If one had to guess at what 'activists' wanted, from informal knowledge of the networks, one might suggest that variation of image might deemed to be of more, or equal, importance, since what might constitute a 'positive' image is a matter of some debate. For instance, so-called 'positive' images of physical activity or demonstrations of 'independence' from a non-disabled perspective are viewed with extreme caution by many disabled activists.

However, the separation did provide a useful if crude framework in which to look at some of the ways in which the views of disabled people might diverge.

SKALLAGRIGG: **PROGRAMME DETAILS**[3]

Skallagrigg was first transmitted in 1994 as part of the BBC's Screen Two series. The play is based on a book of the same name and is the story of Esther, a teenager born with cerebral palsy, who, following the death of her mother, has been left in an institution. When her father decides to reclaim her, Esther is determined to begin her quest for the Skallagrigg, a mythical figure and the hero of stories told by disabled people in hospitals all over the country. He is said to have taken care of a disabled boy called Arthur when he was abandoned in an institution. As Esther's search gathers momentum she becomes increasingly convinced that the stories are based on a real Arthur, tortured and persecuted for the last fifty years by Dilke, a cruel hospital attendant. Esther, her father and her friends team up as a most unusual search party, who eventually 'find' Arthur. The play won a BAFTA award for Drama in 1995.

DISABILITY AND THE MEDIA (SECTION 1)

In broad terms, there were three ways in which broadcast media seemed to impose upon the lives and perceptions of disabled people – and ultimately on the attitudes of the able-bodied to people with disabilities and disability issues:

– in terms of the media's portrayal of the lives of disabled people;

– in terms of the media's power to change perceptions at an individual level…

Journey to Knock[4] did change my attitude. It made me think, it could happen to anybody

(Woman, able-bodied, London)

– in terms of the collective force for social change which media coverage of issues and individuals' lives was expected to be able to effect.

The third issue, the impact of the media on social change, cannot legitimately be covered here but the first issue, the role of the media in provoking reflection and in the construction of social identity, and the collective force of such reflections on a mass scale, are addressed.

In general, there was very little disagreement between able-bodied and disabled respondents in terms of the preferred role for the media. That is, both groups agreed that it was difficult for those living with a disability (either as

'poor souls' or, at the other end, 'denied legitimate access to employment or other means to independent living') to secure sufficient resources to live comfortably – not in the sense of 'middle-class comfort', but in terms of being able to afford special modifications (to home or car). Without political pressure, it was felt that the disabled community was a low priority. Thus the cerebral argument goes, individuals and organisations lobbying for funds have an important role to play. The controversy entered into this 'greatest good …' argument, when the media were seen to be exploited in the lobbying process, and/or when lobbyists and activists were felt to define broadcasting as the central issue, rather than looking at the content of specific programmes in terms of their entertainment value, their educative value and the level at which they provide information – on and for people with disabilities. That is, the controversy began when mass media were seen to be used for 'organisational' ends, rather than to perform their primary role of enabling contributions to the debate.

I think it rather worrying that you have groups of individuals – which is what in essence such groups [charities] are – using their access to the media to either applaud themselves, or to promote their pet soapbox. I feel the issue is much more whether there are any wheelchairs in Eastenders, or whether we can ever change the 'Chanel' girls [newsreaders] for a spectrum of real people.

(Woman, wheelchair-users group, Kensington)

At the very start of the research, it became clear that the biting issues were ones of survival and very personal, confrontational attitudes rather than media portrayal. Indeed, it was extremely difficult for respondents, both the able-bodied and those with disabilities, to cite roles in which disability was addressed. A few key characters and programmes were mentioned – Nessa in *Eldorado*, *Journey to Knock*, *Telethon*, *My Left Foot* and 'those Sunday morning programmes' – indeed the list was very short. So, for both able-bodied respondents and those with a disability, it was felt that media portrayal reflected very accurately the situation in 'real life' – i.e. disability was difficult to find, or confined to 'specialist' (unpopular and inaccessible) slots. It was interesting that in asking viewers to watch *Skallagrigg* (reported on in the second part of the Paper), we were forcing a number of respondents to find and watch a programme slot and a programme they may have thought to be 'interesting' in theory, but which in practice they would not have watched.

Attitudes towards the media's actual and prescribed role varied according to the disabled respondent's own attitudes towards their disability, and the way in which they constructed their personal identity and reflected their social identity. That is, for some, the priority for broadcasting in particular – although this was applied to all mass media – was to portray the 'real' attitudes on the side of both those living with a disability (even if this meant showing them in an unflattering light) and the able-bodied (even if this showed someone as un-realistically tolerant and understanding). For others, the priority was to try and emphasise the 'best practices' current. For yet others, there was an absolute requirement that only the positive side of disability was portrayed, and that the worst of society's discrimination and prejudice should be shown, to hint at the flavour of what people with disabilities have to confront every day. For some in each group, it was important that no one

forget that the television is a personal means of entertainment and enjoyment for all, whether disabled or not.

I think it's often forgotten that we all watch a lot of television – yes we do. It's more difficult to go out, so I know I'll sit at home and just want to be entertained. I think that's important. We're an important group in that sense too.
(Woman, wheelchair-users group, Kensington)

As argued throughout this report, it is important to recognise that the group on which we impose the definition 'disabled' does not necessarily collude in that definition, and that the 'disabled' actually represent a varied group, dependent upon their definition of their personal identity and their perception of the nature of disability. The portrayal of disability in broadcast media, therefore, also faces a similar dilemma: the 'personal' definitions of disability and the social and conceptual cohesiveness of the group, 'the disabled'.

For some able-bodied people too, 'the disabled' is not a group to which one can belong, but an abstract social grouping, which one never really knows or comes into contact with. Even those who had some experience dealing with someone with a disability saw these people in terms of 'having some problems', rather than consigned to membership of the group 'the disabled'.

I never think of somebody who is a manic depressive as disabled. My brother is a manic depressive (institutionalised at one point), but I never think of him as disabled, that's just him.
(Woman, able-bodied, London)

RESPONDING TO DISABILITY
Building on the distinctions made in the above section, we will argue that the

views of the range of respondents interviewed under the umbrella term 'people with disabilities' varied to a large extent, depending upon the level to which they had integrated the notion of 'disabled' into their own personal identity. Certainly, all respondents felt they had suffered to a certain extent through social prescriptions of their situation as a 'disabled person'. However, their own personal response varied a great deal and, on that basis, so did their attitudes towards and their requirements of, broadcast media. The following definitions are necessarily sketchy and debatable. Nevertheless, we would argue that they do give some framework to help understand the perspectives and concerns of the small number of respondents with disabilities we interviewed.

GROUP ONE: 'ACTIVISTS'
This group not only accepted 'disabled' as part of its personal identity, but positively valued and embraced it. They did this deliberately, in an attempt to redefine the social construction of disability – to try to instil positive, assertive and independent values into what was seen essentially as limited, negative and passive social definitions. This group tended to be politically motivated to change attitudes through whatever means possible, whether part of a group or not. In asserting disability as such a central part of their personal identity, they hoped to positively change the construction of disability imposed on them by society.

The role – or potential role – for the media in this 'identity-raising' exercise was felt to be powerful. The remit that this group tended to give broadcast (and other mass) media was an extremely tight one.

Since their sense of personal identity was extremely sharp, this group shied away from programme-makers' attempts to help the general public understand the inner feelings – warts and all – of someone living with a disability. Rather, the firm conviction was that broadcasters and programme-makers should use their considerable power to ensure that positive images alone be portrayed.

I love my life as a disabled person, but society won't accept that.
(Woman, wheelchair user, Kensington)
And the argument put forward was that any 'tarnished' or 'less than heroic' emotions and actions were inappropriate.

I don't think it does disabled people any good, nor the general public any good, to see that he (the lead character in Journey to Knock**) had to hide his (wheel)chair so that he could pick up a girl.**
(Woman, wheelchair user, Kensington)

Any portrayal of someone with a disability which had the underlying assumption that they were 'dysfunctional' and should be 'made better', i.e. able-bodied, was severely criticised.

I query why we have to look for a cure for disabled people [referring to the 'fairy story' of classic narratives]. It's the presumption of able-bodied people that they can make my life better by taking away my disability.
(Woman, wheelchair user, Kensington)

For this powerful and vocal group, disability issues mirror other struggles in terms of 'rights': the black power movement, the women's movement and gay rights. For them the issue is one of civil liberties and the need to change perceptions of disability from pathology and 'poor souls' to positive and productive contributory ones.

Although society was drawn as the culprit in negative images of disability, once the discussion of mass media was initiated there was a strong reactionary stance taken by this group. That is, the media were felt to have potential for powerful good, or for supporting the profound limits put on disabled people's participation in society. Since the mass media were felt to have done little to promote disability rights, and to help in the redressing of the balance, it was felt important that they use their considerable power to make reparation.

It does have a responsibility – it's lies most of the time, and I think it must take some responsibility for this 'poor soul, there, there' attitude.

(Woman, wheelchair user, Kensington)

The range of programmes and types of media coverage included in this requirement were wide and varied, encompassing advertising, mainstream programmes and soaps, full-length drama and drama series, specialist programmes (including *Link* as well as individual, one-off documentaries), and 'minority' programmes similar to those such as the *In the Pink* series for the gay and lesbian community. This, in addition to the comment:

If we could say there was a disabled person in *Eastenders*, a disabled newsreader, a blind person in this or that, then a Christy Brown type story came in, we wouldn't worry about it . . . but it's the 'tragic but brave' bits, or 'they are exceptional people with exceptional talent' . . .

(Woman, wheelchair user, Kensington)

This group was particularly resistant to anything which portrayed the disabled person as either helpless, or someone to be pitied: that is, they required that both the disabled and able-bodied characters seen interacting with the people with disabilities, focus on the positive and assertive aspects of the role:

It's the 'oh poor him', it makes me absolutely sick. The media twist things and we end up looking like poor helpless souls. I would never talk to the media.

(Woman, wheelchair user, Kensington)

Interestingly, radio seemed to produce less of a reaction, partly because it was perceived as less powerful, but also less intrusive and more 'intelligent' than the 'popular' medium of television. It was also seen as more egalitarian because of the potential anonymity of the disability because of the lack of visual images.

On radio they don't know if you're in a wheelchair.

(Woman, wheelchair user, Kensington)

This group also felt that since the media, and television in particular, had such potential for change, and that since they had colluded in the continuing powerlessness of disabled people by the manner in which people with disabilities are portrayed, they should be available to the disability lobby – to raise issues, educate on 'civil rights' and generally raise the collective and individual consciousness; to suggest there was a coherent stand to be taken by disabled people as a group.

Moderator: I spoke to a woman in Glasgow who felt that television was an escape for her, that she wasn't disabled when she watched television, she felt moved out of her wheelchair.

Respondent: Well, she doesn't know what to think, she doesn't know what she should think.

(Woman, wheelchair user, Kensington)

Suggestions made included attempting to impose quotas for the inclusion of disabled actors and actresses, roles portraying disability and numbers of programmes addressing the issues, and generally supported the positive discrimination of the media in favour of people with disabilities.

These respondents felt that it was important that people with disabilities should be directly involved in the decision-making process in relation to programmes addressing any disability issues, and that disability, when raised in a programme, should be fully and completely addressed.

I think there is far too much tokenism, I think if they are going to take on board disability, then they need to spend time showing all aspects.

(Man, manic depressive, London)

This group found humour extremely problematic – unless it was humour utilised by a person with a disability against society as a whole, for instance, laughing about society's attitude towards, and understanding of, disability issues and the lives of disabled people.

There was an absolute requirement that disabled roles should primarily be positive. They should be people who 'break through' against the prejudice and limitations imposed upon them by mainstream society. The role of Nessa in *Eldorado* was therefore controversial, since she was portrayed as a 'normal' teenager, with unreasonable temper tantrums and moods rather than as a very positive role model, coping with the negative attitudes displayed towards her. (Incidentally, it was also felt that portraying her living circumstances as 'normal' was highly unrepresentative and over-optimistic, in terms of the number of ramps around her home and school, which made life relatively easy for her.)

The portrayal (described as 'condescending') of the heroic efforts of disabled people to overcome their disability (rather than society's attitudes towards their disability) was severely criticised. Not only were such roles and portrayals objected to on the grounds of their tokenism, they were felt to try to sustain the assumption (considered 'patronising') that all disabled people would ideally like to be exactly the same

as the able-bodied, and that all seek a cure. For this group of respondents, this underlined the perception that able-bodied pity disabled people for simply 'not being like us'. *Scallagrigg*, discussed in the next section, was praised for its uncompromising approach, especially when compared with *Journey to Knock*, which was criticised on the grounds of an underlying assumption that anyone 'confined' to a wheelchair is to be pitied, because they would rather rejoin the ranks of the able-bodied.

It was felt that the more rigid 'positive images only' stance described here could be moderated in time and a broader approach taken. But this was only possible once the social identity of people with disabilities was felt to be more positive and assertive – and the portrayal of people with disabilities in mainstream broadcasts was a far more frequent occurrence. This group of activists also felt it to be important that 'the disabled' agree to the definition, and accept its 'identity', and, on a practical level, join together to form pressure groups, aimed at empowering both themselves and people with disabilities who felt isolated. On the other hand, there was a resentment (although some understanding) of those who chose to reject or resist the identity of 'disabled'. There was a feeling that the disabled people who chose this route were limiting the furtherance of the 'disability movement' as much as able-bodied people.

I think until disability has been de-stigmatised then there will always be people who are reluctant to accept that they have a disability and to participate in any movement.

(Man, Parkinson's disease, Worcester)

GROUP TWO: 'RELUCTANT' DISABLED
Although the title of this group of respondents appears rather pejorative, it

is an accurate description of how they perceived their situation. That is, they certainly saw themselves as disabled – and felt, regretfully, that society labelled them as such. However, the identity of 'disabled' had little that was positive, valued or empowering for them. Rather, they felt they were 'blocked' by social perceptions of disability, and the lack of knowledge and understanding that society displayed towards them… In its lack of understanding, society attempted to hide away disability, and it was as a result of lack of understanding, and reluctance to confront both disability issues and the disabled person, that disability had such a negative set of connotations.

In terms of perception of the media, this group felt that the media could help change definitions of social identity by creating empathy and inculcating more understanding of disabled people.

If you saw more disabled people on television, maybe people would be a bit more sympathetic, and not so frightened.

(Woman, blind, Glasgow)

In terms of broadcasting, this group felt that the priority was on truth and not on 'issues' in the political sense. They were resistant to the idealised views demonstrated by the group of activist respondents in terms of their positive approach to disability (which was perceived as unrealistic). This group believed that television was, to some extent, an escape from which they could construct their own view of the 'real world' and ignore the limits placed upon them in their own interaction with it.

This small group of respondents felt strongly that the idealised views of the 'activists' were misguided. They felt that only portraying positive, competent and assertive images of people with disabilities perhaps did not help them. That

is, they felt that it was only by understanding the real implications of the limits society placed upon them – through portrayal of what their lives were like – that these limiting actions and attitudes would be addressed and changed by society in general. This group valued the more general role of television in terms of escapism. They felt that, should television concentrate on the more unrealistic, idealised definitions of disability, it would make communicating what they felt to be real disadvantages much more difficult. Their requirement was that broadcast images show disabled people as normal people who happened to be 'disabled'. That is, that television show such characters as normal – including how difficult life can be for people with disabilities. This group also thought portraying the moments of 'triumph' should be shown, when people overcame both society's attitudes towards them and the limitations of their disabilities.

I think the most exciting type of stories are those where they show you that even though you're disabled, you can still have a normal life – you can break through all the difficulties and the prejudice and make a life for yourself.

(Man, manic depressive, London)

For this group, roles such as Nessa in *Eldorado* were actually valued very positively. Not only was she depicted as a disabled person dealing with the disadvantages thrown at her by society, it also showed her being depressed at the attitudes shown towards her. Similarly, the hero in *Journey to Knock* was also 'human', behaving badly as well as positively.

In general, this group felt that, given the number of people who were disabled in society, there was an insufficient presence of both disability issues and

people with disabilities on television – especially people with disabilities not using a wheelchair. However, the role of television was primarily one of personal entertainment, rather than a tool for social change.

GROUP THREE: 'RESISTING' DISABILITY

This third group can be characterised as those who simply see themselves as 'having problems – perhaps just a bit more severe than other people's problems'. This group was extremely reluctant to accept 'disabled' into their own perception of themselves, although they may have had to accept society's definition of themselves as disabled.

I'm registered disabled, but I don't think of myself as disabled.
(Man, Parkinson's disease, London)

As part of the support structure which they may have constructed to allow them to live 'normal' lives, this group was sometimes in contact, or had professional relationships, with 'disability' professional workers. But they could also reject the general term 'disabled', seeing this group as far too diverse to warrant a collective term – particularly if they were allocated to this group themselves.

What on earth would I do in one of those groups [disabled support groups]. I've absolutely nothing in common with them.
(Man, schizophrenic, London)

I couldn't go along to one of her groups, not with mental people.
(Woman, wheelchair user, Glasgow)

I could understand that perhaps groups based around talking therapies could be of some benefit to those with physical disabilities – however, I would be resistant for myself to mixing with such groups.
(Man, manic depressive, London)

Scallagrigg, courtesy BBC

This group was composed of the elderly (or those with some sort of 'disfigurement') and included some who were wheelchair users and others who were profoundly deaf and blind.

I (just) can't work at the moment.
(Woman, blind, Glasgow)

I'm just the same as I was, only I'm probably dying a bit quicker.
(Man, Parkinson's disease, London)

I used to feel sorry for them... I just can't think of myself as like them.
(Woman, wheelchair user, Glasgow)

In terms of their personal identity, then, these respondents were unwilling to take the route of the civil rights movements which formed the 'role models' for the activists. For them, there is not a qualitative difference between themselves and a society which is mainly able-bodied – rather they see themselves as quantitatively less able to live independently. This group, therefore, felt that there was no need for a code of conduct or set of rules concerning the depiction of people with disabilities. Rather, they assumed that the normal rules of courtesy and common sense would protect those who were 'dealing with problems' as well as people with disabilities. However, they assumed that their definition of their similarity to 'mainstream society' would also apply to those that they would call 'disabled', and that to make a 'special case' of disabled people and disability issues would be both patronising and erroneous.

This group of respondents felt extremely strongly that 'quota' systems and positive discrimination only serve to underline and underwrite an inaccurate and unfair set of definitions. Rather, they argued that there should be 'something for everyone' and that this should apply across the board, whether living with what everyone (including the subject) would define as a disability, a 'problem', or 'good health'.

This group shared the able-bodied respondents' protests that they would find a programme such as *Scallagrigg* difficult to watch, precisely because it was about 'disabled people', i.e. 'not me'.

Indeed, this group felt angry about the rights of those they termed 'busybodies' to prescribe the media portrayal of people with disabilities. That is, this group of respondents felt 'the busybodies' had lost the 'middle ground' and 'a sense of humour'. They felt that there was a tendency for people who did not rightly understand their situation and their response to their situation, to make guesses about what they would and would not find 'offensive' or 'upsetting'. Their attitudes, they argued, meant that the whole of their sense of humour – and the reality of life with a 'problem' (in comparison with a disability, which may be a much more serious and limiting 'condition') was missed out and not portrayed on television. On the one hand the dramatic opportunities of disability were seen to be exploited – in terms of melodrama, 'larger than life' heroes and villains, evil and deranged creature, madmen, and more than anything, wheelchair users – while the 'normal people with a problem' were felt to be left off screen, 'in case they offend anybody' . . .

Background assumptions informing disabled and able-bodied respondents' reactions to *Scallagrigg*

The disabled respondents we have called 'activists' expected the programme to put forward powerful, positive images of disabled people and their struggle. The key background assumption for them was that Esther, as a wheelchair user, indicated the programme would be about disability, would confront mainstream 'cosiness', and 'stir up the can of worms' of able-bodied people's passivity towards disability issues.

The main point [was . . .] that there is established guilt in the way in which people with disabilities are/were treated, but the programme treated the subject in a predictable 'cosy' way.

(Woman, disabled, self-completion questionnaire, Cwmbran)

I particularly disliked the [. . .] patronising attitudes of some of the characters. All disabled parts should have been acted out by *truly* disabled. Richard Briers made Arthur look like a 'doddering old fool', which he was not.

(Woman, disabled, self-completion questionnaire, Edinburgh)

The feeling was that the negative attitudes, necessarily portrayed, should be those of people in authority and the able-bodied . . .

Why was the rapist not a (staff member)!? Why did it have to be a patient. Nasty sex/violence done by nasty patient. In truth more likely to be STAFF!

(Man, disabled, self-completion questionnaire, Wellingborough)

. . . and that able-bodied people should be confronted by their own deteriorating body.

[The main point was] hopefully that we all end up old and therefore the same. If you lot get it right for us now, you will get it right for yourselves.

(Man, disabled, self-completion questionnaire, Wellingborough)

For those we have described as 'reluctantly' disabled, wheelchairs were also the first point of 'scene-setting'. That is, in seeing 'wheelchairs', this group expected the drama to be concerned with 'oppression', victimisation, society's attitude towards people with disabilities, but from a sympathetic, 'isn't it dreadful?' type stance, rather than the more confrontational stance above.

It did not show the problems we have to face, or the able-bodied's some-times negative attitudes towards us [. . .] Should have shown the problems we have to face in more detail. Seemed there was only one negative person in the whole programme, with regard to Esther, and that was her grandmother.
(Woman, disabled, self-completion questionnaire, Essex)

This group also felt that some sort of resolution was required – that society, or its symbols in the play, had to show some developing understanding, and 'change of heart' and/or mind to provide a symbol of hope for their own future.

I found it very depressing indeed. What happened at the end? You don't know whether Arthur went back into the home or another one, what happened to Esther, the baby, the warden. [. . .] All these awful things happened and you don't really understand why.

Those who we would describe as 'resisting' the incorporation of 'disabled' into their identity shared many more perceptions and attitudes with the able-bodied respondents than with the other two groups of disabled respondents. That is, they too saw the icon of 'wheelchairs' and interpreted the programme as being about 'seriously disabled people' – 'not like me'.

You've got to feel sorry for them.
(Man, disabled, depth interview, Edinburgh)

Among this group there was also some hostility to a group perceived to be 'so handicapped' even though the re-spondents themselves were categorised as disabled.

The main point was that they are just like us. They don't realise they are as bad as they are.

(Woman, disabled, depth interview, Winchester)

Certainly all groups, except the activists, expected the portrayal of a group of vulnerable people.

The able-bodied respondents, in contrast, tended to categorise disabled people into three groups: what they call 'cripples', or wheelchair users, 'normal people' with a problem, and 'mad' or 'disturbed' people. Again, although only a supposition based on a relatively small sample, this categorisation can help explicate the deep-seated definitions which informed the reactions to the programme:

1. Wheelchair users were seen as the archetypal 'disabled' people. They were visibly different to others, had 'real' problems, the authenticity of which it was difficult to question. They were felt to be sufficiently 'different' to able-bodied people to be less threatening – something had 'happened to them to make them that way' either at birth, or in an accident.

When you see a wheelchair, you think about how lucky you are. I wouldn't like to have to cope with that. You've got to admire them.
(Woman, able-bodied, depth interview, Cheam)

2. The second group were described as 'normal people, like you and me, only they're living with a problem'. This group included the elderly, people with less serious mobility problems, people with learning difficulties, or anyone with a non- or only partly-visible disability, who the able-bodied respondents could easily feel were 'normal people'. This group was contrasted with the group above, and the group thought to be portrayed in the programme.

3. Finally, there was the group described as 'disturbed' or 'mad' people. This group

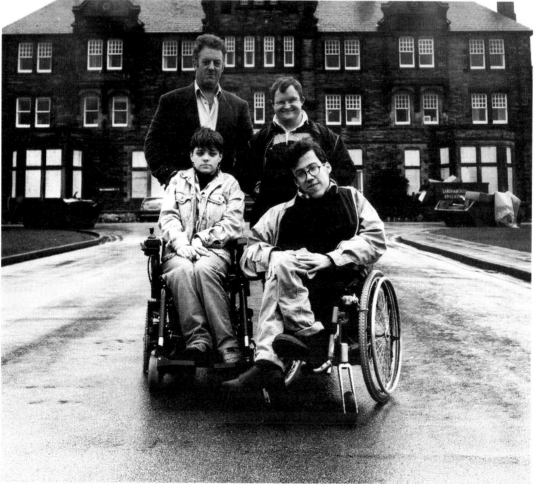

was perceived as threatening by both the able-bodied and the non-activist samples. That is, their disability is a non-apparent, controversial one, with unknown origins and no known 'cure'. It is partly a disease, partly a mental condition.

Arthur's flashbacks I found disturbing and depressing, probably because they reminded me of just how thin the dividing line is between normal 'sane' people and others.
(Man, disabled, self-completion questionnaire, Wellingborough)

One of the key elements of reactions to *Skallagrigg* was that the audience – both able-bodied and disabled respondents – expected that the programme was going to be concerned with *physical* disability and instead, when watching the programme, they felt it was concerned with the much more threatening group of 'disturbed' or 'mad' people.

This helped to explain the antipathy towards Esther and her friends' language and assertiveness, and the deep discomfort expressed in relation to the mini-bus outing – where Esther's father (struggling to come to terms with society's attitudes and his own feelings for his daughter) happily takes out a party of the young people from the institution into the 'real world'.

I found that scene utterly unbelievable. They wouldn't let someone like him – two minutes before, he couldn't understand what she was saying – take a whole coach load of them out on a jolly outing. It just doesn't ring true.
(Man, disabled, depth interview, Edinburgh)

I found it totally unbelievable that any institution would have allowed someone who was untrained and who had no knowledge of the needs and care of disabled people and who couldn't even communicate with his own daughter, to be given charge of three disabled teenagers, and then to be allowed to go tearing up and down the country in the quest for the Skallagrigg.
(Woman, able-bodied, self-completion questionnaire, Essex)

The issues underlying the difficulties and discomfort with the programme, therefore, centre around the removal of 'distance' from the viewer, the easy resolution of the key character's dilemma, and the perception of a threatening change in power in terms of the relationships between the characters in the programme.

The combination of the above factors served to leave the respondents interviewed qualitatively feeling they had been threatened, and they were not sure what response they should make. Given the programme's billing and scheduling, they felt that any complaint would be unreasonable – *particularly* unreasonable because the programme was attempting to deal with issues both worthy and under-represented. Rather, their discomfort emerged and was justified by them in relation to specific scenes: where Arthur was taken into the institution; the love-making scene between Arthur and Linny; the scene where Esther's father takes her and her friends out in a mini-bus; the scene where Arthur is raped; the scene where Arthur is beaten up by the warden; and the ending.

Notes

1. Introductory section of the report, p. 3.
2. Ibid, p. 4.
3. Appendix B of the report, p. 91.
4. *Journey to Knock* was a film made by the BBC (from a play by William Ivory), in which three Englishmen in wheelchairs go on a pilgrimage to a shrine in Ireland. It featured non-disabled actors and was transmitted on 18 September 1991.

Scallagrigg, courtesy BBC

Mat Fraser in Jo Pearson's film *Freak Fucking Basics*
(The Arts Council of England, 1995)

Part Five

Product and control

Introduction

Freak Out, (BBC, 1995) courtesy of David Hevey

The Broadcasting Standards Council's Scallagrigg study 'Perspectives of Disability in Broadcasting' (see Part 4 Chapter 12) raised the question of how ready the disabled and non-disabled audience is to see more uncompromising disability images. For many disabled people, however, such a consideration is irrelevant, believing that only exposure itself will make the audience 'ready'.

What is also currently argued is that the product is likely to be different where disabled people are in control or actively involved in the process of production, whether it is of the advertisement, the photograph, the play, the film or the television programme.

PRODUCT AND CONTROL

David Hevey opens this final section with part of a contribution which explores issues around disabled people controlling and influencing arts and 'output'. This piece is followed by a number of

short contributions on aspects of power: **Stephen Dwoskin** encountering movie industry censorship; **Jerry Rothwell** talking about a community video project; and **Gill Whalley** outlining a video project with a group of people with learning difficulties, who at one point disowned the outcome. **Stephen Dwoskin** followed one of his films to an Italian Festival of disability films, only to find that most people were non-disabled, including selectors of the films and winners. **David Hevey** then returns to describe a struggle for participation at a conference on advertising and disability. A counter-conference set up a working group which in turn led to researcher **Colin Barnes** making some recommendations on portrayal and language in his paper *Disability Imagery in the Media*.

Ann Pointon's final overview links disability rights to the constant problem of 'access'; a word used in the widest possible sense.

5.1

Controlling Interests
David Hevey

Extracts from 'From Self Love to the Picket Line: Strategies for Change in Disability Representation', *Disability & Society* vol. 8 no. 4.

DAVID HEVEY is a television producer, photographer and writer, and parent. His start in photography was as a 'smudger' (a seaside photographer) at a time when he was also studying fine art. His book *The Creatures Time Forgot*[1] is a study of photography and disability imagery and includes a detailed dissection of charity advertising. On a personal level he describes the painful process of 'coming out' as disabled and being able to acknowledge and add the open experience of epilepsy to those other parts of him, the 'post-study working class, the second-generation Irish, the artist, the Marxist', and 'the feminist man'. Also described in detail in *The Creatures Time Forgot* is his conscious process of empowering his disabled photographic subjects, a practice which translates into his later experience as an independent television producer and in his work in the BBC's Disability Programmes Unit.

In these two extracts from the paper 'From Self Love to the Picket Line' Hevey seeks to lay out a 'strategy for the future of disability arts and culture', given, as he states, that the history of representation has been one of exclusion of disabled people from control and of oppressive, negative representation in the hands of others. He perceives the disability arts movement as the first sign of a post-tragedy disability culture but suggests that there is a lack of theory or theories of an alternative process. He offers five elements in what might begin to constitute such a theory.

In the history of disability representation or 'arts and disability', we find a history of representation that was not done by us but done to us. The beginning of a strategy for the future of disability arts and culture, then, is to start to examine some key cultural norms within that history of (mis)representation which still surround us today and which have to be challenged and destroyed.

To begin with, these key norms would include the historical fact that disabled people have not had an input, let alone a controlling interest, in culture and representation done in our name. In addition, we could say that the general history of disability representation is one of oppressive or 'negative' forms. And this has happened precisely because disabled people are excluded from the production of *impairment-based* disability culture and excluded from the dominant 'disability' discourses.[2] We are excluded from most history but particularly, and perversely, from the history of 'disability representation'. Disabled people have been the *subject* of various constructions and representations throughout history but disabled people have not controlled the *object* – that is, the means of producing or positioning our own constructions or representations.

To say this, then, leaves us with the position that historical representation

209

has been either absent or negative, and disabled people want something positive. That last sentence seems to me to be the current position of much disabled-led (but including non-disabled people and organisations) thinking on disability representation. This is a Walls of Jericho situation whereby it is believed that the oppressive representation will fall if we only repeat and repeat the word 'positive' in place of 'negative'.

Where once disabled people would be represented in a state of subconscious oblivion (that is, portrayed as unaware of themselves and their situation), we are now witnessing a small current of 'positive' images coming into circulation of the grinning disabled. This is an extremely superficial gain but it is nonetheless currently considered 'positive'. Debates, indeed strategies, have thus hung on this negative/positive divide, with little or no definition of the terms or of the nature of the struggle over political representation. Of course, among many problems in the call for 'positive' images of disabled people is that it lacks a clear definition of just what we want to be positive about? Are we positive about impairments? Are we 'positive' about being oppressed or discriminated against? Or are we positive about naming that struggle between people with impairments and disabling society?

The current 'strategy for the future' in disability cultural production, then, is to produce something 'positive'. To say the least, this is a weak position for the disability movement to find itself in, let alone accept, so let me outline an analysis of a different route or strategy.

First, we have to go back into the belly of the beast and look at just what is being represented in general disability representation. What is it that unites practically the entire discourse, from Greek theatre to James Bond villains to charity advertising to all the Richard III's, Ravens[3], and so on? *In a word, it is that disablement means impairment and impairment means social flaw.* Thus, we can say that the basic rule of oppressive disability representation is that it is predicated on the social non-worth of an impairment or the person with an impairment. This social construction is naturalised within representation by characters who carry this 'flaw' *on their body* but who hide society's and history's contempt for the disabled person by vocalising a self-loathing or a self-destructive pattern. That is, they naturalise disability as dysfunction, and they consequently act out society's wish or rule by destroying themselves. They hold a cracked mirror up to nature and behold their/our imperfect and flawed reflection. This is the *Tragedy Principle*, [...which] positions a flaw on the body related to the deepest possible social fall. Where impairment enters, the character is proven to be socially dead.[4] Whether in television, theatre, cinema, fine art or charity advertising, the tragedy principle uses the impairment as a metaphor and a symbol for a socially unacceptable person and it is this tragedy principle which is the bone-cage surrounding historical and current disability representation. It is this impairment-as-social-flaw that we mean when we say 'negative' representation and it is this that we have to end. This will be difficult because such readings have become 'natural' within representation.

These forms of disability representation naturalise the exclusion of disabled people from societies organised on labour power as a key commodity in economic production *and* these representations become the target for the ridding of fears by non-disabled people for their own bodies' decline or loss of power. It is important, however, in terms of creating radical and new forms of disability representation, to acknowledge that it is *both* the organisation of economic production as *well* as the projection of (non-disabled) negative desire, which contains disabled people within oppressive cultural representation.

The fall of the tragic character into either a real (that is, narrated) death or a (again, narrated) living death will aid the disavowal, the catharsis, of the non-disabled audiences' ever-present fear for the loss of their own 'able-bodiedness'. 'The Disabled' is a non-disabled construction, a representational framework no more real than a hologram but which has to contain two properties if it is to have any cathartic meaning for society. To repeat, these two 'able-bodied' cathartic needs are: (1) the ridding or disavowal of health, fitness and other physical /functional issues pertaining to the ability to work; and (2) the disavowal of the presence of death and mortality. This is how 'negative' representation serves 'able-bodied' people. Its *positive* active purpose is in supporting the 'able-bodied' management of these two fears. This positive role explains the physical and psychological resistance so many users, like impairment charities, have to changing these models of representation.

So, what is to be done? If we are to move beyond this state of affairs, the cultural task for disabled artists and culture workers is threefold. First, how to 'reclaim' impairment away from a social flaw. Secondly, how to shift disability representation off from the body and into the interface between people with impairments and socially disabling conditions and, thirdly, how to create aesthetic forms which are seen to deal with this successfully (i.e. which can be internalised by disabled people in struggle).

So far so good. However, an analysis of the mechanics of historical and oppressive *tragedy/impairment/disability* represen-

tation is not in itself sufficient to change those forms of representation. What is necessary in the first instant is a shift in the surrounding social relations and economic conditions. Finkelstein has written on the shift from 'phase two' to 'phase three' within the shaping of social disablement.[5] As an extremely broad overview, the shift from heavy manufacturing (Phase 2) through the electronics and cybernetics revolution (Phase 3) is creating the conditions for a different position for disabled people in society and this theoretical position is being borne out. We have had three Tory governments that have been and still are committed to the rolling back of the 'nanny state'. One aspect of this has been the 'care in the community' programmes which has seen the closure of many long-stay institutions and which has resulted in large numbers of disabled people re-entering the social arena, but still having to struggle for basic rights to access. Within this, the UK disability movement has grown. A particular, and in representational terms crucial, development of this new activism (and which links it to other movements based on class, women, colour, etc.) is the *de-biologisation* of disability. That is to say, the issue of disability, like other issues pertaining to women and blacks and gays and lesbians and so on, is shifting its focus *away from the body and on to society.*

Although the disability movement has taken the initiative in articulating this shift, it is a shift which is affecting all sides of the disability issue. For example, and again as Finkelstein has pointed out, the dominant form of oppression of disabled people is shifting from the medical 'cure or care' model to an administrative model. While this may mean that disabled people are shifting from institutions to ghettoes, it nevertheless heralds an age when disabled people *are not to be cured as such*. Despite liberal panic over this new agenda, it presents greater possibilities for the emancipation of disabled people.

Since this shift is happening within the social disability movement, it clearly creates conditions for its emulation within disability representation and the disability arts movement. Indeed, the shift from 'arts and disability' to disability arts' is proof of this movement. The disability arts movement is the first sign of a post-tragedy disability culture. To state this clearly, the disability movement is the articulation that (a) impairment and disability are no longer focused as one, and (b) they are no longer *exclusively* focused on the body. The disability arts movement is the only area which is dealing with the cultural vacuum which now exists given this shift.

However, as much as we have gained the initiative, there are still problems which face the disability arts movement and which need to be unravelled. One in particular is that we currently lack a theory or theories of an alternative process. The final part of this paper, I hope, begins one.

1. Gazing where? Moving off the body

We need to define what we mean by 'disability representation'. Do we mean the representation of impairment, or do we mean the representation of social constrictions, or do we mean the recording of the interface between the two? Artistic and cultural disabled-led practice which positions its gaze towards this interface begins to reflect the struggle.

2. Changing the meaning of impairment

We need to 'reclaim', in light of the shifts of disability-definition (from medical model to administrative model, from institution to care in the community, from arts and disability to disability arts),

the cultural meaning of impairment. We need to undo the tragedy principle and to undo the notion of impairment as flaw. This is clearly linked to (1) above, since what is being projected on to the person with an impairment by 'able-bodied' culture is in itself changing. However, the point of radical art and culture is to create a political poetic of the self and the group. We will be able to redefine our impairments away from flaws by making culture and art which shows *the process* of our transformations. The left has traditionally made a mistake within representation by positioning 'positive' images against 'negative' ones, picket lines against victims. However worthy this has been (and necessary in places), our purpose should be to create work which records the process of change, not just two 'negative' or 'positive' poles.

3. The control of meaning

Our artworks and cultural works must tell *both* of the issue and of themselves. This is critical. Again, learning from the mistakes of other oppressed peoples struggle, particularly the class movements, we must not assume that any reading of any artwork is *in itself* permanent or natural. The best new image in the world can have its meaning altered by adding a different text in or around it.[6] In the final analysis, negativity or positivity within any given cultural form only exists within the *positioning* of the piece. It is not implicit in the surface of the work. Its meaning can be altered by its altered context. The success of our counter-culture is in our ability to *position* meaning.

4. The act of showing must also be shown

Brecht in particular dealt with the relationship between real struggle and the metaphorical or symbolical illumination of struggle in art. In the Brechtian aesthetic, the real struggles of life and oppressed peoples cannot be shown, as it were, naturally. Naturalism as an aesthetic may work as a tool of catharsis – we may suffer with those we see suffer – but it does not illuminate methods for action after the catharsis. Therefore, what is needed is a critical relationship within the story-telling or story-showing *within and between* the form and the issue. In our case, we can position meaning by engaging and reinterpreting forms as well as reinterpreting contents. This is to acknowledge that the representational forms themselves are conveyers of messages but are not innocent of the struggle. The point of new methods with new messages is that they convey the sense of a new order (or at least the decline of the old one). This links itself to the three previous parts because it displays a process which *metaphorically* or *symbolically* represents change.

5. The success or failure of a new form

Again, radical drama theory, particularly that of the 70s involving class politics and gay and lesbian politics (and, of course, both at once), dealt with the extremely critical issue of the relationship between producer and consumer. The success of new forms of disability representation can be judged, in my estimation, by their consumption by disabled people and their ability to mobilise disabled people into action. One of the main characteristics that has distinguished all radical art, from that of the Soviet revolution to the art of South Africa, from the art of our movement to the work of the AIDS practitioners in the United States, is its proximity to an *active* audience. However, there is the problem of the romantics' notion of pure art devoid of social responsibility. Some people engaging in the issue of disability representation have tried to affect the taste of non-disabled audiences and supporters, rather than engage in a

political creativity within and about the disability struggle. Picasso said that taste was the enemy of creativity and, eventually, those disabled artists who pursue that path of affecting taste will find their work stagnate, since they are facilitating an outsider's vision of themselves. This is a mistake, though understandable because we have profound lack of role-models in this area. If people entering this issue align their aesthetics and texts to a field which operates between their sense of self and their relationship to the movement, the changes to both will create the base of their continued aesthetic change and growth.

In conclusion, the strategies for change lay in an analysis of what has gone before *and* a cultural intervention in what is socially happening to disabled people. This dialectic is our terrain. Within this dynamic, we can affect and create cultural forms and an agenda which bring the non-disabled world to us, not we to it.

Notes

1. David Hevey, *The Creatures Time Forgot: Photography and Disability Imagery* (London: Routledge, 1992).
2. By the word 'discourse', I mean an exchange or flow of information within a given social form or context. Basically, an information exchange.
3. Graham Greene's anti-hero in *Gun for Sale*.
4. V. Finkelstein, 'Disability: An Administrative Challenge?' (The Health & Welfare Heritage), in M. Oliver (ed.), *Social Work: Disabled People and Disabling Environments* (London: Jessica Ainsley, 1991).
5. V. Finkelstein, *Attitudes and Disabled People: Issues for Discussion* (New York: World Rehabilitation Fund, 1980).
6. See, in particular, the representational theory of Victor Burgin, who has worked extensively on 'scripto-visual' reading and meaning of representation, in V. Burgin (ed.) *Thinking Photography* (London: Macmillan, 1982), and V. Burgin, *The End of Art Theory: Criticism and Postmodernity* (London: Macmillan, 1986).

Whose Film?

Stephen Dwoskin

Extracts from 'Missing Pieces', *DAM* vol. 2 no. 1, Spring 1992.

STEPHEN DWOSKIN was born in New York and has lived in Britain since 1964. He is an avant-garde film-maker, who has also tutored in graphic design, film and television. He is the author of *Film Is* and *'Ha, Ha!' (La Solution Imaginaire with Photograph)*,[1] and has made over thirty films. A number of these have had a disability theme, including the award-winning *Outside In* (1981) and *Behindert* (1974). *Outside In* was based on his own surreal exchanges (encounters) between disability and non-disability. His most recent film *Trying to Kiss the Moon* is also autobiographical.

In 1992 Dwoskin was commissioned by Channel Four to make a film, *Face of Our Fear*, the proposal for which he had submitted many months earlier. The final decision to commission was made shortly before the channel's *Disabling World* season of programmes on disability was launched, as part of which the channel wished to transmit his work. The film was completed on time, but without important clips of film. As production progressed refusals to allow the use of film clips, and even stills came on all sides from the film companies. This extract describes the total censorship that film companies are able to exercise over their product.

I launched myself into the film with some serious questions and grave doubts about whether I could make the unrealistically short deadline for such a complex subject. Channel Four, who had commissioned the script, had been sitting on it for over nineteen months after they had received the final draft. Starting was a drawn out affair since I had an idea of trying to offset the usual negative image of disabled people by incorporating positive images created by disabled people themselves. Finding disabled persons to take part was only marginally time-consuming and those who agreed to take part were completely sympathetic. The real difficulties occurred from the able-bodied people who were around – ranging from sheer awkwardness when in the presence of the disabled people to complete depression at the idea of seeing people with disabilities.

Since the theme of the film evolved around the history of the visual stigma of disability and its presence in today's society, it meant dealing with the media itself since they are the most direct users of the negative image. In fact, much of the media exploits the images of disability – tabloid newspapers, magazines television and cinema – so I began to seek film clips to use within my film as prime illustrations of this and as concrete evidence of the argument. Four of the major American film companies (MGM, MCA, 20th Century-Fox and Warner Bros.) refused outright to allow any use of their films. This ban extended even to the use of still photographs from any of their films. So an image of Lon Chaney from the 1925 version of *The Phantom of the Opera* was not permitted – even though horror and movie books regularly use this image. No image from *What Ever Happened to Baby Jane* nor *Coming Home* nor *Moulin Rouge* nor *Moby Dick* nor *Mad Max II* (he wears a calliper in the film) nor Vincent Price in *House of Wax* (where Vincent plays an evil mad killer who pretends innocence by using a wheelchair) nor *Chamber of Horrors*. *The Fugitive* (where Dr Richard Kimble hunts for the one-armed killer) was not allowed simply because the word 'fear' was in the title of my film.

The cowboy film *Warlock*, which the *Radio Times* recently described as a mature and serious western, has Anthony Quinn limping around on a calliper and proving to be a sneaky killer. A clip from this film was also not permitted. The pan I wanted to use was when the motivation for him being a killer is revealed – when he confronts his old love played by Dorothy Malone with the fact that he would like to go back with her (he has been killing or having killed her various other lovers out of jealousy). She responds with great venom: 'Do you think I could have ever loved a cripple?' Yet this point – the point that he is both evil and sexually unattractive because he is a 'cripple' – has no direct relation to main narrative of the film. The main narrative hinges around Henry Fonda coming to clean-up the town of Warlock. My desire to use this particular kind of example was that it graphically demonstrated the ease with which the media employs negative stereotyping of disabled people embroidered into a larger more familiar narrative – in this case a Western – and presents it as 'entertainment'. (Most people know 'warlock' means male witch!)

Having been prevented from using this film clip of *Warlock*, I began rapidly to seek an equivalent example. The very next day I was flipping late night TV only to catch the end part of an episode of *The Equalizer*. There in this detective drama was some supposedly disabled guy mournfully lying in a bed (with that acted blank stare of depression) while the wife, feeling 'sexy', tries to fondle him. 'No I can't', he says. She is rejected and retreats. Later, this very same woman reaches a suicidal 'death wish' and places herself in the line of a gunman since her life is no longer worth living. Her identity and womanhood have been removed by her disabled husband's impotency. Later the husband is forced by the able-bodied hero to rescue her – that is, he becomes a 'man' again! I never found out what the title of the episode was; I did get the date of programme but I was again not allowed to use anything from *The Equalizer*.

Even more than those films or programmes employing disability as a central theme (such as *Coming Home* or *Raging Moon*), films like *Warlock* or TV programmes like *The Equalizer* use the negative images of disability as a matter of fact. This position is accepted by the viewer (and probably by the makers) without question since the main focus is on the primary narrative – that is, the cowboy film or the detective thriller, or whatever – and the disabled images become a dramatic shorthand and are readily accepted as that. This is far more dangerous and maintains the stigma more subversively.

I was surprised just how frequently this occurs. I was less surprised about the fact that almost all the presentations of disabled persons are done solely to support the able-bodied characters. Seldom, if ever, are the disabled presented with any credible existence; instead they exist only to give a credible and heroic position to the able-bodied. Seldom are the disabled characters women. They are usually men when it comes to mobility disabilities. It seems

Stephen Dwoskin, of director *Face of Our Fear,* on location, courtesy of Channel Four

woman are reserved only for such disabilities as blindness (as in *Wait until Dark*) or facial scaring (as in *A Woman's Face*). Yes, women also have the hearing difficulties, as in *Johnny Belinda.* However, while I was putting together my film the BBC did a three-part drama titled *Goodbye Cruel World*, about a woman who got a fictitious ailment called 'Way's disease'. Claimed to be based on a real disease, it dealt with 'courage' and 'heartwarming' drama, as the woman attempts to start a charity to research the disease. Ostensibly this is what it was supposed to be about – trauma as drama. It did, as it went along, begin to concentrate on the husband's plight rather than on the woman's.

There were many more examples of this blatant exploitation of disabled people: a 'funny' comic drama called *Road to Knock* (terrible); a reincarnation of the *Heidi* story; and the charity telethon-type shows. Disabled people are certainly being paraded around in the name of entertainment. However, the biggest hypocrisy I found was when I tried to use a film clip of *My Left Foot*. The woman from Granada said, 'No! Not even a still. The film has nothing to do with disability.'

It is about Christy Brown I was told. I said that Christy was a disabled person and wrote about himself as such. 'No' was still the answer. Yet Channel Four was showing the film at the launch of the *Disabling World* week. I was also stopped from using anything from *Sunrise at Campobello* – about President Franklin Roosevelt having polio. In the end I wondered what Christy and Franklin would say about all this! Then I wondered if I was doing the right thing.

Notes
1. S. Dwoskin, *Film Is* (Peter Owen, 1975) and *Ha, Ha! (La Solution Imaginaire) with Photography* (New York: The Smith, 1993).

5.3

Whose Project?
Jerry Rothwell

From 'Means of Production', *Mediawise, Mental Health Media Quarterly*, Winter 1990/91.

Jerry Rothwell is a community media worker and co-ordinator of Fastforward, a Mental Health Media project which supports the use of video and multimedia by people with learning difficulties.

Over the last few years, there has been a great upsurge in the establishment of video projects, with the aim of 'giving disabled people a voice'. Some of these are excellent; others in reality allow little opportunity for creative or expressive development by the disabled people involved. Valley and Vale is a film and video workshop that has been working with disabled people for some time, and their video *A Trade in Wind* was made with people who have experienced mental distress. Jerry Rothwell outlines usefulness of community video in empowerment.

I approached the younger man, who held a notebook in his hand, to which he frequently referred. 'What is your name?', he inquired. I gave it, and he referred to his book and verified my statement. 'I am very anxious to leave this asylum,' I said. 'I am not mentally ill. I have no delusions, nor am I suffering from any form of insanity.' The superintendent here heard my voice, and turning round, placed his hand on my shoulder. 'This was a very bad one,' he said. He drew me away from the commissioner, who was already addressing another patient, and my opportunity vanished, my hopes sank to zero.

The label of 'mental illness' often brings with it a denial of the right to be heard. The woman who wrote this account in 1909, Marcia Hamilcar, had been waiting for weeks for this opportunity to make her case to the commissioners responsible for the asylum in which she was held, on their irregular visits. Marcia Hamilcar was fortunate in that she, at least, had access to a pen and notebook, in which she could record the everyday injustices she faced and voice her own opinions of them. These notes ultimately became the basis of her book, *Legally Dead: Experiences during Seventeen Weeks Detention in a Private Asylum.*

Today the classification of 'mental illness' can still carry this invalidation of your opinions, suspension of your civil rights and lack of consultation about the issues that directly affect your welfare. Video and broadcasting have perhaps taken over from publishing as the dominant media through which we can communicate perspectives and opinions about our society. But most of us are restricted from participating in this particular cultural forum by prohibitive costs, legislation, professionalisation and the commercial and political interests which surround it. The theme of mental health has long fascinated film-makers, but despite the large number of films and television programmes which deal with the subject, there have been few opportunities for people who have been classified as 'mentally ill' to represent themselves and their interests on screen.

In the last thirty years there have been various responses to this media monopoly by disenfranchised groups: the guerrilla television of the 60s, film workshops of the 70s and the independent media sector of the 80s, encouraged by the promised commitment of the emerging Channel Four. At the beginning of the 90s, however, community video – which enables views and experiences which are not usually seen in the media – is at a low ebb. Workshops have been encouraged by funders to look upon themselves increasingly as media trainers (for those wanting to work full-time in the film and TV industries) directing money and energy away from facilitating grass-roots production. Correspondingly, there has been a disillusionment with poor-quality community videos and the lack of effective distribution.

However, successful community video productions can play a significant role not only in voicing those opinions that are usually unheard, but in empowering those involved to participate in developments and decisions that affect their lives. My own experience as a video worker working with survivors to produce and screen *A Trade in Wind* has affirmed this.

The video was made by two people who have experienced mental distress, working in conjunction with Valley and Vale, a community arts team in South Wales. The aim of the project was to enable them to address mental health issues using video. 'Madness' is a cultural , social and political definition which needs to be publicly questioned by those who find themselves on the wrong side of it.

The project began by using discussion and role-play to explore the experiences of people in the group and their contact with psychiatric institutions. Participants then learned basic skills in video production to enable them to turn these ideas into a short video, which they were able to use to initiate debate about the participation of survivors in the planning of mental health services and to campaign for their right to discuss their own treatment.

Gaining technical skills and having editorial control over the video was a crucial feature of the project. The views of those who have experienced mental distress are increasingly being sought by broadcasters and the makers of training films on mental health issues. While this is to be welcomed, it is not a substitute for real power over the production of those programmes. Too often, interviews are used to give an appearance of consultation in programmes which neither challenge the marginalisation of survivors in the organisation of services, nor question the prevailing medical and administrative orthodoxies.

Screening the video has been as important as the process of producing it, it has allowed us to draw attention to people who are often remote and inaccessible to the groups they service: administrators, policy-makers, trainers and broadcasters. Each screening has been introduced by the makers of the tape and been followed by a discussion about the issues it raises. As well as giving the group confidence, this has also given them a forum to put across a user's perspective to mental health professionals. The video enables the group to put their own experiences on the agenda, to start a dialogue, to work towards the redressing of the power imbalances that exist in debates about mental health issues – between therapist and 'client', administrator and 'patient', those whose work requires the use of labels and those who are labelled.

Whose Video?
Gill Whalley

From 'Who's in Charge around Here', *Fastforward News* (Mental Health Media), Autumn 1994.

Gill Whalley has worked with children and adults with learning difficulties for the last twelve years. This includes teaching, project development work and working with self-advocacy and women's groups. She is presently working as a tutor for the Open University.

Video has opened many opportunities for people with learning difficulties to explore issues and use their voice. This piece by Gill Whalley follows the progress of a self-advocacy project with people with learning difficulties in which she was involved. It shows the complexity in the processes of negotiation which genuinely ensure involvement, and the degree of sensitivity that is essential if disabled people involved in such projects are not to feel 'used' or actually become 'used' rather than 'users'.

There is a natural link between video and self-advocacy work. As a medium, video is accessible and immediate. It provides many self-advocacy groups with the opportunity to communicate their views to wider audiences and to produce their own videos in ways which can be validating and empowering. For this to be meaningful, however, it is vital that groups control and direct the actual process of video-making.

Using the language of self-advocacy is very easy. In my experience, however, any work that attempts to be genuinely student-led is fraught with conflict and compromise. Video, maybe because of its immediacy, often seems to bring these issues to a head.

In this contribution, I want to describe the making of a video and pack, entitled 'No Means No' which was produced by a group of women with learning difficulties in Walsall. The group started meeting two and a half years before and had worked on a range of issues to do with women's safety and sexuality. The impetus for the work had come from the women's own, often very negative experiences. In terms of our way of working, the processes within the group were always seen as vitally important. Everything we did was designed to develop the women's confidence and self-esteem.

Fairly early on, the women were keen to share their work with other women with learning difficulties. There are obviously many pressures on women with learning difficulties to internalise and individualise their experiences. Within each session we would work on messages that the group might want to give other women to try and break down

Photo courtesy of Kate Green

this sense of isolation. Very quickly the idea of making a video developed and in January 1993 we were lucky enough to secure the funding to make this a reality. At the same time the women received a grant to organise their own women's safety conference for other women with learning difficulties.

Central to all of this work was the issue of power. It was vital that control of the materials and the conference should stay with the group, that the video remained a vehicle for the women to say what they wanted to say. As workers we saw our role as being to protect that process. This entails a way of working that can be slow, fragmented, disjointed and incredibly time-consuming. Trying to fit that into a time limited framework of deadlines and external agendas can prove complex. Maintaining the purity of the process against these pressures and constraints was agonising and at times impossible.

The group had a very clear sense of what messages they wanted the video to communicate but our way of working was also shaped by the pressure of wanting to produce the video for the conference. Eventually the group made the decision that they would employ a worker to film and provide the technical expertise for the video. The worker was interviewed and provided with a clear remit by the group who were to direct and retain editorial control of the final video.

While this model offers advantages, it has the potential for many problems. Some of these are practical. Very early on, the video hit technical problems when borrowed equipment failed to work. This meant that both the material and the time left to work with was severely restricted. The editing process can be highly complex – at times inaccessible to students. All the time I was acutely aware of the power of both my own and the video worker's interventions and of the tremendous significance they carried with the group.

The first version of 'No Means No' carried all the technical problems that had been encountered when filming. In addition, the women's group felt uncomfortable with the actual content. Some of these tensions were around the different perceptions of the professional's role: how far should and can the group process go in editing the final video? While it had initially been agreed that the group should have ultimate control, how far could this go in practice? It became obvious that there were many issues which really needed unravelling.

To the group, however, the video no longer felt theirs. Once we had reached this stage it was clear that it needed to be reshot. Eventually we were able to do this.

We worked with the same model of professional video workers, shooting under the direction of the group, but this time within the framework of a very tightly written contract – spelling out the different roles and responsibilities and defining the decision-making processes we wanted to observe.

Despite all the problems that had gone before it, the video was remade with enthusiasm. The women have a tremendous feeling of pride in the final product, and a strong sense of owning both the video and photo pack that accompanies it. They have undoubtedly gained skills and confidence through this work. However, it is useful to place these gains in a wider context. The pack contains a picture of a woman holding a condom, which became the subject of a complaint from the woman's father, a complaint which resulted in a formal investigation from the Authority. During the course of this investigation, the woman concerned, one of the group's most active members, changed her mind and said that she had never wanted to participate in the group in the first place. The packs had to be changed to remove her picture and a legal disclaimer placed on every page as well as on the video.

People with learning difficulties are probably one of the most powerless and disadvantaged groups in society. In many areas of their life they are marginalised, manipulated or ignored. The work we do has perhaps to be seen against this context: apparent steps forward can in reality be tenuous and insecure.

Video, however, provides people with learning difficulties with an invaluable tool to not only express themselves but to experience that communication in positions of control. Controlling and owning the video-making process is probably easier to write and talk about than to do – in practice, maybe it becomes about degrees of involvement, tinged with pragmatism and compromise, a process which involves constant struggle. Within that process, however, there are undoubtedly many gains and benefits for the students themselves.

Whose Festival?

Stephen Dwoskin

From 'The Others and Too Much', *DAM* vol. 3 no. 1, Spring 1993. For biographical notes see Part 4, Chapter 14.

The 'festival scene' – even those festivals planned around disability films or videos – are not really organised with a real expectation that disabled people will come along. 'Access', as everywhere, is usually an afterthought, but more surprising is that lack of distinction that non-disabled people make in their own products 'about disability' and those made by disabled people. Stephen Dwoskin encountered what was probably a fairly familiar scene in Italy in 1992.

Last December (2–5 December 1992) produced the First Festival Europeo Cinema Handicap, held in Turin, Italy. To this curious title was added 'Noi, Gli Altri', meaning 'We, the Others', which made it all sound more like a festival of Spaghetti Westerns.

Since they were showing three of my films, they were evidently not showing Spaghetti Westerns. Attempts, before the festival, to get some basic information were extremely enigmatic and, like the Italian post, very irregular. However, since I have a good friend in Turin, I eventually got some answers to questions such as did they want the films as film or on video? Did they have an accessible hotel? At this point I discovered the festival was being organised through the office of 'Assessorata Assistenza Sanita' of Turin – something like the Social Service Department over here. This explained the long delays in communication and the absence of concrete film information. I did discover that it was funded by the City and Province of Turin and the European Commission of Social Affairs, with the collaboration of EUCREA (European Association for Creativity by and with Disabled Persons).

Once there, I soon realised that it was neither like a film festival nor was most of the work made by people with disabilities. All the films were on video and were presented by video projection – a process causing extra visual fatigue and the softening of images. These screenings were arranged between those films in competition and those out. The criteria used to make the selection are beyond me. They certainly had nothing to do with either the date of the film, the nature of the content, nor the length. There were fourteen films in competition, seven of which were Italian, the majority being short films. There were twelve films out of competition, including Jo Pearson's *All in Your Head*. Only the films in competition had simultaneous translation; there was no signing nor subtitling.

Undoubtedly, the most disturbing thing about this festival of 'Handicapped

Cinema' was the fact that most of the films were made by non-disabled people about disabled people. As such, they were mostly documentaries and recordings of therapy or theatre groups for disabled people. Examples of the competition material presented included the very commercial-looking *Ruckblick*, a film of the Amici Dance Group's performance of their stage production. The Amici Dance Group includes some performers with disabilities. (*Ruckblick* was listed as a British entry although it was a Japanese production and directed by a non-disabled British director). Another film, from The Netherlands, *Tekens Op De Vloer* (title not translated into English), followed the making of a dance performance with a mentally handicapped person. These two examples were runner-ups for one of three prizes. The winner of the first prize was a messy and sexist Italian film entitled *Note a Margine* (not translated) about a disabled male who supposedly has no mobility, gesture or verbal communication getting sexually interested in the young and pretty nurses (and vice versa). It was made by another non-disabled director, and certainly won the first prize of five million lire (£2,500) for local political reasons. Of the films in competition deserving more attention in this documentary framework was a French film called *Orphée et Eurydice*. It was well made in film terms, and allowed the performers to be seen with autonomy, feeling and sensitivity – not, as in other cases, performers in rehabilitation centres.

After a couple of days I began to consider that this festival was perhaps exploitative and political rather than a serious attempt to spotlight the work of disabled people. In the first place, there were very few disabled people involved, either as guests, as film directors, or as organisers. There were few disabled people in the audience, but the overall audience attendance was, in any case, small. As far as I could tell, I was the only disabled film director. Only the British and the French had disabled representatives from EUCREA (Sian Vasey was the British representative). One member of the jury, from France, was a wheelchair user. The films were from only four of the twelve EC countries (Britain, Italy, Holland and France), so it wasn't representative of Europe. Out of a total of twenty-six films projected (in and out of competition), fourteen were Italian (and one somehow or other was from the USA). And yet there were also EUCREA representatives attending from Spain, Belgium, Luxembourg, Portugal, Greece and Germany.

In the end, this First Festival Europeo Cinema Handicap became a mini-pastiche of a *festival à la conférence*. On the final day, and in pink marble surroundings, the awards were given. Speeches were made, and some fancy attempts to show clips from the prize-winning films was endured. Prior to this were some long discussions, laid out like some UN conference, but addressing familiar problems – such as lack of access – and declarations that it will be better somewhere, someday. There were no serious discussions on the cinema. A relatively fair amount of money went into this event and so I reckon that 'We, the Others' referred to the bureaucrats collecting the handshakes. Oh, by the way, I did win a prize. It wasn't among the three prizes. It was a Special Prize resulting from a controversy on the jury – about Cinema and Disability? It is a football cup.

Whose Conference?
David Hevey

Extracts from Chapter 7, 'Revolt of the Species', *The Creatures Time Forgot: Photography and Disability Imagery* (London: Routledge, 1992), pp. 99–104. For biographical notes see Part 4, Chapter 13.

These extracts from *The Creatures Time Forgot* are about the politics of protest – the staking of ownership claims in debates around disability which in the past have been framed by non-disabled people in their own terms. The conference 'Putting People in the Brief' was one such event, taking its title from an advertising agency's executive remark that 'The issue of impact [of charity advertising] on the lives of disabled people has not come up – it's not in the brief.'[1] But while it raised legitimate debate around the subject of disability images in charity advertising, the degree of involvement of disabled people in the debate was questioned; disabled people with particular interests and expertise in this area thought that they too were not in the conference brief. This is an account of how they succeeded in gaining limited participation, then later set up their own conference, called 'Cap in Hand', to initiate more disabled-controlled work around images.

REVOLT OF THE SPECIES

If we are to create political disability imagery which mobilises disabled people into self-love and action, then the dual process of subjective and objective identification is vital. This is a long way from the standard left 'dialectical' imagery of 'struggle' v. 'victim' observed abstractedly (the Miranda syndrome), which essentially fails because the viewer can pity but not become. The position of total victim is unlivable. As James Baldwin put it, 'The victim who is able to articulate the situation of the victim has ceased to be a victim; he, or she, has become a threat.'[2]

So, how does this work in the disability *realpolitik?* Arguably, one of the key battles for the disability movement on the issue of disability representation came when the King's Fund Centre organised a conference on disability imagery entitled 'Putting People in the Brief' in 1989. This was to be the back-up and confirmation of the consultancy paper entitled 'They Are Not in the Brief' written by non-disabled disability consultant Susan Scott-Parker. Both 'dealt with' disability representation but, as both titles suggest, the nearest this came to being named was in a 'they'. The issue of disability imagery in charity advertising was to be discussed and several prominent members of both the charitable and advertising sectors were invited. Certain disabled people were invited while others, who had clearly been involved in the politics of disability representation but who might widen the remit beyond the 'reformist' agenda of the day, were not.

This, however, changed. Some of us who were not initially invited to the seminar called a meeting to which disabled people who had been invited and disabled people who had not been invited to the King's Fund Conference came. Non-disabled allies like Camerawork attended.[3] It was important to build on the

Photo courtesy of David Hevey

links between the disability movement and allies and prevent the charities, to use Aneurin Bevan's joke, from claiming medals from the battles they lost! I wrote a series of demands which the group endorsed. These we intended to distribute at the conference if we did gain admittance, or to distribute from a picket line if we didn't.

We demanded that any charity advertising guidelines should be written and controlled by disabled people and we pointed out that charities and ad agencies would never change their advertising without the employment of disabled people in positions of power at all levels of the process. We insisted that a fundamental shift of power to disabled people and away from charity had to be based on the social model of disability and 'be adopted throughout the concepts and thinking of charities'.[4] The demands continued to state that the disability issue was one of rights, not of charity, and that the charities and their advertising were not incidental nor were they working for us. They were a key site of struggle when they 'project through their very influential poster-campaigns negative stereotypes of isolated hopelessness'.

The eight-point paper continued to take apart the smug self-congratulatory feel of the day, and ended with the demand that the King's Fund Centre support disabled controlled solutions to charity advertising and not sponsor yet more non-disabled control dressed up as help. As I put it at the time, 'Remember, Othello was black, not blacked-up!'

An ad hoc committee was formed by disabled people and planned to picket the seminar to force changes. However, those of us who were initially considered non-desirable were suddenly invited. Although still a significant minority, the day was an important struggle and a success from our point of view. It undoubtedly created a lot of animosity but resulted in the King's Fund Centre agreeing to fund the Disabled-Only Ad Hoc Group (renamed as the Media Images Group and affiliated to the British Council of Organisations of Disabled People) to set up a steering group and commission a research document outlining a code of ethics for the portrayal of disabled people in charity advertising and the media. This report by Colin Barnes pulls together ideas of what makes a disability image negative or positive within the media, then it outlines the structure by which disabled and non-disabled people can read the signs. This structure will provide markers for complaints, for example. There is no doubt that this document will provide an important text for controlling future charity advertising.[5]

It appears that the mountain has indeed come to Mohammed. However, although image guidelines and ethics are an important area of disability intervention, it has to be remembered that as a critical response to an oppressive form, they are unlikely to contain a process for the counter-formation of alternative imagery. Their site of struggle is still within 'the belly of the beast', critiquing images set within oppressive structures. That notwithstanding, and given that 'ethics' are unlikely to contain the depth of critical analysis that other photographic theory and practice contain, they are none the less a political step forward because they are mobilised by the 'task' of the disability movement, whereas the previous photographic theory described, no matter how important it might be, is generally not. Codes, ethics, critiques and so on which seek to change non-disabled controlled disability/impairment imagery are welcomed because they establish the issue of representation in many parties' minds, but their ability to shift the balance of power towards disabled people and disabled people's cultural representation is unlikely to be within the ethics themselves.

And, of course, the setting-up of non-statutory codes, ethics and voluntary self-regulation by charities and others may be particularly welcomed, but probably further softened, by non-disabled people. Most charities and voluntary sector organisations recognise that there is no way forward other than reform, but they do so under silent protest. The 'bargain', if we are not extremely careful, will be struck.[6] The bargain, as Paul Longmore has pointed out, is that the access struggle is not named, physical barriers are not named, and the disability 'problem' is discussed in the realm of 'attitudes'.[7] The positive representation bargain, with the charities' endorsement of the code of ethics, is that they will 'positively' represent impairments if we agree not to represent charities as disablers! The representational bargain met its historical height with the acceptance by the American people of disabled president Franklin Delano Roosevelt. Of the 35,000 photographs of President Roosevelt, only two (and these were never published) showed him seated in his wheelchair.[8] Roosevelt and the media correctly understood the power of photography in the representation, or not in this case, of disablement and constructed a structured absence of his impairment or disablement worthy of Stalin's exit of Trotsky from images of the Bolshevik Revolution. There can be no doubt that Roosevelt, from the time he contracted polio in 1921 to his death in 1945, not only acquiesced in this vision of himself but acquiesced 'positively'. The reformation of oppressive imagery is only important (or, at least, more than superficially) if it is linked to wider social issues, such as access.

Codes of ethics have to be clear whether they are asking non-disabled organisations to be 'positive' about the impairment or 'positive' about the disablement and what a positive (or, for that matter, negative) relationship to each really is. 'Positive' should mean the naming of the site of struggle and the group's or individual's relationship to it. 'Positive' should not be the denial, disavowal or suppression of the struggle and oppression. Of course, the reality of positive imagery is that it is not a free-floating self-referential form. Its meaning is anchored in its context, distribution and *task*. Therefore, the issue of disability representation has to be tied to the general movement for rights. If non-disabled organisations do support our representational struggles, and there are clear signs that this is happening,[9] then we have to build into this support a 'clause' whereby image-politics become a part of the struggle for access, not an excuse for it. Otherwise, the replacement of the issue of 'attitudes' for the issue of access will be echoed by the replacement of plastic images for physical access.

Clearly, we are in an inherently passive and unstable position if we remain *exclusively* in the approval/disapproval relationship to charity and media disability imagery. In a sense, this position is the classic position of most viewers and consumers of photographic imagery, even those who take their own images. Barthes wrote that photography and the photograph, like original (that is, historical) theatre, record the relationship of the dead to the living. In photography, all that is photographed is dead in the sense that it has passed on.[10] The visual moment reflected back to us is a reflection of something past. It is from this position of reading, which must affect all those who consume imagery, that the roots of the passification of disabled people in relation to oppressive disability imagery are entwined with the existing physical marginalisation which the charities and other forms of non-disabled representation practise. There is nothing fatalistic in this position, the important thing is to be aware of it and to question what is to be done about it.

The role of disabled groups such as the BCODP Media Images group is clearly to challenge the 'tragedy principle' of the media and charity portrayal of disabled people. However, the pressure-group position is not enough. Disabled people have given notice of a refusal to occupy the victim position. We, as disabled people, have become a threat. This threat has to be converted into power and analysis. Not for nothing is the lesbian symbol a double-headed axe. We need a two-pronged approach. One head of our axe is the 'ethics' pressure cited previously. The other might be the further intervention in the image discourse from the position of the subject. The root of this process lies more in radical drama theory than photographic theory.

Notes

1. Susan Scott-Parker, 'They Aren't in the Brief', a discussion paper for the King's Fund Centre (London: The King's Fund Centre, 1989).

2. Quoted in Jo Spence and Rosie Martin, 'Photo-therapy: Psychic Realism as a Healing Art?', TEN-8 no. 30, Autumn 1988, p. 2.

3. Camerawork Gallery also organised the disabled-only conference, 'Cap in Hand', February 1991 in response to the King's Fund Centre Conference.

4. The ad hoc group's eight-point paper to the King's Fund Centre, drafted by David Hevey.

5. Colin Barnes, *Disabling Imagery and the Media: An Exploration of the Principles for Media Representations of Disabled People* (Halifax: Ryburn with BCODP, 1992).

6. Mary Johnson, 'The Bargain', *The Disability Rag*, September/October 1988, pp. 5–8.

7. Ibid. p. 6.

8. Hugh G. Gallagher, FDR's *Splendid Deception* (New York: Dodd Mead & Co., 1985).

9. A glossary of some of the organisations which have given substantial economic support for the entire *Creatures* project (which comprises the book, a national poster series, a touring exhibition, a training pack and a seminar) includes the Arts Council of Great Britain, the Greater London Arts, Camerawork Gallery (London), the Rowntree Foundation (UK), etc. All of them are non-disabled controlled.

10. Roland Barthes, *Camera Lucida: Reflections on Photography*, trans. Richard Howard (London: Fontana Paperbacks, 1984), p. 31.

Media Guidelines
Colin Barnes

From Part Three, 'Principles for Media Representations of Disabled People', of *Disabling Imagery and the Media: An Exploration of the Principles for Media Representations of Disabled People* (Halifax: Ryburn with BCODP, 1992).

Colin Barnes lectures in the School of Sociology and Social Policy at Leeds University. He is a researcher for BCODP (the British Council of Organisations of Disabled People) and is author of *Disabled People in Britain: A Case for Anti-Discrimination Legislation*.[1] He has a particular interest in education and is involved with the Integration Alliance, an organisation promoting inclusive education.

Disabling Imagery in the Media **came from the research project that followed the two conferences, 'Putting People in the Brief' and 'Cap in Hand', discussed in Part Five, Chapter Six. It was published as a 'first paper' so that its recommendations are useful rather than the definitive or last word on the subject.**

In the first part of this chapter, Barnes looks at changing disability language. There are in fact numerous 'guides to the representation of disabled people in the media' within broadcasting organisations or published by organisations both *of* and *for* disabled people. However, many are simple sets of 'don'ts' and no guide is of more than booklet size, although some[2] give more explanation around terminology than others.

In the USA there is a Media Access Office (MAO) as a central point of reference and activity, and some of the problematic language such as 'physically challenged' and 'differently able' (not generally accepted or promoted here but delightful to journalists who need to brighten up their columns) are US imports. However, it is notable that in more recent work from the States there appears to be more rigour in the discussion around terminology.[3]

The current limited concentration on language in Britain is partly a recognition that though important, it is not the most active element in change. More importantly, it is seen as having a distracting effect when the major item on the disability agenda is civil rights legislation. Nevertheless, disabled people are sensitive to language and the debate around changing language is of intrinsic interest and relevance to many. And Barnes helpfully makes clear (for those people who are still uncertain and confused) what the difference between 'disabled people' and 'people with disabilities' is, and why some disabled people using the social model might strongly prefer the former over the latter. In the second part of the chapter, Barnes sets out some principles that he thinks would move the representation of disabled people in a more positive direction.

THE LANGUAGE OF DISABILITY

Society's misconceptions about disabled people are constantly being reinforced by disabling terms like 'cripple', 'spastic', and 'idiot'. Of course there is nothing inherently wrong with these terms, it is simply that their meaning has been substantially devalued by societal perceptions of disabled people; in short, they have been turned into terms of abuse. Their continued use contributes significantly to the negative self-image of disabled people and, at the same time, perpetuates discriminatory attitudes and practices among the general public.

In the same way that lesbians, gay men, black people, members of minority ethnic groups and women have identified the power of language in the promotion of heterosexism, homophobia, racism and sexism, so too disabled people are sensitive to the ways in which words cultivate institutional discrimination.

Consequently, a major aim of the British Council of Organisations of Disabled People (BCODP) and the disability rights movement in general is the elimination of disablist language in books, in libraries, in schools and in the media. Therefore, all those who work in the communications media are asked to alert themselves to unacceptable terminology and refrain from using it.

Unfortunately this is not as simple as it sounds because many of the terms commonly used in relation to disability are used interchangeably and mean different things to different people. Much of this confusion stems from definitions of disability devised by non-disabled people who work in official bodies like the Office of Populations Censuses and Surveys and the World Health Organisation. Based on able-bodied assumptions about the experience of disablement these organisations define disability as the relationship between impairment and handicap. 'Impairment' refers to a defective limb, organ or mechanism of the body; 'disability' is the resulting lack of function; and 'handicap' denotes the limitations on daily living that result from disability.

Rejected by disabled people and their organisations these meanings individualise and medicalise the problems associated with living with impairment. Their whole focus is on the individual and their perceived inadequacy – restrictive environments and disabling barriers are effectively ignored. They ensure that disabled people are held responsible for any difficulties they encounter during the course of their daily lives.

In contrast the British Council of Organisations of Disabled People (BCODP) favour an approach similar to that developed by the Union of Physically Impaired Against Segregation in 1976, and later adopted and adapted by the Disabled People's International (DPI) – the first international organisation controlled and run by disabled people – in 1981. Hence, although increasingly recognised as attributable to social causes also,[4] the term 'impairment' refers to individually based functional limitations – whether physical, intellectual sensory or hidden – but 'disability' is the loss or limitation of opportunities to take part in the normal life of the community on an equal level with others due to physical and social barriers.[5]

This shift of emphasis not only makes the problem of terminology much simpler, but also identifies the main cause of disability – a highly discriminatory society which penalises those who do not conform to able-bodied perceptions of normality. 'Disablism', therefore, refers to prejudice, stereotyping or 'institutional discrimination' against disabled people.

It also means that the phrase 'people with disabilities' is incorrect – people

Disabled women reject the Guardian's helpless Britannia advert,
courtesy of Brenda Prince/Format

have impairments, they do not have disabilities. Additionally, though the tendency to place the noun 'people' before 'disability' is viewed positively because it emphasises the fact that individuals with impairments are in fact people – something which historically has been denied – it has a number of important implications which need to be explained.

First, 'people with disabilities' assumes that disability is the property of the individual and not of society. Here the terms 'disabilities' and 'disability' refer to a medical condition; and 'person with a disability' can easily be substituted by 'person with cerebral palsy' or 'person with multiple sclerosis', etc. As we have seen, disabled people and their organisations have rejected the implications of

the medical model of disability.

Secondly, by linking 'disability' to 'impairment' this phrase conveniently sidesteps the consequences of institutional discrimination against disabled people – poverty, dependence and social isolation – and, by implication, the need for change.

Thirdly, it is an explicit denial of a political or 'disabled identity'. Since the emergence of the disability rights movement the word 'disabled' before 'people' or 'person' has come to signify identification with this collective identity. Phrases such as 'people with disabilities' undermine that identity.

Referring to disabled people as 'handicapped' stems from the notion that the whole of life is a competition – as in horse racing or in golf – and implies that

and disability are not the same thing and should never be confused.

Emotive terms like 'afflicted', 'stricken', 'sufferer' and 'victim' in sentences relating to a particular condition or impairment must be avoided. They are subjective and place the writer's set of values on the individual or group being described. Examples include: 'afflicted/stricken with polio', 'multiple sclerosis victim/sufferer'. Also phrases like 'confined to a wheelchair' or 'wheelchair bound' are inappropriate. Wheelchairs empower rather than confine – they are a mobility aid just like a pair of shoes.

Finally, it should be noted that this list is not exhaustive and occasionally meanings are subject to change. When in doubt check with an organisation controlled and run by disabled people. Information about these organisations can be obtained from the British Council of Organisations of Disabled People.

they will not do well. Also 'handicap' has allusions to 'cap in hand' and begging. Neither term is acceptable to the disabled community.

Use of phrases such as 'the impaired', 'the disabled', 'the handicapped', 'the blind', 'the deaf', 'the deaf and dumb', 'the crippled' tend to dehumanise and objectify disabled people and should be avoided. It is also offensive to label someone by their impairment. For example: an 'epileptic' or an 'arthritic'. Where it is absolutely necessary to refer to an individual's impairment it is better to say 'has epilepsy' or 'has arthritis'.

Words and phrases that characterise disabled people as dependent or pitiable and/or which perpetuate the myth that disabled people are incapable of participating in the life of the community should also be avoided. For example: the meaning of 'invalid' is clear – in-valid. In general terms it connotes illness. Illness

THE PORTRAYAL OF DISABLED PEOPLE IN THE MEDIA

Recruitment of disabled people

Following the recommendations made at the 'Cap in Hand' conference, there must be more effort to recruit disabled people to work in mainstream media organisations. Disablist imagery will only disappear if disabled people are integrated at all levels into the media.

Disability equality training

There is an urgent need for more disability equality training (DET), organised and sponsored by disabled people and their organisations for all media employees. To combat negative portrayals of disabled people media personnel must be fully aware of the implications for society of their continued production. There has been some encouraging signs over the last two years in some areas of the media, but there is still much room for improvement.

Accessible media content

Media personnel should strive to ensure that all media content is produced in accessible forms for disabled people. For example, all TV programmes should be accompanied by sign language and subtitles for deaf people and all print media should be widely available in braille or on tape for blind people. This provision need not encroach on mainstream services but their availability should be well publicised. Such a policy sends a clear signal to the non-disabled community that disabled people are valued members of society and must be integrated accordingly.

Language and terminology

All media personnel must be aware of the disabling impact of language and avoid using inappropriate terminology. This is particularly relevant to journalists and reporters because of the psychological effects of discrimination; many disabled people have internalised their oppression to the extent that they describe themselves in stereotypical and derogatory ways. Often emotive words have become so indelibly linked to specific impairments, reinforced by the subjective judgments of 'carers' and others, that they are used unconsciously. Hence, intelligent and sensitive reporting is sometimes necessary so that the true feelings and beliefs of disabled people are revealed rather than simply the regurgitation of familiar clichés.

The employment of disabled actors

Where possible all portrayals of disabled characters in the media should be played by disabled actors. As it is no longer acceptable for white actors to play black people, it should also be unacceptable for non-disabled actors to play disabled characters. Since there may be a shortage of disabled actors it is important that writers, producers, directors, agencies and advertisers put pressure on colleges and drama schools to take positive steps to recruit and train more disabled people for the acting profession.

Advice and consultation

Authors, scriptwriters, journalists, reporters and advertisers have a responsibility to check the accuracy of their work before it is made public. In order to avoid inaccuracies they should seek advice from organisations controlled and run by disabled people. Information about these organisations can be obtained from the British Council of Organisations of Disabled People.

Accurate portrayals

i. disabled people and discrimination

When portraying disabled people in the media it is important to remember that the general public has little insight into the environmental and social barriers that prevent them from living full and active lives. Living with disability means being confronted with environmental and social barriers daily; any portrayal of disabled people, in whatever context, which does not reflect this experience is both grossly inaccurate and a major cause of their continued existence.

ii. disabled people and charity

Avoid depicting disabled individuals as receivers of charity. Show disabled people interacting with both disabled and non-disabled people as equals; giving as well as receiving. Too often disabled individuals are presented solely as recipients of pity.

iii. disabled people and individuality

Shun one-dimensional characterisations of disabled people. Wherever appropriate, portray disabled people as having individual and complex personalities with a full range of emotions and activities. In common with all human beings, disabled individuals experience a variety of emotions such as happiness, depression, anger, etc., and play an assortment of roles including lover, parent, provider, etc.

This variation should be accurately reflected in media portrayals of disabled people.

iv. disabled people and evil

Avoid presenting physical or intellectual characteristics of any kind as the sole determinants of personality. Be particularly cautious about implying a correlation between impairment and evil.

v. disabled people and disability voyeurism

Refrain from presenting disabled people as objects of curiosity. Disabled individuals should be presented as members of an average population or a cast of characters. Disabled people are generally able to participate in all aspects of community life and should be portrayed in a wide variety of roles and situations.

vi. disabled people and comedy

A disabled individual should not be ridiculed or made the butt of a joke (blind people or people with visual impairments do not drive cars, play darts or bump into everything in their path; despite the myth making of some script writers, rather limited comedians and unscrupulous mainstream advertisers).

vii. disabled people and sensationalism

Avoid the sensational in portrayals of disabled people. Be especially cautious of the stereotype of disabled people as either the victims or the perpetrators of violence.

viii. disabled people and the super cripple

Resist presenting disabled characters with extraordinary abilities or attributes. To do so is to suggest that a disabled individual must over-compensate and become super human to be accepted by society.

ix. disabled people and will-power

Avoid the 'stiff upper lip' type story-line that implies a disabled character need only have the 'will' and the 'right attitude' to succeed.

x. disabled people and sexuality

Avoid showing disabled people as sex-ually abnormal. Do not portray disabled individuals as sexually dead or as sexually degenerate. Show disabled people in loving relationships expressing the same sexual needs and desires as non-disabled people.

xi. disabled people and the disabled population

When depicting disabled people in the media ensure that they are representative of the sexual, racial, ethnic, gender and age divisions in the disabled population as a whole.

Notes

1. C. Barnes, *Disabled People in Britain and Discrimination: A Case for Anti-Discrimination Legislation* (London: C. Hurst and Co. with BCODP, 1991).
2. See, for example, *Disability and Television: Guidelines on Representation for Producers* (Channel Four, 1992).
3. See Jack Nelson, 'Broken Images: Portrayals of Those with Disabilities in the American Media', and Mary Johnson, 'Sticks and Stones: The Language of Disability', in Jack A. Nelson (ed.), *The Disabled, the Media and the Information Age* (Westport, CT: Greenwood Press, 1994).
4. P. Abberley, 'The Concept of Oppression and the Development of a Social Theory of Disability', *Disability, Handicap and Society* vol. 2 no. 1, 1986, pp. 5–19.
5. Barnes, *Disabled People in Britain and Discrimination*.

Rights of Access
Ann Pointon

For biographical notes see Part 3, Chapter 2.

The following piece tries to draw together many disparate but 'relevant' ends. While access has been the one of the themes of the book, we have not offered a substantial discussion in relation to new technology which is enhancing access but is fast changing; nevertheless it will briefly be mentioned in relation to its usefulness for people with sensory impairments.

This piece also links facets of 'access' (whether of access to the built environment or to employment options) to the importance of civil rights legislation for disabled people.

Finally, it comes full circle to issues raised at the start of the book around access to image.

RIGHTS OF ACCESS

'Access' is the disability buzz word of the 90s, but is almost mythic in its elusiveness. Disabled people shout it, write it, demand it, while non-disabled people protest that they have put those ramps in place so why all the fuss? Non-disabled arts and media professionals with some experience of 'access' may also add that they now interpret a number of theatrical performances; subtitle television programmes; provide audiotapes in many museums and galleries; and have even discovered audio-description. Yet, still, disabled people are saying that access as an issue has scarcely been addressed; that it is selective, limited, 'special'; and that it is always costed half-way down the line.

In a barrier-free dream, boundaries would break down. There would be no distinction, for instance, in audience access and access for workers; the product and its channel of transmission would be technologically accessible; and so too would be the means of making that product.

In the recently enacted Disability Discrimination Act (1995), two sections are intended to be effective in preventing discrimination in employment and in the provision of goods and services. The act is not as far-reaching as the Americans with Disabilities Act (ADA) of 1990, or the private members' Civil Rights (Disabled Persons) Bill, which was rejected in Parliament, despite an effective parliamentary campaign and a parallel campaign of demonstration and direct action. Nevertheless, it will raise access questions in a sharper way than before, for all broadcasters and, in the long run, will change assumptions. Currently, for instance, broadcasters like Channel Four are subtitling over 30 per cent of their output, in a process of moving to meet the 50 per cent minimum by 1998 demanded by the Broadcasting Act 1990. One might speculate that this modest but ground-breaking percentage will move upwards as the Disability Discrimination Act starts to affect organisations' long-term planning.

What is obvious is that before Deaf or disabled people can offer adequate critiques or develop the widest understanding of a medium, they need to be able to 'read it'.

ACCESS TO THE PRODUCT: CLOSED CAPTIONS

In terms of access to the commercial product for Deaf people there are some signs of progress. In the USA, for instance, the ADA benefited Deaf people quite crucially in forcing suppliers of television sets to build-in a decoder chip for 'Closed Captions' in sets of over 13 inches, whereas in Britain a video caption decoder must be purchased.

Closed Captions is a system for subtitling ordinary videotapes, giving access to feature films to deaf people who have a decoding system. As George Cole, writing in *Home Entertainment*[1] describes, the system was developed by the National Captioning Institute (NCI), a non-profit making organisation in America, and 5,000 movies have already been captioned (at a cost of around £1,600 per title), with over 400 video titles available in the UK. Captions are converted into codes and placed on an unused picture line, and as deaf viewer Karen Hudson says in the *Home Entertainment* article:

I thought I was managing just fine, and then along comes the caption reader. No longer do I have to stick to visual films full of action and little dialogue. I now watch films that before I would've passed over as boring, such as *Philadelphia* and *Four Weddings and a Funeral*.

. . . AND SIGN LANGUAGE

More recently in Britain, £50,000 of National Lottery money has been awarded to Derby's Royal School for the Deaf to help build Europe's first sign language video library. This is the final phase in the establishment of a £1 million National Sign Language Video Centre, which already has a video studio and editing suite.

The number of theatre performances given with sign interpretation is also growing, although some Deaf people would say this is outpacing the availability of sufficiently skilled interpreters, in what is a very specialist and artistically demanding interpretative role.

ACCESS TO THE PRODUCT: AUDIODESCRIPTION

For people with visual impairments, progress has been slower. Few organisations of any kind, let alone theatres or cinemas are able to provide information in tape, braille or large print.

As far as direct access to the 'product' is concerned, audiodescription is a method whereby visual information is added in sound form to a performance, the first work for which was done in the theatre. For people with visual impairments, audiodescription is already available in some twelve theatres in Britain with important silent information such as gesture, facial expression, and scene being given over headphones.[2] The system was pioneered in the USA by Cody and Dr Margaret Pfanstiehl, with information described by Cody to Margaret, who is blind. And in Britain, playwright Norman King, who was losing his sight through diabetes, introduced audiodescription, first in amateur productions at the Robin Hood Theatre, Averham, then later convincing director Mark Piper of its value for the Windsor Theatre Royal.[3]

Audiodescription is now available with a growing number of feature films, although it is generally non-commercial film theatres which are moving to equip cinemas with the necessary equipment and customer headphones. It has been estimated that in film and television some 50 per cent of information is given visually, so clearly the addition of an audiodescription track makes a substantial difference to the enjoyment of visually impaired cinemagoers.

However, the provision of an audiodescription service on television is a greater technological challenge and progress in Britain is linked to the European Audetel Project which has been investigating the technological problems. A pilot study here with partners BBC/ITV/ITC and the RNIB is also being followed up, in which 100 people were given decoders for a specified research period in which audiodescribed programmes were shown. Already a body of knowledge is being built up and training programmes planned for audiodescribers.[4]

PHYSICAL ACCESS

Problems of access to a location, such as cinema or theatre are easier for non-disabled people to grasp, and many theatres now have access details in their programme leaflets. In the cinema, progress has been much slower, with cinema exhibitors not applying for access grants (for instance through ADAPT – Access for Disabled People to Arts Premises Today), while theatres, museums and galleries take much greater advantage of such help.

Even the National Film Theatre, some fourteen years on from the *Carry on Cripple* season, has such limited access for wheelchair users that it would be difficult to run another disability season in this location.

ACCESS AS STANDARD

But access for the audience is only part of the access issue; being part of an 'audience', while important, is just one of a disabled person's possible roles.

Would-be film and programme-makers, performers, media workers and administrators of every kind want to be able to get to the conference or meeting on time (not twenty minutes late via the kitchen, the goods lift, the guard's van or in the arms of 'two strong men and true'); if Deaf, they want access to what the participants are saying, and, if visually impaired, they will need to have the necessary documents in an accessible form. But in the film and broadcasting industry, as in society generally, sophisticated technology is available to disabled people in only the most limited ways.

The new British 'arrival' at disability as a rights issue may fundamentally change the climate for disabled people. Millee Hill, for instance. comments on a vast difference in approach to disabled people's rights in North America compared to the UK. As she says:

Disabled people are more visible, part of ordinary life there – they don't stand out. The US has the most progressive of attitudes. A lot of that can be put down to their anti-discrimination legislation. It shows on the buses and subways. Canada has a Human Rights Charter – and it shows in the way you're treated, in people's friendliness, willingness to help. Here's the difference: at university in Canada, one of my courses was going to be in a room up a flight of stairs. They changed the class to the ground floor. In the same situation studying in the UK, four men were recruited every time to haul me up. I was in fear of my life in case they slipped.[5]

ACCESS TO IMAGE

It may indeed be particularly difficult for the industry that recycles negative images of disabled people (whether of horror, helplessness, sexlessness, etc.) to separate those images and their metaphorical use from the real disabled people on the street who are its subjects

I don't know any tax lawyer who's an idealist.

Tom Cruise in *The Firm*, CIC Video, closed captions by NCI

and its objects.

Attempts to change these images by film- or programme-makers are not without their contradictions. Longmore[6] describes a number of television dramas that have attempted to include access issues, civil rights or prejudice in the narrative, but have reverted to the treatment of access as an act of generosity that non-disabled people should perform (for instance in an episode of *Alice*, 1984). And film biographies made for TV such as that of Jill Kinmont (*The Other Side of the Mountain* [1977] and *The Other Side of the Mountain, Part II* [1979]) turn on the traditional account of overcoming severe disability, while ignoring Kinmont's struggle to combat discrimination in education and employment.[6]

Longmore gives numerous examples but he identifies more positive developments in advertising starting in the mid-80s, with a number of disabled people appearing in ads for Levi Jeans, McDonalds and Kodak. This trend has yet to bite in British advertising, where the print media is still drowned in charity-

generated images, only some of which have started to edge away from the 'helpless victim' approach, and disability in television advertising is virtually absent. A generally positive attempt by Fuji to include a disabled character in a campaign came to an abrupt end.[7]

Given the variation of experience among disabled people themselves, there is of course no guarantee that in their 'product' there would be no place for the old negative themes and images. According to Darke, disabled people cannot be expected to produce 'loads of right-on stuff'; they will want to make entertainment, some of which may be deeply suspect in disability terms.[8] What could be anticipated, however, is that there would be a much greater range of product, images and treatments of disability on the market.

And there is an increasingly politically aware voice. Not only is there more film and other art output made by disabled people available, and this critical mass of work is valuable in itself, but one can begin to see ways of building up frameworks of analyses that take legitimate and conscious account of the film-maker or artist's encounter with and progress through the experience of disability.

A recent side-by-side review by Paul Darke of two new documentary shorts made by disabled people (Stephen Dwoskin's *Trying to Kiss the Moon* [UK], and Billy Golfus's *When Billy Broke his Head and Other Tales of Wonder* [USA]) interestingly identifies the very different autobiographical approaches of the two men. An experienced film-maker, Stephen Dwoskin, says Darke:

offers us in this, his latest movie, fragments of his life (a life) through old b&w, and colour, home movies and photographs; all beautifully interwoven with inserts from his long line of avantgarde films, personal remi-

'Fortress Falling' courtesy of Sue Elsegood

niscences, extracts from letters to and from friends and family, and apparently disparate images... The *disability* aspects of the film are never explicit but constantly strike at the core of the lives that many of us have led... Dwoskin's residence in Europe has given him the edge over most Stateside disabled film-makers by enabling him to escape from the need to assert one's self as 'normal', and to instead explore the self as being the sum total of his life experiences and not his desires or dreams... There is no linear charac-terisation of the individual, and as such (and as is life) it is both anti-realist, and more realist than any other film I have ever seen. Dwoskin is one of the few people, let alone film-makers, to appreciate the sig-nificance of personal history in the location of the individual in the present; a history that is transformed as the present unravels itself.

In contrast, but also highly rec-ommended by Darke, is Billy Golfus's *When Billy Broke His Head and Other Tales of Wonder.*

As an American film-maker, totally submerged in American culture, Golfus's film, unlike the Eurosensitive Stephen Dwoskin, is very much about the individual. The film's individualism, and somewhat voyeuristic stance takes on the mechanics of disability, gives it a zest of enthusiasm and outraged indignation that carries the viewer along.

Golfus's film is a road movie, or, more precisely, a rights of passage movie; not into adulthood but an awareness of disability politics (the social model of disability, to be exact) by someone who is newly disabled. The manner in which Golfus achieves this, like Dwoskin's *Trying to Kiss the Moon*, is through the recollections and reminiscences of friends, family and new acquaintances. But Golfus's aim and method – which is as equally valid as Dwoskin's – is quite different: Golfus wishes to validate himself as a person who is now, as a disabled person, invalidated by a disabling society.

Golfus, newly disabled in a motorcycle accident, travels the breadth of the USA, meeting the leading lights of the American Disability Movement (ADAPT etc.) and questioning them about the socially constructed nature of disability. One of the problems that I know some viewers will have is the voyeuristic manner in which some of the interviews take place... Plus, as an American, Golfus is very much about asserting his 'normality', or ordinariness. This is a very American production – the antithesis of Dwoskin's film, with its European sensibility – concerned with emphasising the individualistic (and capitalistic) abilities and concerns of the American disabled person as a member of a dispossessed group, who isn't getting his fair share of the nation's spoils or equal treatment. And as much as Golfus is (rightly) concerned with portraying disabled people as a dispossessed group, it is in the American manner of emphasising what the individual can do ('we are really normal people inside' kind of philosophy) against what, and how, the individual experiences their life in relation to others (as in the Dwoskin film). Golfus is concerned with showing what disabled people can do over and above any philosophy or theory of the self.[9]

DISCOVERY

Quite apart from different cultural and artistic approaches, a key difference between these two films is the stage in the experience of disability which both film makers have reached. Golfus is still in the stage of discovery of rights, and indeed of 'disability and community'. As a non-disabled person, one might be attracted to both films, and as a disabled person, these different and quite legitimate starting points would make absolute and non-contradictory sense. But what of other layers and boundaries? As a white disabled woman, one might say that these are the experiences of men and something else remains to be said; as a black disabled person, one would certainly notice the absence of Black participants and images in both; as a Deaf person one might first seek the subtitles.

For people with sensory impairments the technological and linguistic barriers are fundamental. As Rosie Ilett says in 'The Sisters Are Doing It Themselves', for deaf people who use sign language and want direct access to information, the medium is the message. 'Unless performers and information providers are actually from the deaf community itself the full communication needs of deaf people will not be understood and the experiences of deaf people will not be incorporated and reflected.'[10]

But a holistic approach to access is still to come, and it is dependent in a large part on a major shift in the dominant view of disabled people as 'other'. This shift, and the surrendering of some power, is a painful process but unavoidable if a philosophy of 'special' provision for these 'sad' (or 'repellent') beings is to be replaced by a norm of equality of participation in the community.

As Tom Shakespeare argued in 1993, the issues of meaning and representation have been raised, but (with the exception of Jenny Morris's work in her book *Pride Against Prejudice*) have not been effectively explored or developed within British disability theory.[11] One could add to this, as at the beginning of this book, that nor has such exploration or development taken place within British media theory.

Shakespeare argues too that the social model analysis of disability has neglected issues of cultural meaning and representation, and he sees the future as having to go beyond 'reliance on over-deterministic Marxian analogies' and towards other sources such as structural anthropology, psychoanalysis and, crucially, feminism.

His three-fold strategy would centre on the need, first, to develop work around imagery and representation. This might use approaches such as those adopted by Hevey and Barnes to expose stereotypical views and distortions of disabled people ('nailing the lie') both as a negative process of resistance and positive campaigns to present alternative images based on strength and pride. Secondly would come a focus of attention on 'environmental processes and social relations which create disability; graphic representations of our exclusion and segregation'. Thirdly, the non-disabled world would become a focus of attention, in order 'to expose the myth of the whole and complete and unflawed body; that is, we must problematise the normal.'

One could argue that this process has already in fact begun, and there are alluring prospects of exciting work, both practical and theoretical, particularly for the next generation of disabled people. And it is worth adding that while this drive for actual and perceived autonomy is in our own creative hands, there certainly should be space for non-disabled allies in this process of social change and radical transformation.

Notes

1. George Cole, Article in *Home Entertainment*, June 1995.
2. Alison Silverwood, Audiodescription, *DAM*, vol. 2 no. 4, Winter 1992.
3. Ibid.
4. See Bibliography for Audetel reports.
5. M. Hill, *London Disability News*, May 1993, p. 4.
6. Paul K. Longmore, 'Screening Stereotypes: Images of Disabled People in Television and Motion Pictures', in A. Gartner and T. Joe (eds), *Images of the Disabled: Disabling Images* (New York: Praeger, 1987).
7. Emily Bell, 'Fuji: Every Picture Tells a Story', the *Observer*, 22 July 1990.
8. P. Darke, Booklet notes to Bristol Watershed's *Screening Lies*, Disability Film Season, June–August 1995.
9. P. Darke, 'Autobiographies of Discovery', *DAM* vol. 5, no. 2, Summer 1995.
10. R. Ilett, 'The Sisters Are Doing It Themselves', *DAM* vol. 4, no.4, Winter 1994.
11. Tom Shakespeare, 'Re-presenting Disabled People', review of three books in *Disability and Society* vol. 8, no. 1, 1993.

Select Bibliography

Background

Barnes, C., Disabled People in Britain: A Case for Anti-Discrimination Legislation (London: Hurst/British Council of Organisations of Disabled People, 1991).

Driedger, Diane, The Last Civil Rights Movement: Disabled People's International (New York: St. Martin's Press, 1989).

Gillespie-Sells, K., and Ruebain, D., Disability: Double the Prejudice and Double the Struggle (London: Channel Four, 1992). [Booklet on gay/lesbian disability issues]

Gregory, S., and Hartley, G., Constructing Deafness (Milton Keynes: Pinter/Open University, 1991).

Keith, Lois (ed.), Mustn't Grumble: Writing by Disabled Women (London: The Women's Press, 1994).

Lane, Harlan, When the Mind Hears: A History of the Deaf (Harmondsworth: Penguin, 1988).

Morris, Jenny, Disabled Lives (London: BBC Education, 1992). [Booklet]

Morris, Jenny, Pride Against Prejudice: Transforming Attitudes to Disability (London: The Women's Press Ltd, 1992).

Oliver, M., The Politics of Disablement (London: Macmillan Education Ltd, 1990).

Pagel, M., On Our Own Behalf: An Introduction to the Self-Organisation of Disabled People (Greater Manchester Coalition of Disabled People, 1988). [Booklet]

Rieser, R., and Mason, M., Disability in the Classroom: A Human Rights Issue (London: Disability in Education, 1992) [2nd edn from: 78 Mildmay Grove, London N1 4PJ]

'Representation and Disabled People', Disability and Society vol. 9 no. 3, 1994 [Special Issue].

Swain, J., Finkelstein, V., French, S., and Oliver, M., Disabling Barriers, Enabling Environments (London: Sage Publications/Open University, 1993).

Taylor, G., Bishop, J. (eds), Being Deaf; the Experience of Deafness (Milton Keynes: Pinter/Open University, 1991).

Equal opportunities and access

ADAPTations to Access-ability (Dunfermline: ADAPT Trust, 1995).

Arts and Disability Directory, 3rd edn (London: Arts Council of Great Britain, 1994).

The AUDETEL Project, Audio Description of Television for the Visual Disabled and Elderly, Final Report: Volume I, Strategies for Manufacturing and Networking; Volume II, Optimisation of an Audio Description Service for Visually Handicapped and Elderly People. Human and Technical Factors; Volume III, The Production of Audiodescribed Programmes. Optimisation of the Production Process, and Guidelines for Describers (Independent Television Commission, 1993).

Aspis, S., Laws about Our Rights [Booklet written for people with learning difficulties available from: Instrument House, 207–215 Kings Cross Road, London WC1 9DB].

Cooper, Ray, Eliminating Shadows: A Manual on Photography and Disability (London: Paddington Printshop, 1990). [From 1, Elgin Avenue, London W9 3PR]

Delin, A., and Morrison, E., Access – Guidelines for Marketing to Disabled Audiences (London: The Arts Council of Great Britain, 1993).

Doyle, B., Disability Discrimination: The New Law (Bristol: Jordans, 1996).

Focus – Access to Training in Film and Video for Disabled People, Conference Report (BBC Equal Opportunities Department, 1990).

Earnscliffe, J., In through the Front Door – Disabled People and the Visual Arts: Examples of Good Practice (London: The Arts Council of Great Britain, 1992).

Gearing Up for Good Practice: Access to the Arts – A Study of Good Practice at the London Coliseum, Occasional Paper No. 3 (London Boroughs Disability Resource Team, 1990).

Morrison, E., Equal Opportunities – Policy into Practice: Disability (The Independent Theatre Council, 1990).

Report on the Initiative to Increase the Employment of Disabled People in the Arts (London: Arts Council of Great Britain, 1993).

Media general

Bettelheim, Bruno, The Uses of Enchantment: The Power and Importance of Fairy Tales (Harmondsworth: Penguin, 1978)

Gross, L., and Katz., Ruby, J., Image Ethics: The Moral Rights of Subjects in Photographs, Film, and Television (New York: Oxford University Press, 1988).

Home, A., Into the Box of Delights: A History of Children's Television (London: BBC Books, 1993).

Masterman, L., Television Mythologies: Stars, Shows and Signs (London: Comedia/Routledge, 1984).

Petrie, D., Cinema and the Realms of Enchantment: Lectures, Seminars and Essays by Marina Warner and Others (London: BFI Publishing, 1993).

Renov, M. (ed.), Theorizing Documentary (London: Routledge, 1993).

Root, J., Open the Box (Comedia/Channel Four, 1986).

Media – Disability

Anderson, R.G., Faces, Forms, Films: The Artistry of Lon Chaney (New York: Castle Books, 1971).

Armstrong, K., and Moore, W., 'Shut Out by the media', Journalist, October 1985.

Asch, Adrienne, and Fine, Michelle 'In Search of a Heroine: Images of Women with Disabilities in Fiction and Drama', Women with Disabilities: Essays in Psychology, Culture and Politics (Temple University Press, 1988).

Barnes, C., Disabling Imagery and the Media (Halifax: Ryburn/BCODP, 1992).

Broadcasting Standards Council, Perspectives of Disability in Broadcasting: Research Working Paper II (London, 1995)

Bogdan, R., Freak Show: Presenting Human Oddities for Amusements and Profit (Chicago and London: University of Chicago Press, 1988).

Bogdan, D., and Biklen, R., 'Media Portrayals of Disabled People: A Study in Stereotypes', Interracial Books for Children Bulletin vol. 4 nos 6/7 (1982).

Burleigh, M., 'Selling Murder: The Killing Films of the Third Reich', Chapter 6 in Death and Deliverance: 'Euthanasia' in Germany, 1900–1945 (Cambridge: University of Cambridge Press, 1994).

Collett, R., Access to Image Photo Work Book: Disability Photography Issues (Bradford: Valid, 1992). [Available from: Valid, 17–21 Chapel Street, Bradford, BD1 5DT]

Croton, G., and Pascoe, C., International Year of Disabled People, 1981: BBC Programmes on Mental and Physical Handicap, 1970 to 1980 (London: BBC Education, 1980).

Cumberbatch, G., and Negrine, R., Images of Disability on Television (London: Routledge, 1992).

Darke, P., 'The Elephant Man: An Analysis from a Disabled Perspective', Disability and Society vol. 9 no. 3, 1994.

Davies, K., Dickey, J., and Stratford, T., Chapter 4, Out of Focus: Writings on Women and the Media (London: The Women's Press Ltd, 1987).

Erickson, W., and Wolfe, D. (eds), Images of Blind and Visually Impaired People in the Movies, 1913–1985: An Annotated Filmography with Notes (New York: American Foundation for the Blind, 1985).

Fleming, M., and Manvell, R., Images of Madness: The Portrayal of Insanity in the Feature Film (London: Fairleigh Dickinson University Press, 1985).

Gartner, A., and Joe, T., Images of the Disabled: Disabling Images (New York: Praeger, 1987).

Hevey, D., The Creatures Time Forgot: Photography and the Construction of Disability Imagery (London: Routledge, 1992).

Howell, M., and Ford, P., The True History of the Elephant Man (Harmondsworth: Penguin Books, 1980).

Johnson, M., 'Sticks and Stones: The Language of Disability', Chapter 2 in Nelson, J. A., The Disabled, the Media and the Information Age (Westport, CT: Greenwood Press, 1994).

Karpf, A., Doctoring the Media: The Reporting of Health and Medicine (London: Routledge, 1988).

Kent, D., In Search of a Heroine: Images of Women with Disabilities in Fiction and Drama (USA: Temple University Press, 1988).

Klobas, L.E., Disability Drama in Television and Film (Jefferson, NC: McFarland, 1988).

Longmore, Paul K., 'Screening Stereotypes: Images of Disabled People', Social Policy vol. 16 no. 1, Summer 1985.

Longmore, Paul K., 'Screening Stereotypes: Images of Disabled People in TV and Motion Pictures', in Gartner A., and Joe, T. (eds), Images of the Disabled: Disabling Images, (New York: Praeger, 1987).

Nelson, J. A., The Disabled, the Media and the Information Age (Westport, CT: Greenwood Press, 1994).

Norden, M. F., The Cinema of Isolation: A History of Physical Disability in the Movies (New Brunswick, NJ: Rutgers University Press, 1994).

Pointon, A., Disability and Television: Guidelines on Representation for Producers (Channel Four, 1992).

Rieser, Richard (ed.), Invisible Children: Report of the Joint Conference on Children, Images and Disability, 1 March 1995 (London: Save the Children/Integration Alliance, 1995).

Shakespeare, Tom, 'Cultural Representation of Disabled People: Dustbins for Disavowal', Disability and Society, March 1994.

Schuchman, J. S., Hollywood Speaks: Deafness and the Film Entertainment Industry (Urbana, University of Illinois Press, 1988).

Scott-Parker, S., They Aren't in the Brief – Advertising People With Disabilities (London: King's Fund Centre, 1989).

Skal, D. J., The Monster Show: A Cultural History of Horror (London: Plexus, 1994).

Smith, Steve, and Jordan, Antionette, What the Papers Say and Don't Say about Disability (London: The Spastics Society, 1992).

Sutherland, A. T., Disabled We Stand (Souvenir Press, 1981).

Van Zoonen, L., Feminist Media Studies (London: Sage, 1994).

Video Directory: Ability and Disability (London: Mental Health Media Council, 1993).

Poetry

From Dark to Light: An Anthology of Poetry and Words from Survivors' Poetry (London: Survivors's Poetry, 1993)

Re-Write: An Anthology of New Writing (London: Shape 1994).

Napolitano, Sue, A Dangerous Woman (Greater Manchester Coalition of Disabled People, 1995).

Journals

Access by Design (quarterly). Centre for Accessible Environments, Nutmeg House, 60 Gainsford Street, London SE1 2NY.

British Deaf News (monthly). British Deaf Association, 38 Victoria Place, Carlisle, CA1 1HU.

Coalition (quarterly). Greater Manchester Coalition of Disabled People Carisbrook, Wenlock Way, Gorton, Manchester M12 5LF.

DAM (quarterly; previously Disability Arts Magazine). Ceased publication 1996.

Disability and Society (Quarterly). (Previously Disability, Handicap and Society.) Carfax Publishing Co., PO Box 25, Abingdon, Oxon OX14 3UE.

Disability Now (monthly). Scope (previously the Spastics Society), 12 Park Crescent, London W1.

Dail Magazine. c/o London Disability Arts Forum (LDAF), 34 Osnaburgh Street, London NW1 3ND.

Select Filmography and List of Programmes

A Christmas Carol, 1911, J. Searle Dawley, US
Afraid of the Dark, 1991, Mark Peploe, Fr/GB
And Now Tomorrow, 1944, Irving Pichel, US
Asylum, 1972, Peter Robinson, US
Bad Day at Black Rock, 1954, John Sturges, US
Ballad in Blue, 1964, Paul Henreid, GB
Beau Bandit, 1930, US
The Best Years of our Lives, 1946, William Wyler, US
The Big Parade, 1925, King Vidor, US
Blind Fury, 1989, Philip Noyce, US
Blind Terror, 1971, Richard Fleischer, GB
Blink, 1994, Michael Apted, US
Born on the Fourth of July, 1989, Oliver Stone, US
The Boy Who Stole a Million, 1960, Charles Crichton, GB
The Bride of Frankenstein, 1935, James Whale, US
Charlie Chan at the Olympics, 1936, US
Chamber of Horrors, 1966, Hy Averback, US
Children of a Lesser God, 1986, Randa Haines, US
City Lights, 1931, Charlie Chaplin, US
Coming Home, 1978, Hal Ashby, US
Creature from the Black Lagoon, 1954, Jack Arnold, US
A Dangerous Woman, 1993, Stephen Gyllenhaal, US
The Dark Angel, 1925, George Fitzmaurice, US
Dark Eyes of London, 1939, Walter Summers, GB
Dr. Terror's House of Horrors, 1964, Freddie Francis, GB
Duet for One, 1986, Andre Konchalovsky, US
Dumb and Dumber, 1994, Peter Farelly, US
The Elephant Man, 1980, David Lynch, US
The Enchanged Cottage, 1945, John Cromwell, US
Eyes in the Night, 1942, Fred Zinneman, US
Eyes of a Stranger, 1980, Ken Wiederhorn, US
Flesh and Fury, 1952, Joseph Pevney, US
For a Few Dollars More, 1965, Sergio Leone, IT/DE/ES
For the First Time, 1959, Rudolph Maté, DE
Forrest Gump, 1994, Robert Zemeckis, US
Four Weddings and a Funeral, 1994, Mike Newell, UK
Frankenstein, 1910, J. Searle Dawley, US
Freaks, 1932, Tod Browning, US
The Fugitive, 1993, Andrew Davis, US
Goldfinger, 1964, Guy Hamilton, GB
The Great Escape, 1962, John Sturges, US
The Heart is a Lonely Hunter, 1968, Robert Ellis Miller, US
House of Wax, 1953, André de Toth, US
The Hunchback of Notre Dame, 1923, Wallace Worsely, US
The Hunchback of Notre Dame, 1939, William Dieterle, US
It's a Gift, 1934, Norman Z. McLeod, US
Jennifer 8, 1992, Bruce Robinson, US
Johnny Belinda, 1948, Jean Negulesco, US
Kitty, 1929, Victor Saville, GB
The Lawnmower Man, 1992, Brett Leonard, GB/US
The Longest Day, 1962, Ken Annakin/Andrew Marton/Bernhard Wicki/Darryl F. Zanuck, US
Long John Silver's Return to Treasure Island, 1954, Byron Haskin, US
The Lost Weekend, 1945, Billy Wilder, US
Mad Max II, 1981, George Miller, AUS
Magnificent Obsession, 1954, Douglas Sirk, US
A Man on the Beach, 1956, Joseph Losey, GB
Mask, 1985, Peter Bogdanovich, US
The Men, 1950 Fred Zinneman, US
Midnight Cowboy, 1969, John Schlesinger, US
The Miracle Worker, 1962, Arthur Penn, US
Moby Dick, 1956, John Huston, US
Monkey Shines, 1988, George A. Romero, US
Moonraker, 1979, Lewis Gilbert, GB/FR
Moulin Rouge, 1952, John Huston, US
My Left Foot, 1989, Jim Sheridan, GB
Night Song, 1947, John Cromwell, US
No Road Back, 1956, Montgomery Tully, GB
No Trees in the Street, 1958, Lee Thompson, GB
Of Mice and Men, 1992, Gary Sinise, US
Passion Fish, 1992, John Sayles, US
A Patch of Blue, 1965, Guy Green, US
Patton, 1969, Franklin J. Schaffner, US
The Penalty, 1920, Wallace Worsley, US
Peter Pan, 1953, Hamilton Luske/Clyde Geronimi/Wilfred Jackson, US
Phantom of the Opera, 1925, Rupert Julian, US
Pocketful of Miracles, 1961, Frank Capra, US
Pollyanna, 1960, David Swift, US
Pride of the Marines, 1945, Delmer Daves, US
Proof, 1991, Jocelyn Moorhouse, AUS
The Raging Moon, 1970, Bryan Forbes, GB
Rain Man, 1988, Barry Levinson, US
Rambo, 1985, George Pan Cosmatos, US
Reach for the Sky, 1956, Lewis Gilbert, GB
Saboteur, 1942, Alfred Hitchcock, US
See No Evil, Hear No Evil, 1989, Arthur Hiller, US
Spellbound, 1945, Alfred Hitchcock, US
The Spy Who Loved Me, 1977, Lewis Gilbert, GB
The Story of Esther Costello, 1957, David Miller, GB
23 Paces to Baker Street, 1956, Henry Hathaway, US
Tell Me That You Love Me Junie Moon, 1969, Otto Preminger, US
Tiger in the Smoke, 1956, Roy Ward Baker, GB
Tim, 1979, Michael Pate, AU
Torch Song, 1953, Charles Walters, US
Treasure Island, 1950, Byron Haskin, GB
Voices, 1973, Kevin Billington, GB
Voices, 1979, Robert Markowitz, US
Union Station, 1950, Rudolph Mate, US
The Unknown, 1927, Tod Browning, US
Victim, 1916, William S. Davis, US
Wait until Dark, 1967, Terence Young, US
Warlock, 1988, Steve Miner, US
The Waterdance, 1991, Neil Jimenez, US
West of Zanzibar, 1928, Tod Browning, US
Whatever Happened to Baby Jane, 1962, Robert Aldrich, US
Whose Life Is It Anyway, 1981, John Badham, US
Without Warning: The James Brady Story, 1991, Michael Toshiyuki, US

Witness in the Dark, 1959, Wolf Rilla, GB
Woman in Red, 1984, Gene Wilder, US
Young Frankenstein, 1974, Mel Brooks, US
You'd Be Surprised, 1926, Arthur Rosson, US

Shorts

Behindert (Hindered), 1974, Stephen Dwoskin, GB/WGer
Face of our Fear, 1992, Stephen Dwoskin, GB (for Channel Four).
The Fall, 26 April 1991, (Arts Council/BBC)
Outside In, 1981, Stephen Dwoskin, GB/WGer
Trying to Kiss the Moon, 1995, Stephen Dwoskin, GB
When Billy Broke His Head . . . and Other Tales of Wonder, 1995, David E. Simpson, US

Television: drama and docudrama

Dramas with deaf/disability theme and including one or more deaf/disabled actors:

. . . And Your Name is Jonah, 1976, CBS
The Count of Solar, 2 February 1992, Tristram Powell, BBC
Deptford Graffiti, 16 December 1991, Philip Davis, Channel Four
Horizon: Joey, 9 December 1974, Brian Gibson, BBC
On Giant's Shoulders, 28 February 1979, Anthony Simmons, BBC
Pictures in the Mind, 6 April 1987, Nigel Evans, Channel Four
Raspberry Ripple, 1 April 1988, Nigel Finch, BBC
Skallagrigg, 9 March 1994, John Chapman, BBC

Dramas and drama series with non-disabled actors

Goodbye Cruel World, serial from 6 January 1992, Adrian Shergold, BBC
Ironside, series 1967–75, USA
Journey to Knock, 18 September 1991, David Wheatley, BBC
Keeping Tom Nice, 15 August 1990, Ruth Caleb, BBC
Tumbledown, 1988, Richard Eyre, BBC

Television: factual

Long running or regular disability/deaf series

From the Edge, 1992 to date, BBC2
Inside Out, 1995 to date, Channel Four
Link, 1976 to date, ATV/Central/Carlton for ITV
Listening Eye, 1984–1991, Tyne Tees TV for Channel Four
One in Four, 1986–1992, BBC2
Over the Edge, 1993 to date, BBC2
People First, 1992–1995, Channel Four
Same Difference, 1987–199, Same Production Company for Channel Four
See Hear, 1981 to date, BBC1
Sign On, 1992 to date, Tyne Tees TV for Channel Four

Short disability series

Against the 9–5, 1994, BBC
Contact, 1976, BBC
D'art , 1992, YTV for Channel Four
Disabled Lives, 1992, BBC
Don't Just Sit There, 1988, Ideas Factory for Channel Four
Go for It, 1989, Ideas Factory for Channel Four

The Handicapped Family, 1980, BBC
The Invisible Wall, 1995, BBC
Lost for Words, 1979, BBC
Old School Ties, 1995, BBC2

Documentary features

Breaking the Rules, 19 July 1994, Impulse for BBC
Forty Minutes: I, Alison, 10 March 1988, Ann Paul, BBC
Link: We Won't Go Away, 24 November 1981, Patricia Ingram, Central for ITV
Man Alive: Alison, 3 December 1981, Ann Paul, BBC
Man Alive: Very Independent People, 26 March 1981, Ann Paul, BBC
QED: Breaking the Silence, 6 April 1988, Malcolm Brinkworth, BBC
QED: On His Own Two Feet, 20 May 1991, Malcolm Brinkworth, BBC
Open Space Special: Rights Not Charity, 13 October 1988, BBC
The Skin Horse, 1983, Nigel Evans, BBC
The Tin Lids: Childhood 1991, Anglia
The Tin Lids: 30 Years On 1991, Anglia
Cutting Edge: Looking After Mum 1993, Channel 4

Index